Using
Computer Color
Effectively

Using Computer Color Effectively

An Illustrated Reference

L. G. Thorell / W. J. Smith

HEWLETT PACKARD

Prentice Hall, Englewood Cliffs, New Jersey 07632

Library of Congress Cataloging-in-Publication Data

Thorell, L. G. (Lisa G.)
   Using computer color effectively: an illustrated reference/L. G.
Thorell, W. J. Smith.
      p. cm.
  Bibliography: p.
  Includes index.
  ISBN 0-13-939878-3.
  1. Color computer graphics. I. Smith, W. J. (Wanda J.)
II. Title.
T385.T4956 1989
006.6—dc19   88–18613
                               CIP

Editorial / production supervision: Sophie Papanikolaou and **bookworks**
Interior design: Sophie Papanikolaou and Anne T. Bonanno
Cover design: Anne T. Bonanno
Manufacturing buyer: Mary Ann Gloriande
Page layout: Gail Collis

© 1990 by Prentice-Hall, Inc.
A Division of Simon & Schuster
Englewood Cliffs, New Jersey 07632

The publisher offers discounts on this book when ordered
in bulk quantities. For more information, write or call:

Special Sales
Prentice-Hall, Inc.
College Technical and Reference Division
Englewood Cliffs, NJ 07632
(201) 592-2498

Printed in the United States of America
10 9 8 7 6 5 4 3 2 1

ISBN 0-13-939878-3

Prentice-Hall International (UK) Limited, *London*
Prentice-Hall of Australia Pty. Limited, *Sydney*
Prentice-Hall Canada Inc., *Toronto*
Prentice-Hall Hispanoamericana, S.A., *Mexico*
Prentice-Hall of India Private Limited, *New Delhi*
Prentice-Hall of Japan, Inc., *Tokyo*
Simon & Schuster Asia Pte. Ltd., *Singapore*
Editora Prentice-Hall do Brasil, Ltda., *Rio de Janeiro*

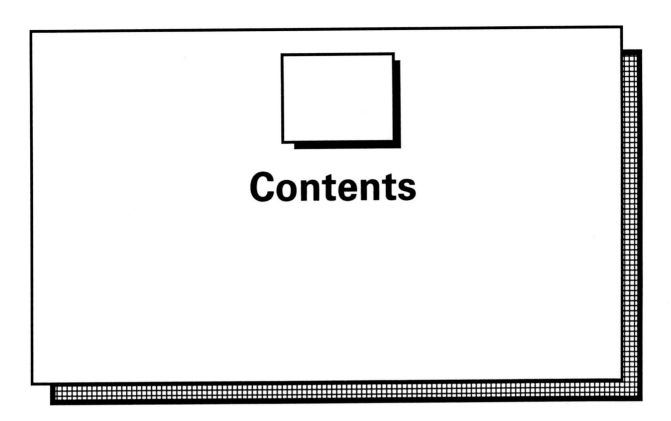

Contents

Transferring Color to Hard Copy 43

Color Coding 69

Computer Color Applications 83

PART II TECHNICAL ASPECTS OF VISION AND COMPUTER COLOR

6 Color Vision 103

7 Color Image Quality 121

8 Color, Visual Comfort, and Performance 141

Preface

The painter of the future will be a colorist such as there has never yet been.

Vincent Van Gogh

If the premise that user interface is theater is true, then color is a major stage prop. However, like many elements of user interface with computer devices, color is an obscure quality. Even for those skilled in good user interface design, the principles underlying color perception are often poorly understood. A hypothetical example will illustrate this point and show how the inappropriate use of color can affect the impression of product quality.

A hardware engineer is anxious to show his executive management his newly developed, high resolution, large capacity color display and printer. When the engineer assigns colors to the images on the display, the text has poor legibility, the colors are difficult to discriminate, and there are unintended depth illusions. When he transfers the screen images to hard copy, these problems are less apparent but the colors do not match those on the screen. In addition, the unimportant messages presented in low contrast colors on the black background screen become emphasized because they are a high contrast on the white paper printout. The engineer's attempt to demonstrate the quality of the display and print images is a disappointment to all.

The purpose of this book is to describe how to use computer color effectively and reduce the likelihood of unfortunate situations like the one just described. This book provides answers to questions frequently asked by designers and users about assigning and manipulating color on computer displays, plotters, printers, and film recorders. The questions address practical, technical, and aesthetic issues. Examples are:

- "How can color be used to improve communication in a business presentation?"
- "How can colors be used in computer graphics to produce special effects?"
- "How can color quality be measured?"
- "How many digital-to-analog conversion levels are necessary?"
- "What color combinations will be most attractive?"

Many of the answers to these and other questions can be found in technical publications from physiologists, psychologists, physicists and human factors engineers. However, the answers are either difficult to find, too cumbersome to invite quick reading, or not easy to understand for those not specializing in these fields.

The major objectives of this book are to consolidate this information into an easily accessible form and to minimize theory while maximizing practical applications. It is written primarily for programmers, engineers, and technical writers, for it is with these individuals that the access to computer color begins. However, it is also written for creators of business graphics, artists and anyone who is involved in the design and use of computer color images. We assume our readers have a wide range of academic and experiential backgrounds with different impressions of the world and different vocabularies. However, they all have similar visual systems.

The information assembled in this book is from selected state-of-the-art color vision research. Unfortunately, there is an abundance of outdated and inaccurate information in publication and in particular in non-technical media. The intent of this book is to present concisely validated research findings pertinent to computer color perception and to describe how these findings are applied to produce effective color output.

The book is divided into three sections. *Part I, Computer Color*, includes a basic introduction of the importance and advantages of computer color images, a brief overview of color physics and vision fundamentals, descriptions of computer color devices, and computer color applications and coding. *Part II, Technical Aspects of Vision and Computer Color* provides a more detailed and technical description of color perception, and discussions of color and visual comfort, color representation systems, and color manipulation with software. *Part III, Color Application Guidelines*, is a condensed summary of color use tools based on the information presented.

Part I, Computer Color, includes five chapters. *Chapter 1, The Benefits of Computer Color*, describes how color can have an impact on user performance and gives examples of research which show tasks in which color is most beneficial. *Chapters 2 and 3, Displaying Computer Color*, and *Transferring Color to Hardcopy*, present a general overview of the current technologies which display computer color (soft copy) images and which produce a permanent (hard copy) version of them. In particular, *Chapter 2* describes the physics of light, basic principles of color vision, light emissive and light reflective display technologies, and advantages and disadvantages of input devices that allow manipulation of color. *Chapter 3* describes devices that transfer computer color to hard copy (e.g., plotters, printers, and camera systems). It includes some techniques that can be used to enhance and expand plotted and printed color. This chapter also discusses the impact of inks and paper quality on color appearance and briefly describes manual photography and film recording used to transfer soft copy to 35 mm slides. The chapter concludes with a discussion and table comparing these devices. *Chapter 4, Color Coding*, describes ways in which color conveys a meaning or produces an effect. *Chapter 5, Applications of Computer Color*, describes how color is used in scientific research, education, engineering, business and entertainment.

Part II, Technical Aspects of Vision and Computer Color, also includes five chapters. *Chapter 6, Color Vision*, explains the basic principles of color perception so users can understand its effects on visual and mental processing. It describes the perception of light, its interpretation as color, and the interaction of the physical properties of light and psychological properties of color. It also covers the limitations of the eye with regard to color perception and factors that influence its efficiency. *Chapter 7, Color Image Quality*, describes how different forms of imagery affect the perception of color and how color has an impact on image recognition and quality of image appearance. It specifically describes how image lightness and contrast, size, shape, location, duration, and ambient light affect color perception. It also shows how color can impact acuity and response speed. *Chapter 8, Color Visual Comfort and Performance*, addresses ergonomic issues of color displays and visual comfort. The primary goal of this chapter is to present state-of-the-art research results on issues like visual comfort, color adaptation, screen background brightness, screen glare, and flicker. *Chapter 9, Specification of Color*, describes how the properties of color can be represented in three-dimensional spaces and two-dimensional diagrams assigned values. It shows how this organization has evolved into different systems of specification that allow for measurement, comparison and prediction of color appearance. *Chapter 10, Manipulating Color on Displays*, provides a general overview on how programming assigns and manipulates color. It describes some sophisticated techniques for modifying and expanding colors. It also gives examples of color use in image processing for specialized applications like satellite, medical, and geological imaging.

Part III, Color Application Guidelines, contains one chapter, *Chapter 11, Computer Color Guidelines* which summarizes guidelines on effective use of color for computer images based on the visual principles described in previous chapters. It shows several examples of color palettes that conform to these guidelines on both black and white background media.

Our intention is to structure the content of the book so that the reader can quickly obtain a general overview of the major topics, principles of color vision and the application of color to computer images by reading the figure captions and *"Useful Facts"* at the end of each chapter. *References* are listed at the end of each chapter.

All the figures not attributed to other sources were created on a Hewlett-Packard raster graphics display capable of producing 4096 colors. The images were then transferred to hard copy by a matrix camera, film recorder, plotter, or printer. Images transferred to paper or transparency were manually photographed. The film used in the matrix camera was Kodak Kodachrome ASA 64 color slide film; the film used for the manual photographs was Ektrachrome ASA 160 for tungsten light.

We would like to extend our appreciation to a number of people who helped make this book a reality and enhanced its accuracy and ease of understanding. We would first like to thank Hewlett-Packard's management for their interest, support, and encouragement. Those personally involved with the project included: *Cyril Yansouni* (formerly of Hewlett-Packard) who provided the initial funding, and *Jack Magri, Chuck House, Wayne Grove*, and *Steve Joseph*.

Our thanks next goes to the engineers, secretaries, industrial designers, and technical writers in Hewlett-Packard who provided technical and comprehensive reviews of the book and many constructive comments: *Ross Allen, Patty Angelos, Larry Barbara, Lee Boswell, Jim Boyden, Joyce Farrell, Roland Haitz, Larry Hubby, George Kaposhilin, Alain Klein, Nic Lyons, Chris Marshall, John Meyer, Larry Rowland, Jayne Schurick, Michael Slack, Paul Sorenson, Myron Sun, Anna Wichansky, and Evelyn Williams*. These individuals represent Corporate Engineering, HP Labs, and divisions which develop plotters and printers (in San Diego, California), personal computer systems (in Sunnyvale, California) and software (in Sunnyvale and Pinewood, England), engineering workstations (in Ft. Collins, Colorado), and optoelectronics (in San Jose, California). We would also like to thank *Bryan Stahmer* for his ideas on initial artwork, *Rich Marconi* for his assistance with the matrix camera, and *Judy Flamer* and *Vicki Rode* for their help in converting the screen designs to 35 mm slides.

Other professionals we would like to thank are *Dr. Terry Benzschawel* (Artificial Intelligence Laboratory, NyNex), *Dr. Fergus Campbell* (Cambridge University, England), *Peter dePavloff* (de Pavloff Marine Engineering, San Francisco), *James McMullen* (Graphics Consultant, San Francisco), *Avi Namen* (University of Toronto, Canada), *Anny Rouillard* (Rouillard and Associates, Interior Architecture, San Francisco), and *Dr. Harry Synder* (Virginia Polytechnic Institute). A very special thanks goes to *Dr. Gerald Murch* (Tektronix, Oregon) for his many reviews, suggestions, and encouragement.

Finally, we would like to acknowledge *The Compage Company* (San Francisco) for their advice, organization, early copy editing, and months of patience in blending early versions into a unified manuscript.

In closing, we dedicate this book to engineers, programmers, technical writers, graphics artists, and all those who use computer color. We hope that it will show all readers how to effectively and creatively use computer color.

Lisa Thorell
Wanda Smith

1

The Benefits of Computer Color

The colors in painting are, as it were, blandishments to lure the eyes, as poetry is a lure to the ears.

Nicolas Poussin

Color Vision and Computer Images

Color is more than just a blandishment to lure the eyes. The ability to see color allows us to perceive the brilliant colors in a sunset, the subtle colors of twilight. Its perception can be so enjoyable that we may not realize it serves other important purposes. For example, it has played a major role in our survival for millions of years by enhancing our ability to see dangerous shapes before they see us (see Figure 1.1).

Color perception allows us to distinguish both natural images and artificial ones created by computer output devices. When color is applied to display or hard copy media, it optimizes the use of our natural ability to detect images, which has evolved over millions of years.

Monochrome versus Color

Because computer color images more closely represent the appearance of real ones, they are generally superior to black and white (*achromatic*) or single color (*monochrome*) presentation (see Figure 1.2). In addition to enhancing realism, the appropriate use of color enhances the location, association, grouping, coding, and memory of images.

Until recently the widespread use of achromatic (or monochrome) visual displays and hard copy images has been primarily due to inability to produce high fidelity color because of technical difficulties in output technologies. The rapid increase in the use of color in various forms of media (for example, movies, television, and recently newspapers) attests to its popularity. The more recent increase in color computer displays used for careful visual analysis (for example, for medical diagnosis and structure analysis) attests to its usefulness in image interpretation. In fact, computer displays that do not offer color output appear to be experiencing the same fate as their black and white predecessor, the achromatic television.

Figure 1.1 *Color Perception and Survival* Color perception helps us distinguish dangerous shapes like this scorpion fish whose spines are venomous. (*Photo courtesy of George Crispo.*)

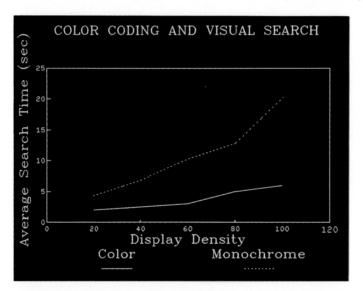

Figure 1.2 *Color vs. Monochrome Effects on Performance* Finding color coded objects is faster than locating images which are in monochrome. (*Adapted from Smith, 1967.*)

The increasing use of color in computer media requires that it be correctly applied to optimize visual perception and image interpretation. The information presented in the following pages is intended to assist in this process.

Uses for Color

Many computer color images that look like artistic renderings actually represent complex functions. For example, color often reveals the structure and relationships of information. Although fractals may look like patterns similar to those woven into middle Eastern carpets (see Figure 1.3), each color represents the number of times a mathematical expression repeats itself (see Chapter 5).

Figure 1.3 *Fractal* The different colors represent different iterations of a mathematical (geometric) formula. (*Courtesy of Nic Lyons of Hewlett-Packard.*)

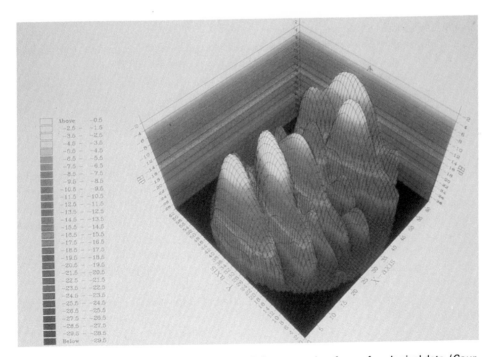

Figure 1.4 *Computer Colored Representation* Color mapped surfaces of geological data. (*Courtesy of UNIRAS and created with UNIRAS software.*)

Computer color has other functions which may not be immediately obvious. For example, the quality of computer color images can be so realistic that they look like photographs. However, the colors assigned to these images often represent more than a replica of their natural appearance. They may represent different elevations (see Figure 1.4) or nonvisible wavelengths of light (see Chapter 10).

Color Vision and Computer Images

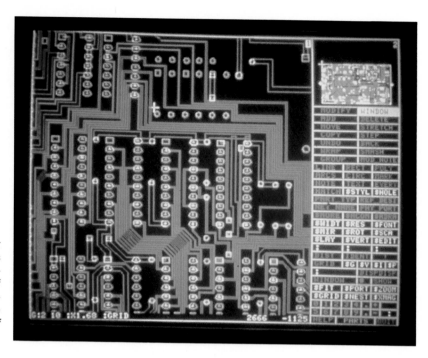

Figure 1.5 *Color in a Complex Screen* Color separates circuits (cyan) and component holes (magenta) and segregates commands of an engineering design editor. The upper right is a miniature view of the printed circuit board. (*Courtesy of Hewlett-Packard.*)

Computer images are becoming more complex. Color can help organize this complexity (see Figure 1.5). It can order and classify menus, associate related icons, and enhance or subdue active and inactive windows.

Color thus adds more than just an aesthetic factor to computer images (see Figures 1.2 to 1.5). Field and laboratory studies show the positive effect of color on response time, error rate, and learning. It thus significantly impacts users' performance with computer display systems as shown in the following research.

Color Research

Because color vision plays such an important role in our lives, there is an extensive amount of research on its effects. The research includes the study of many interacting variables involved in color perception and extends over almost 100 years. Some of the interacting variables involved in color perception and computer display hardware and software design are listed in Table 1.1.

The relationship between the many variables and factors involved in color perception and its study are not simple. Color research is helping to identify these variables, how they interact, and how they affect our ability to see color. This information is useful in developing guidelines for the effective application of color (see Chapter 11) to computer imaging.

Color Research Disciplines

Color vision research occurs in many fields including optics, physiology, psychophysics, and human factors engineering. Since color science is multidisciplinary, it includes terms and theories from all these disciplines. For example, physiologists identify and describe the neural structures of the brain responsible for seeing light. They study color vision by recording the responses of neurons at different areas in the visual system. Their findings are useful in understanding the "wiring" of the visual process and, in particular, of color vision (see Figure 1.6).

TABLE 1.1

Variables Contributing to Computer Display Color Quality

Visual	Hardware	Software
Color	Chromaticity of display primaries	Color space algorithm
Hue	Wavelength	
Saturation	Purity	
Lightness or brightness	Light intensity	Gamma correction
Perceptual difference between colors	DAC levels	Frame buffer and color map
Contrast sensitivity	Spatial and luminance contrast	Virtual color controls
Legibility	Resolution	Anti-aliasing
Flicker	Refresh rate Phosphor decay Brightness	

Psychophysicists study other aspects of color perception. They present specific patterns to observers and measure the resulting visual responses. Their goal is to study the relationship between the input (for example, light patterns or physical units of light) and the output (for example, visual responses or units of color sensation). One of their research methods is to present two lights to an observer and ask for a report of when a light which varies in brightness matches another light of fixed brightness (see Figure 1.7). This type of experiment helps determine the relationship between intensity and perceived brightness. Their results show that doubling the intensity of light on a computer display does not result in it appearing twice as bright (see Chapter 6).

Physicists precisely characterize light in both physical and mathematical terms. Their terms and methods are useful for technically describing and measuring light and controlling it on computer devices. Their tools are typically used by development engineers in designing and testing products like color displays and hard copy devices (see Chapters 2 and 3).

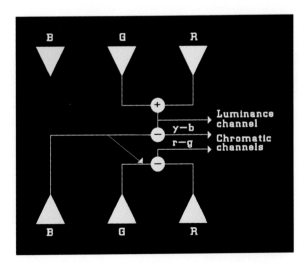

Figure 1.6 *Schematic of Neural Connections Used in Color Perception* Diagram showing how the three different cones (red, blue, and green) in the eye are connected to calculate color. (*Adapted from Boynton, 1979.*)

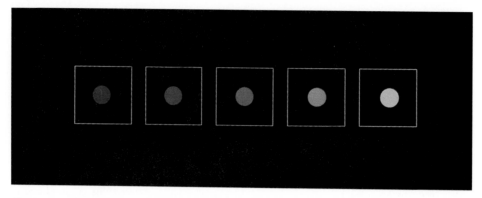

Figure 1.7 *Appearance of Doubling Intensities* Although the intensity of each of the sequential yellow circles is doubled, each intensity does not appear twice as bright.

Human factors engineers study color perception by determining how it affects user performance. They will typically ask a test subject to complete a task which involves colored and noncolored images (see Figure 1.8). Their measures include performance responses like search time, response time, error rate, and learning time. For example, a human factors engineer may compare the time to search for items on a monochrome with that on a multicolor display. Their findings help establish product design guidelines, standards, and testing criteria. They also evaluate the relationship between responses to colors on computer displays and their hard copy reproductions.

Although these scientists and engineers have different reasons for studying color perception, their findings all enhance the understanding of visual mechanisms and help determine the importance of color. For example, the cell responses recorded by the physiologist underlie the reports of visual sensations measured by the psychophysicist. In turn, the research of the psychophysicist contributes to understanding visual performance measured by the human factors engineer. The visual performance measures are useful in determining the effectiveness of computer color.

Laboratory Research

Most color vision research is conducted in a laboratory; some is conducted in the field. The advantage of laboratory research is that variables which affect research results in various ways can be controlled whereas controlling variables in the field is usually a

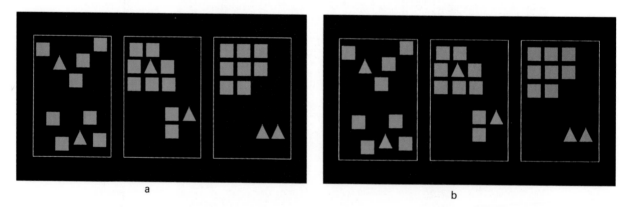

a   b

Figure 1.8 *Monochrome versus Color to Enhance Detection* a) Locating the triangles is difficult when they are the same color as the squares and randomly located. b)The cyan triangles are faster to find in the organized array (middle panel) than in the random arrangement (left panel). The cyan triangles are fastest to locate when separated from the squares and grouped to-gether.

difficult, if not impossible, process. The following describes examples of research in both environments.

COLOR CODING AND PERFORMANCE   One of the most useful applications of color in computer images is as a color code (see Chapter 4). In color coding, colors are assigned different meanings (for example, red for an error message, green for normal system messages). Human factors research comparing color with other visual codes like shape, brightness, size, and type font show that color is a superior form of coding. In particular, it results in the best performance when searching for an item, grouping items, and tracking a moving object.

SEARCH TASKS   One of the first activities in any visual search task is to locate images in a scene. Typical search tasks in computer applications include looking for a particular file in a listing, a keyword on a page, or a data point on a graph.

In a typical search study, symbols of different colors are randomly scattered in a scene. Test subjects must find specific colored symbols as quickly as possible. Search responses are recorded when the subjects respond, for example, by pressing a key when finding the target. Usually, a computer records the time from presentation of a target to the response (for example, key depression), subjects errors, and calculates performance statistics.

In general, presenting items in color allows a viewer to find them more quickly and with fewer errors. Error rates for noncolor coded images can be four times greater than those coded in color. These advantages increase as the number of items or screen density increases (see Figure 1.9). Search time is fastest when an item is coded in two ways, specifically by color and shape.

FORMATTING AND SEARCH   The format or spatial arrangement of images also affects the speed of finding colored objects. For example, grouping images of similar colors results in faster search times when they are in an organized rather than a random array (see also Figure 1.9).

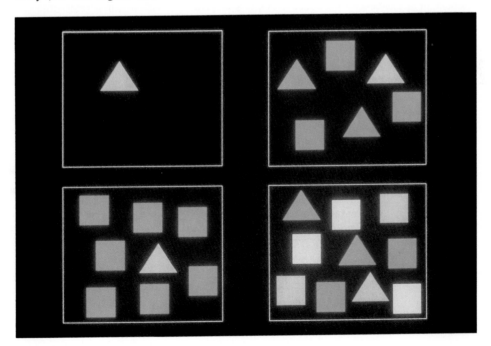

Figure 1.9 *Visual Search as a Function of Color, Shape, and Number of Items*   Search time is faster for shapes of a specific color (for example, yellow triangles in left panels) than when there are many objects of similar shape (top right) and similar color (lower right).

RAPID SEARCH   Rapid search is necessary for many tasks including locating flight information on airport displays, identifying images on radar screens, or reading a medical status indicator on a patient's bedside display. Presenting too many colors or using similar colors slows visual search.

Search time depends on many other factors: the number of items in the scene, the size of the search items, their contrast, arrangement and the ambient lighting. As the complexity of the display increases, search time increases. Table 1.2 lists estimates of search times for high contrast color images viewed in daylight illumination.

Locating a single colored item on an achromatic background is a simple task. The task becomes more complex when irrelevant display images are the same color as relevant ones. In addition, the task becomes more difficult as the number of images and relevant colors increases. However, research also shows that irrelevant colors do not affect search time.

In general, color search studies show that

- Finding a single colored item is fastest on a blank screen or on a screen with items of a different color than the target
- Search time increases if other screen items differ only slightly in color from the target
- Searching takes more time if irrelevant objects resemble the target in both shape and color
- Search time increases as the number of items similar in color to the target items increase
- Search time is not affected by irrelevant colors (provided these colors are not similar to the target color)

COUNTING TASKS   Studies of counting accuracy show that fewer errors occur when objects are coded in color rather than in other codes (see Figure 1.10). These results have been observed by displaying a number of items and asking a test subject to count the number of occurrences of a specific code. The items are visible for a brief time (for example, 100 msec.) to reduce the possibility of a perfect score. Some subjects locate items of a specific color; others locate items coded in a different form (for example, font or underscore).

TRACKING TASKS   Research on the ability to visually locate an image and follow its movement also shows that performance is superior with colored targets (see Figure 1.11). Common tracking tasks include monitoring air traffic on a radar display or finding targets in a video game. In the laboratory, a typical tracking task is following highlighted target items among irrelevant and nonhighlighted items. Moving targets are typically presented in different colors, brightness levels, or shapes.

TABLE 1.2

Estimated Typical Search Rates for Distinctly Colored Items*

Time (sec/item)	Target Items
.03	Digit or character in an ordered array (for example, table)
.30	Set of three digits in a random array
.70	Complex shape in a random array of other shapes

* (From Carter, 1982.)

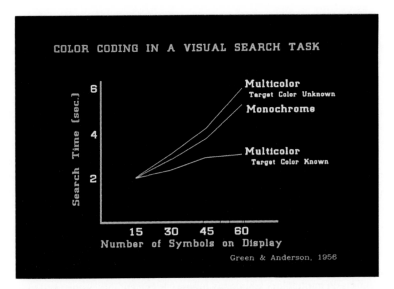

Figure 1.10 *Effects of Color on Search and Counting* Counting color coded items where color is known results in fewer errors than counting items coded in other ways. (*Adapted from Green and Anderson, 1956.*)

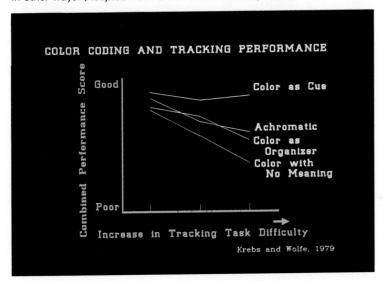

Figure 1.11 *Color in Tracking Tasks* The colors used as a visual cue in tracking result in superior performance. Achromatic highlighting results in about the same performance as organized colored items. Colors assigned without meanings result in the lowest performance. (*Adapted from Krebs and Wolfe, 1979.*)

SUPPORTING FINDINGS   A survey of 42 human factors engineering studies examining the effects of highlighting on visual performance support the findings just described. These studies include a wide range of viewing conditions, experimental methods, and stimulus control. They show that color is superior to brightness, shape, underlining, and other forms of coding. Laboratory research data thus concurs with what is obvious to the visual system: Color is one of the best ways to highlight information.

Field Research

Laboratory research thus demonstrates the performance advantages of color compared with other forms of coding. Careful review of these studies shows the difficulty involved in making equal comparisons between different coding techniques. Most laboratory research of color coding compares types of codes that have very dissimilar features (for example, shape versus color). These differences in stimuli are often considered confounding variables in these studies. In addition, laboratory studies of color perception may not be representative of operating environments. Other variables in the environment that may enhance or reduce color perception are typically not included in these studies. Also, the forms of codes studied in a laboratory may not represent those commonly viewed in computer applications (for example, a small spot of light compared to a screen character or area fill image). Thus, generalizations from these studies may not be valid in more complex environments.

However, almost all studies of color perception in environments outside the laboratory support the finding that color is a superior form of coding. The following is a description of four studies where the tasks include search, counting, and learning. They all compare color to monochrome coding.

FORMS PROCESSING   Prudential Insurance Company of America conducted a study to determine user performance with multicolored versus single color screens. For three months, the performance of two groups of 40 claims processors was measured. One group processed claims on multicolor cathode ray tubes (CRTs); another group used monochrome CRTs. Performance was assessed in terms of training time and accuracy. Worker preference was also surveyed.

A comparison of the performance of the claims processors showed fewer errors and less training time for those using colored displays. Also, most of subjects preferred and rated the quality of the color display superior to the monochrome type. The perceived superiority of the multicolored displays was so convincing that Prudential decided to replace their monochrome displays with multicolor devices, despite the fact that at that time the multicolor devices were significantly (40 percent) more expensive.

MONITORING AIR TRAFFIC   Air traffic control requires fast and accurate visual perception and decisions. It therefore represents a good real-world test of the effect of color on search time and accuracy. In a study at Gatwick Airport in the United Kingdom, test subjects were trained to locate planes on either a color or monochrome display. Those trained with the color displays attempted to locate distinctly colored targets; the other group tried to locate targets highlighted by other methods. All other aspects of the displays (for example, screen resolution and software) were the same. The test results showed that subjects using color displays located aircraft 16 percent faster than those using the monochrome screens. However, unlike the Prudential study, there were no significant differences in training time.

FLIGHT SIMULATION   In a study of test pilot performance, pilots responded more quickly to enemy targets coded by color than by shape. Their response times and error rates for searching and counting threatening and friendly targets were monitored while they performed complex flight maneuvers. Response performance was significantly faster with the color coded threat targets. However, response time of both pilot groups increased as the number of targets on the screen increased.

BUSINESS DECISIONS   In a study of the effect of color on business decisions, students showed that color allowed graphs to be more easily understood and helpful for good decisions than graphs presented in monochrome line styles. Their problem was to allocate portions of an advertising budget to three territories. The solution required interpreting a graph and tabular data. One group analyzed the information in multicolor; another group analyzed the same information in monochrome.

Students viewing the multicolor enhanced charts and tables performed significantly better on the problem: Seventy percent achieved near optimal solutions compared to 33 percent for the monochrome group.

Learning

Color can enhance learning. Red, blue, green, and yellow are the colors most useful for coding information that needs to be remembered. This conclusion is based on several studies. They include studies of diverse populations (for example, New Guinea tribesmen, English children, adults, and monkeys) which show that certain colors (for example, red, blue, green, and yellow) are more easy to learn and remember than others. These colors are also the first color terms expressed in most languages. These terms are called *focal colors*. These four colors also attract attention more than other colors and are generally preferred across all cultures.

People select the same samples of these four colors from standardized color charts to be the "best examples" of a color. They are considered *unique colors* because they possess no secondary hue component and are never confused with other colors. Thus, a unique yellow has no visually apparent red or green properties and is not confused with them; a unique red contains no blue or yellow components and is not confused; and so on.

Inappropriate Applications for Color

While laboratory and field research show that color has certain benefits, researchers agree that color has limitations.

- Search time increases when the color of the target item is similar to the color of other items in the scene
- Visual performance decreases if the color is not meaningfully related to the task
- Spurious use of color (for example, coding color inconsistently) increases the time to find a colored symbol

Use of color must therefore be meaningful and consistent. When used as a code (rather than to separate or group images), it should, if possible, complement its aesthetic application. The inappropriate and overuse of color often occurs in color presentations (see Figure 1.12).

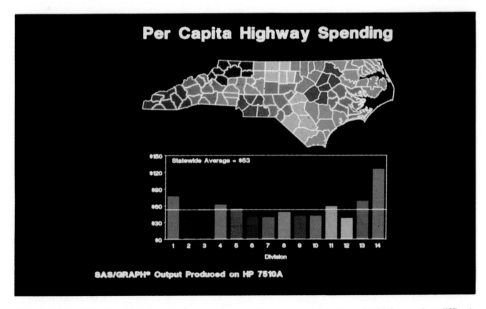

Figure 1.12 *Effective Number of Colors* Many colors are used, some of which are also difficult to distinguish. (*Courtesy of Hewlett-Packard.*)

Other Factors Influencing Responses to Color

Laboratory and field studies thus show that color enhances overall visual performance. Studies also show that many responses to color result from their associations in a particular culture or environment, emotional associations, or inherited characteristics.

Cultural and Environmental Influences

Color has always played an important symbolic role in cultures. However, associations of colors rarely match across cultures. In fact, the meanings of colors can vary significantly (see Table 1.3).

In addition, the association of colors within cultures can vary significantly. Subcultures, such as professional groups, often have specific and very different associations to colors (see Table 1.4). Color assignment appears to depend on the application in which it is used. For example, in the medical field, red designates normal conditions in a computer image like a thermogram. In another type of medical computer image, red denotes an abnormality, such as a malignant tumor. The different associations of color make common understanding of color meanings difficult across and within cultures.

Emotional Responses

Emotions also affect responses to colors. In addition, colors often appear to have an immediate and direct impact on our emotions. Colors seem to stimulate or depress feelings, cause tension or reduce boredom. However, although colors appear to affect behavior, their effects are highly dependent on psychological associations. Regardless of their causes and effects, the emotional impact of colors should not be ignored or discounted because color can affect cognitive processing.

Emotional reactions to color are not consistent, and, thus, predicting their effects is difficult. Causative statements about the emotional effects of color are difficult to validate and often unreliable. Attempts to scientifically establish the effects of color on personality and levels of arousal have also been difficult to quantify. However, a few studies have demonstrated some interesting findings such as the level and types of emotional responses which occur with certain colors. The most intense emotional responses appear to occur with colors at either end of the visible spectrum (for example, violet and red). These results occur in studies of physiological reactions such as electrical resistance of the skin, electrical activity of the brain, and blood pressure. For example, blood pressure increases more when people view red than white and more when viewing white than blue. In addition, both blood pressure and galvanic skin responses appear to be more strongly

TABLE 1.3

Some Cultural Associations of Colors

| Culture | Association to Colors | | | |
	Red	Blue	Green	Yellow
Japan	Anger Danger	Villainy	Future Youth Energy	Grace Nobility
United States	Danger	Masculinity	Safe	Cowardice Caution
France	Aristocracy		Criminality	
Egypt		Virtue Faith Truth	Fertility Strength	Happiness Prosperity

TABLE 1.4

Associations of Color by Professional Groups

| Color | Professional Group | | |
	Process Control Engineers	Financial Managers	Health Care Professionals
Blue	Cold Water	Corporate Reliable	Death
Turquoise	Steam	Cool Subdued	Oxygen deficient
Green	Nominal Safe	Profitable	Infected
Yellow	Caution	Important	Jaundiced
Red	Danger	Unprofitable	Healthy
Purple	Hot Radioactive	Wealthy	Cause for concern

affected by longer wavelengths than by shorter ones. Whereas the effects of color on heart rate appear to depend on recalled associations.

However, these physiological responses to color also appear to reverse themselves very quickly and then diminish. This implies that the emotional impacts of color are most useful for producing immediate and transient effects. In addition, overall preferences to colors are probably more controlled by psychological associations rather than by initial physiological responses.

Innate or Learned Preferences?

Regardless of whether color enhances or reduces visual performance, studies show that people prefer color to monochrome presentations. Responses to and preferences for color appear to be both innately and environmentally determined. Studies of infants and very young children across several widely diversified cultures show that they choose objects in bright saturated colors (such as red, blue, green, and yellow) rather than desaturated ones (such as brown, mauve, gray, pink, pale blue, lime, and lavender). Toy companies, book publishers, television, and advertising agencies take advantage of this phenomenon in designing for infants and toddlers. Computer application programs designed for children should make use of these color preferences.

The same innate attraction to certain colors appears to continue, although to a lesser extent, into adulthood. Even when people reach an age when cultural factors and environmental associations affect color preferences, a general bias toward red, blue, green, and yellow continues. For example, these four colors are the colors most often used in national identifiers (such as national flags) (see Figure 1.13).

Corporate Identities

This basic attraction to red, blue, green, and yellow has been demonstrated for centuries. For example, in the thirteenth century, these colors were used on the shields of messengers (known as heralds) and military legions to identify their affiliation from far distances. The colors of family crests originated from the shields of these messengers.

Corporations, sports clubs, universities, and other professional groups continue to use colored crests or symbols (often called logos) as their trademarks. Some of the most recognized logos of international corporations use either red, blue, green, or yellow. For example, red is the color of the Coca-Cola logo, blue of the Hewlett-Packard logo, red and yellow of the Shell Oil logo, and yellow and green of the John Deere tractor company.

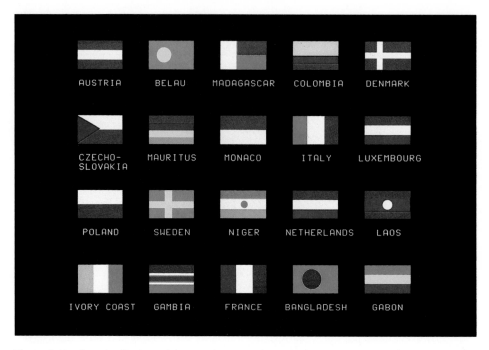

Figure 1.13 *Popular Choices of Colors* National flags with at least one of the four basic colors (red, blue, green, or yellow). (*Adapted from Inglefield, 1984.*)

Corporations use specific colors to attract attention and to ensure memory of their logos, thus helping to create a recognized corporate identity.

The Influences of Fashion

Cultural influences and the dictates of fashion are also significant factors in color preferences. In fact, they can be the dominant selection criterion in choosing a preferred color or product. In highly modernized cultures, color preferences are greatly influenced by fashion and advertising (see Figure 1.14). However, in more primitive societies, color preferences are more affected by basic survival requirements and environmental associations. In these cultures, however, color preferences are also affected by fashion trends.

Color is a primary factor in initial attraction to a product or an advertisement. It is also often the deciding factor in a purchaser's decision to buy a product. Since fashion is always changing, we can expect preferences for colors to follow trends in fashion. For example, the preferences in western cultures for bright colors and brown as a neutral tone during the 1970s has been replaced in the 1980s by the popularity of muted pastels (for example, mauve or teal) and gray as the neutral tone.

An awareness of colors that are currently popular is helpful to maximize the appeal for computer colors. However, relying on fashionable colors for use in computer output may not accomplish the desired response. Unlike fashionable colors, our visual system does not change with time. When visual performance is critical, priority should be given to physiological responses.

Aesthetic Influences

The overall preference and acceptance of colors and their combinations can also be greatly influenced by an individual's "sense of aesthetics." The continued popularity of the color combinations in the paintings of artists like Manet, Van Gogh, and Matisse demonstrate their immunity to popular fads.

Preferences for color combinations and judgments of their aesthetic quality may be

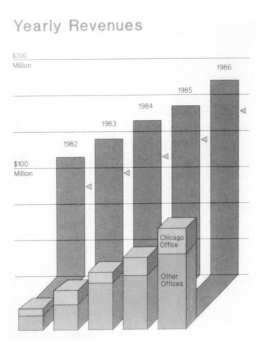

Figure 1.14 *Popular Colors in Business Graphics* Popular colors of the mid-1980s applied to business graphs. (*Courtesy of Hewlett-Packard.*)

based on the degree to which psychological dimensions of color (for example, hue, saturation, and lightness) balance. In general, colors balance when they are not extremes within the same dimension. Thus, color values that are too similar or different are generally less preferred than other combinations (see Figure 1.15). Examples of color combinations

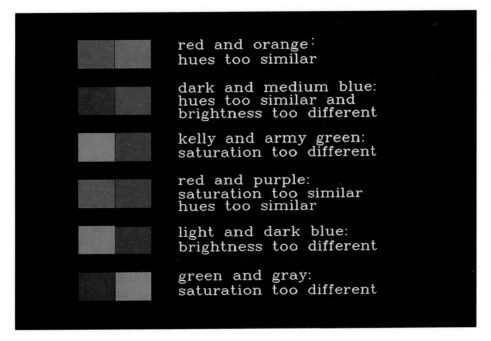

Figure 1.15 *Less Preferred Color Combinations* Color extremes that are very different or similar are generally less preferable than other colors.

that are less preferred and do not fit the balance criterion are: red with orange (hue too similar), dark and medium blue (lightness too similar), kelly and army green (saturation too similar), red and purple (saturation too different), light and dark blue (lightness too different), and green and gray (saturation too different). Although these color combinations are less preferred than others, they are often good candidates for highlighting or subduing information and can therefore influence performance (see Chapter 4).

Color preferences also may be based on the balance between structure and organization of colored images. If colors are located in a clear, orderly, and meaningful manner, they are usually more aesthetically pleasing than colors randomly assigned without a particular coding scheme or purpose. In computer color applications, color ordering is probably the least known or most ignored of all color aesthetic principles.

The following chapters describe techniques that are useful to assign colors to computer images so they will be easily perceived, discriminated, and tailored to specific applications.

Useful Facts

Color as a Natural Information Extractor	Color enhances our natural ability to identify images.
	Much of the nervous system in the brain processes images. Highly specialized cells detect and discriminate color.
Monochrome versus Color	Color is superior to monochrome because it adds another perceptual dimension to images that enhances information processing.
Vision and Computer Color	Understanding how the eye perceives color can help predict the success of computer color.
	The increased use of color in computer output means it will increase in importance as a communication aid. It is therefore essential that the design and use of color be appropriate to the task and visual capabilities of the viewer. Both physical and psychological components of light contribute to color quality.
	Optimal color values for hardware and software components of computer color depend on responses of the visual system.
Advantages of Color	Color can enhance the ability to discriminate and interpret related and unrelated information.
Color and Performance	Laboratory and field studies show that color is a superior coding technique, particularly for location, counting, and tracking of images.

	Search time depends on factors like image size, contrast, and surrounding color values. Large and high contrast images are located faster.
	As the density of items increases, the advantage of color coding increases. However, when the number of colors increases, the advantage of color as a coding technique decreases. Incorrect or inappropriate use of color can degrade performance.
Lab versus Field Research	Field research supports the findings of lab research regarding the effects of color on performance.
Learning	Color can enhance learning.
Color Interpretation	The interpretation of color is influenced by culture, environments, emotional and learned associations, innate physiological responses, and aesthetic appreciation.

REFERENCES

Benbasat, I., A. S. Dexter, and P. Todd, "An Experimental Program Investigating Color-enhanced and Graphical Information Presentation: An Integration of the Findings," *Communication of the ACM*, 29(11), November 1986, 1094–1105.

Berlin, B. and P. Kay. *Basic Color Terms: Their Universality and Evolution* (Berkeley, CA: U. of Calif. Press, 1969).

Bloomfield, J. R., "Visual Search with Embedded Targets: Color and Texture Differences," *Human Factors*, 21(3), 1979, 317–330.

Bornstein, M. H., "Color Vision and Color Naming: A Psychophysiological Hypothesis of Cultural Difference," *Psychol. Bull.*, 80(4), 1973, 257–285.

Boynton, R. M. *Human Color Vision* (New York: Holt, Rinehart, & Winston, 1979).

Cahill, M. C. and R. C. Carter, "Color Code Size for Searching Displays of Different Density," *Human Factors*, 18(3), 1976, 2273–2280.

Carter, R. C., "Visual Search and Color Coding," *Proceedings of the Human Factors Society— 23rd Annual Meeting*, 1979, pp. 369–373.

Carter, R. C., "Visual Search with Color," *J. Exp. Psych.*, 8(1), 1982, 126–136.

Carter, R. C., "Visual Search with Large Colour Codes," *International Conference on Displays for Man-Machine Systems*, 50, April 4–7, 1977, 65–68.

Carter, E. C. and R. C. Carter, "Color and Conspicuousness," *J. Opt. Soc. Am.*, 71(6), 1981, 723–729.

Christ, R. E., "Color Research for Visual Displays," *SID*, 1977, pp. 50–51.

Christ, R. E., "Review and Analysis of Color Coding Research for Visual Displays," *Human Factors*, 17(6), 1975, 524–570.

Christner, C. A. and H. W. Ray, "An Evaluation of the Effect of Selected Combinations of Target and Background Coding on Map-reading Performance," *Human Factors*, 1961, pp. 131–146.

Deken, J. *Computer Images* (New York: Stewart Tabori and Chang Pub., 1983).

Derefeldt, G., U. Berggrund, C. E. Hedin, and H. Marmlin, "Search Time: Colour Coding and Symbol Size," *Colour Coded vs Monochrome Electronic Display Proceedings of a NATO Workshop*, Farnborough, United Kingdom, 1984, pp. 33.1–33.8.

Green, B. F. and L. K. Anderson, "Color Coding in a Visual Search Task," *J. of Exp. Psych.*, 51(1), 1956, 19–24.

Heider, E. R., " 'Focal' Color Areas and the Development of Color Names," *Developmental Psychology*, 4(3), 1971, 447–455.

Heider, E. R., "Universals in Color Naming and Memory," *J. of Exp. Psych.*, 93(1), 1972, 10–20.

Inglefield, E. *Flags* (New York: Arco Publishing, Inc., 1984).

Hunt, V. R., "The Next Generation Air Traffic Control Display," *SID*, May 1986, pp. 20–22.

Keister, R. S., "Data Entry Performance on Color Versus Monochromatic Displays," *Proceedings of the Human Factors Society 25th Annual Meeting*, 1981, pp. 736–740.

Kopala, C. J., "The Use of Color-coded Symbols in a Highly Dense Situation Display," *Proceedings of the Human Factors Society*, 1979, pp. 397–401.

Krebs, M. T. and T. D. Wolf, "Design Principles for the Use of Color in Displays," *Proc. Soc. Information Display*, 20, 1979, 10–15.

Luria, S. M. and M. S. Strauss, "Eye Movements during Search for Coded and Uncoded Targets," *Perception and Psychophysics*, 17(3), 1975, 303–308.

Nourse, J. C. and R. B. Welch, "Emotional Attributes of Color: A Comparison of Violet and Green," *Perceptual and Motor Skills*, 32, 1971, 403–406.

Osgood, C. E., W. H. May, and M. Miron. *Cross-cultural Universals of Affective Meaning* (Urbana: U. of Illinois Press, 1976).

Phillips, R. J. and L. Noyes, "A Comparison of Colour and Visual Texture as Codes for Use as Area Symbols on Thematic Maps," *Ergonomics*, 23(12), 1980, 1117–1128.

Raab, J. S., "Color Display Images Prototyping Requirements," The Aerospace Corp, TOR—0086(6902–061–3), July 1986.

Raker, D. S., "Color Graphics Terminals: A Growth Market," *Digital Design*, Feb. 1983, pp. 46–59.

Robertson, P. J. *Review of Color Display Benefits*. Hursley Park, United Kingdom: IBM TR HF056, Jan. 1982.

Robertson, P. J. *The Use of Colour for Computer Displays*. IBM Technical Report #HF005, 1976.

Smith, S. L., "Color Coding and Visual Separability in Information Displays," *J. of Applied Psych.*, 47(6), 1963, 358–364.

Smith, S. L., "Legibility of Overprinted Symbols in Multicoloured Displays," *J. of Eng. Psych.*, 2, 1963, 82–96.

Smith, S. L. and D. W. Thomas, "Colour versus Shape Coding in Information Displays," *J. of Applied Psych.*, 48(3), 1964, 137–146.

Smith, W. J. and J. E. Farrell, "The Ergonomics of Enhancing User Performance with Color Displays," *Proceedings of the Society for Information Display*, 2, May 1985, 5.1.1–5.1.16.

Taylor, R. M., "Human Factors Aspects of Color and Monochrome Coding in Visual Displays," *IATA* Seminar, July 1977, pp. 4–17.

Von Gehr, G., "Color Takes Off," *Computer Graphics World*, 1973, p. 88.

Waller, R., P. Lefrere, and M. MacDonald-Ross, "Do You Need That Second Color?" *IEEE Transactions on Professional Communications*, PC-25 (2), June 1982, 80–85.

Ware, C. and T. C. Beatty, "Using Color to Display Structures in Multidimensional Discrete Data," *Color Research and Application*, Supplement, 11, 1986, S11–S14.

Williams, L. E., "The Effects of Target Specification on Objects Fixated during Visual Search," *Acta Psychologica*, 27, 1967, 355–360.

2

Displaying Computer Color

There is a mixture of colors whenever various colors are so divided and combined that the eye cannot distinguish these from each other, in which case the eye receives a single impression.

Chevreul

Computer Displays

Computers dynamically present display images and transfer them to static media like paper, transparencies, or 35 mm slides. A good visual interface for a computer display is critical to easily create, manipulate, recognize, and discriminate colored images. A computer display must be capable of producing the resolution and color quality that is appropriate for specific types of images and visual tasks.

Computer displays mainly differ from other imaging media in that they are interactive: The viewer can actually change the image while it is being viewed. The two principal components of a display system are the display and input devices that allow the creation and manipulation of images. Displays are thus the visual interface between a computer imaging system and a user. As such, they are a critical component in the efficiency of the system.

Displays can instantly produce and maintain images because of their ability to generate and store electrical signals in memory. The electrical signals stimulate materials at designated areas on the display surface causing them to emit or reflect light. Images are visible on displays because of the differences in luminance contrast between different areas of the screen.

Knowing the physical properties of light is useful in understanding how computer displays create color and how to use color effectively. The terms which describe the physical aspects of light are useful to describe and measure color appearance and production of computer devices.

The Physics of Light

Light Waves or Particles?

Light is a dynamic phenomenon. However, its dynamic nature is difficult to observe. This is because the physical composition of light consists of extremely small vibrating particles (called *photons*) which are too small for the eye to see. They travel in straight paths and, for a particular medium, at a constant speed. In a vacuum (like outer space), light travels at about 186,000 miles per second. The speed of light decreases and the path of light bends (refracts) as it passes through other media.

Every photon contains a certain amount of energy which relates to the frequency at which it vibrates. Photon vibration is linearly related to energy: higher energy produces faster vibration.

Most light consists of millions of photons. The behavior of masses of photons is similar to a wave in that it is cyclic (consists of a regular pattern of peaks and troughs). The distance from the beginning of one cycle to the next is called its *wavelength*. The description of light from a visual perspective is most easily understood in terms of wavelength because it best describes the stimulus to the visual system.

The Visible Spectrum

If light waves are arranged according to their length, they form the electromagnetic spectrum. Forms of energy from this spectrum include radio waves, gamma rays, X rays, microwaves, and visible light. Visible light is actually a very narrow range of this spectrum (see Figure 2.1) in which only the region between 380 to 770 nanometers is visible (1 nanometer or nm $= 10^{-9}$ meters $= 10^{-3}$ microns). In general, light below 460 nm is perceived as blue, light between 490 to 540 nm as green and that over 610 nm as red.

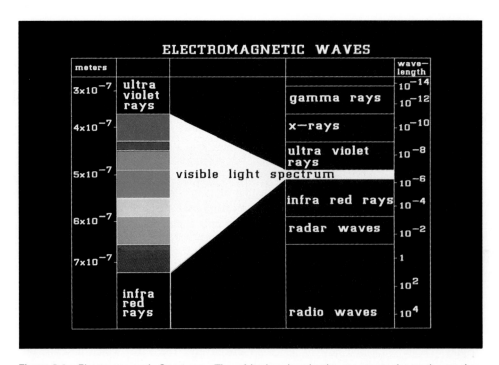

Figure 2.1 *Electromagnetic Spectrum* The white band and color spectrum shows the portion of the electromagnetic radiation that is visible. Short wavelengths are perceived as violet and blue and long wavelengths as orange and red. (*Adapted from Barnes and Noble, 1981.*)

These areas respectively define the short, medium, and long wavelength regions of the visible spectrum.

Light Properties

Light also is described by two other physical properties which can be independently varied and measured: *intensity* (the strength of light) and *purity* (the degree to which the light contains one or more wavelengths). Intensity can be described in terms of either photons or waves. In terms of photons, intensity is related to the number of photons present. In terms of wave theory, intensity describes the amplitude or height of the light wave. The perception of wavelength is hue, the perception of intensity is brightness, and the perception of purity is saturation.

Light composed of a single wavelength or a very narrow band of wavelengths (bandwidth) of the spectrum is monochromatic and, by definition, is 100 percent pure. A pure light consists of photons of identical energy. Except for lasers and other special narrowband light sources, monochromatic light is relatively uncommon. Most light we perceive has a broad bandwidth (consists of many wavelengths). For example, computer displays produce colors which are composed of many wavelengths.

LIGHT EMISSION AND REFLECTION   Objects and display devices either emit or reflect light. Most light emissive sources generate a broad range of wavelengths. Light is usually described by a graph of its spectral bandwidth, a plot of how much radiant energy is present in each wavelength. Plots like these are useful to describe the *spectral distribution* of the color components of displays like a CRT (see Figure 2.2).

Seeing light requires the ability to process photons emitted or reflected from objects. The portion of a light source (for example, the sun or an incandescent bulb) not absorbed by (or transmitted through) an object is *reflected*. In general, reflected light also consists of a continuous band of wavelengths (see Figure 2.3).

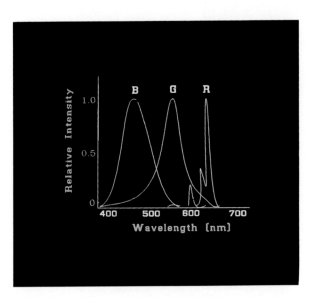

Figure 2.2 *Spectral Distribution of CRT Colors* The bandwidth of CRT colors (blue B, green G, and red R phosphors) is significantly less than the bandwidth of the visual photoreceptors (see Figure 2.5).

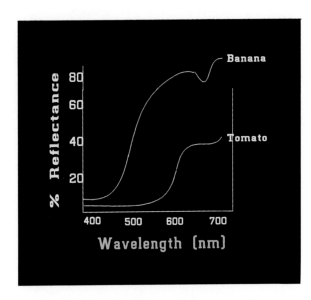

Figure 2.3 *Common Spectral Reflectances* The curves show the spectral reflectance of a tomato and a banana. The amount of perceived color is related to the position and shape of the curve. Its shade (darkness and lightness) is related to the height of the curve. (*Adapted from Wyszecki and Stiles, 1982.*)

QUANTIFYING AND REPRESENTING
LIGHT IN A DIAGRAM

Whether light is reflected or emitted, the color sensation produced can be quantitatively described. A standard means for representing color is the CIE (Commission Internationale de l'Eclairage) diagram (see Chapter 9), a graph which relates the physical energy in a light to its hue and saturation (see Figure 2.4). Hue is arranged clockwise around the horseshoe shape in this diagram. Saturation is the perceptual correlate of purity, and is represented roughly from the center of the diagram (least "pure") outwards to the edge of the diagram (most "pure"). Thus, lights that appear white will cluster near the center of the diagram, while spectrally pure lights are around the perimeter. The CIE diagram only provides a partial description of light—a measure of intensity is also necessary.

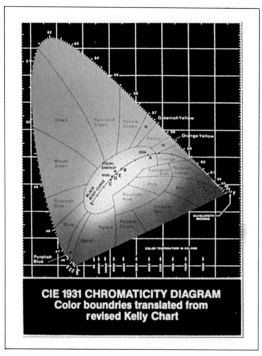

Figure 2.4 *Colors Arranged on the CIE Diagram* Arrangement of hues and saturations on a CIE diagram. (*Courtesy of Photo Research.*)

UNITS OF LIGHT Radiometric measures describe light in terms of its physical energy. For example, *radiant flux* is a measure of the energy (per unit time) generated from a light source in all directions. *Radiance* is a measure of the radiant flux emerging from a surface in a specific direction and is the appropriate measure for computer displays.

The equivalent photometric measure to radiance is *luminance*. There are two perceptual properties related to luminance: the apparent strengths of brightness and lightness. The *brightness* of a light refers to the perception of its lightness or darkness. *Lightness* describes the degree to which a light appears like white or black. A printed page varies in both brightness and lightness; an emissive display simultaneously varies both properties. Thus, increasing the intensity of a CRT color results in a lighter and brighter appearance of the color. Typical luminance units and their conversions are

(continued)

$$1 \text{ cd/m}^2 = 0.292 \text{ fL*} \quad = 0.314 \text{ mL}$$
$$1 \text{ fL} \quad = 6.426 \text{ cd/m}^2 = 1.076 \text{ mL}$$
$$1 \text{ mL} \quad = 0.929 \text{ fL} \quad = 6.183 \text{ cd/m}^2$$

Not all wavelengths are equally effective in stimulating the visual system (see Figure 2.5). People with normal vision are much more sensitive to middle wavelengths than to short and long ones. More precisely, photoreceptors need to absorb fewer photons of a middle wavelength light for detection to occur than is required for short or long wavelength lights. The photometric system of light measurement incorporates this characteristic of visual perception into its calculations.

* fL = foot lamberts, mL = millilamberts, cd = candelas

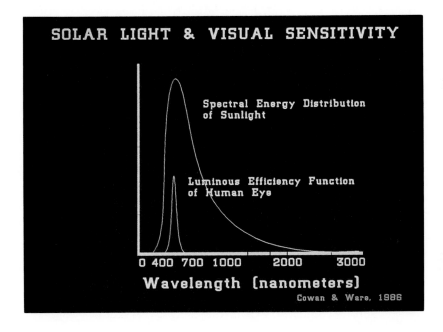

Figure 2.5 *Spectral Sensitivity* The eye is most sensitive to middle wavelengths or yellow-green. The spectral sensitivity function of the eye is shown. Also shown is the spectral energy distribution of the sun. (*Adapted from Wyszecki and Stiles, 1982.*)

Display Technologies

There are two general types of display technologies: emissive (light emitters) and nonemissive (light reflectors). An emissive display produces images by projecting light from the front surface of its screen. Images are visible through its transparent glass cover. A cathode ray tube (CRT) is a well-known example of emissive display technology. A nonemissive display produces images by reflecting ambient light from its screen. A liquid crystal display (LCD) is a common form of nonemissive technology.

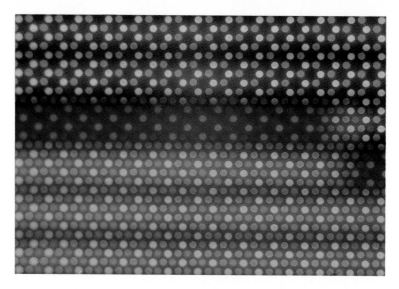

Figure 2.6 *Phosphor Triads* Magnification of a CRT screen shows the arrangement of phosphor triads in a pixel producing different colors. In the top portion of the screen, only the red and green phosphors are lit, producing yellow. In the center, only the blue phosphors are lit. In the bottom, all the pixels are lit resulting in the appearance of gray. (The faint horizontal shadows are caused by the CRT raster.) Viewing the photo at six feet causes the pixels to visually blend into colors and images. (*Courtesy of Gunnar Tonnquist.*)

Pixels and Color Production

Images produced on display screens are composites of individually lighted spots (for example, dots or rectangles). These individual picture elements (*pixels*) are not visible at typical display viewing distances (for example, 50 cm). Instead, a larger image composed of the individual pixels is apparent.

Colored areas on a display screen consist of many pixels. In a CRT, each pixel consists of a triad of phosphor colors: red, blue, and green (see Figure 2.6). The perceived color is a mixture of all the pixel colors in a small region of the screen integrated by the eye at one time.

Pixels adjusted to different light intensities create the appearance of different saturation and lightness values. Displays thus can produce all three of the perceptual components of color: hue, saturation, and lightness (see Figure 2.7).

Cathode Ray Tubes (CRTs)

The CRT is the most ubiquitous of computer display technologies. Its use has rapidly expanded from traditional office applications such as programming and text processing to computer-aided design (CAD), manufacturing (CAM), process control, and medical, environmental, and satellite imaging.

ADVANTAGES AND DISADVANTAGES   The major advantages of CRTs are

- Wide range of color and luminance levels
- High resolution
- High addressing capacity
- Ability to present static and dynamic images
- Diversity of application programs
- Superior system connectivity
- Low cost

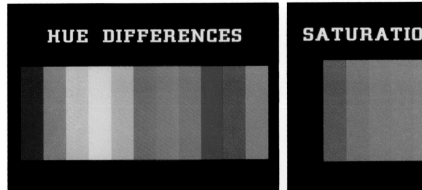

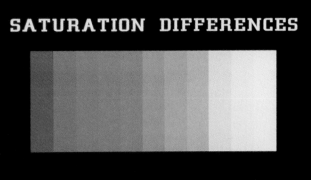

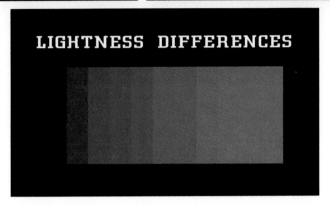

Figure 2.7 *Effect of Beam Intensities on Color Phosphors* The hues, saturations, and lightness values are the result of variations in the intensities of the electron beam on the CRT phosphors.

Their disadvantages include

- Flicker
- Glare
- Short phosphor life
- High power requirements
- Electrical and noise emissions
- Large size
- Weight

CREATING IMAGES ON A CRT   A CRT display produces an image when electrons strike the phosphorescent material lining the front interior of its tube causing them to glow and emit light. The phosphors are arranged in triads of primary colors: red, blue, and green (see Figure 2.8). The *electron beams* are aligned onto the phosphors by perforations in a metal plate called a *shadow mask*. This plate is located just behind the phosphor coating. The perforations help to create a sharp image edge and ensure that the electrons stimulate the appropriate phosphor.

ALIGNING IMAGES   The alignment of electron beams is thus a major component in the appearance, quality, and resolution of a CRT image. If the electron beam is not correctly aligned (misconverged) on the phosphor triads, it causes the appearance of color fringes or double images apparent along the edges of an image. Misconvergence is undesirable because it reduces image resolution. Convergence is important where resolution is critical. Studies have shown that under ideal conditions, misalignments as small as seven minutes of arc can be detected.

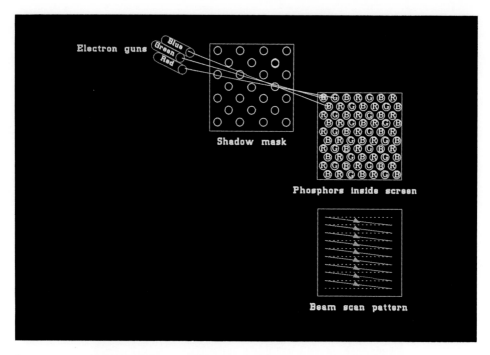

Figure 2.8 *Light Generation in a CRT Tube* Electron beams project through a metal plate (shadow mask) onto the phosphor coating on the screen and repeatedly scan horizontally from the top to bottom of the screen exciting the phosphors. Projection of the electron beams through a shadow mask (right) ensures their alignment.

The amount of misconvergence that is acceptable depends on the characteristics of the image and the technology of the electron gun convergence circuitry. In addition, it depends on the visual angle of the image, the brightness contrast of the image and the visual adaptation of the viewer (see Chapters 6, 7, and 8). The alignment of electron beams (*convergence*) is most obvious on single-pixel wide lines. Studies of single-stroke width character legibility indicate that a 1 to 1.5 minutes of arc limit is a reasonable specification for image registration. This limit applies to color displays with particle electron beam (delta gun) configurations and narrow-line display images. Recent advances in display technology and the availability of on-line convergence allow better control of convergence.

MIXING CRT COLORS Phosphor spots are individually energized by one of three electron beams and are thus selectively lighted. Illumination of all three (red, blue, and green) phosphors in a triad produces white and not lighting any of the phosphors results in black. Stimulating different combinations of the red, blue, or green phosphors in the triads produces a set of secondary colors (for example, lighting blue and green phosphors produces cyan, lighting red and green produces yellow, and lighting red and blue produces magenta). Illuminating different combinations of the three primary colors at varying intensities produces a full spectrum of colors (see Figure 2.9). Each secondary color is brighter than each primary of which it is composed because of the addition of light energy from the electron beams. CRT color mixing is thus an *additive process* (see Box).

OPTIMUM PHOSPHORS From an engineering perspective, important features of CRT phosphors that determine color quality are the phosphor's luminous efficiency, length of time it generates light (phosphor life), and color stability. From a vision science perspective, the important feature is how well the phosphor appears to represent an ideal (unique) red, green, or blue (their ability to stimulate the color sensitive mechanisms of the eye). To optimize color perception, phosphors should correspond with the *unique hues* of color perception. (A unique hue has no other hue components and is not confused

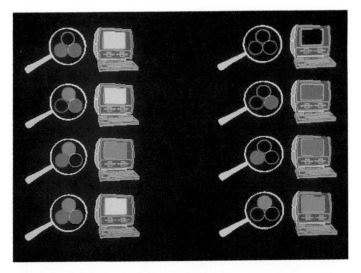

Figure 2.9 *CRT Color Mixing* Each of the small screen representations shows the color result of illuminating different combinations of phosphor triads. Eight different color values (including white and black) can be produced by three primary colors in a simple color display system. (*Courtesy of Hewlett-Packard.*)

COMBINING LIGHTS TO PRODUCE COLORS: ADDITIVE COLOR MIXTURE

Combining lights of different wavelengths produces additional colors and is described as *additive color mixture*. In this process, lights add together to produce a combined spectral distribution (see Figure 2.10).

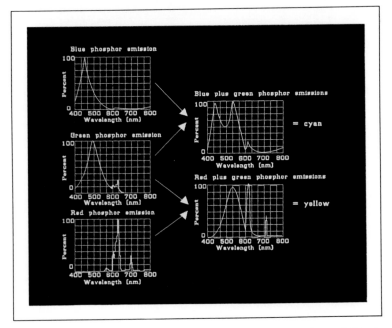

Figure 2.10 *CRT Color Additivity* Spectral distributions of primary CRT colors and two of their combinations: cyan (blue plus green) and yellow (green plus red). (*Adapted from Murch, 1984.*)

(continued)

This process can be represented by the formula

$$\phi_\lambda' = \phi_{\lambda 1} + \phi_{\lambda 2}$$

where $\phi_{\lambda 1}$ and $\phi_{\lambda 2}$ are the light distributions for the two sources and ϕ_λ' is the combined spectral distribution.

Just as the eye integrates (blends) light of small spot sources (for example, one to ten minutes of arc), it integrates the small dots of light emitting phosphors that compose images on computer screens like CRTs into one color.

with other colors (see Chapter 1). Red, green, and blue phosphors whose dominant wavelengths are 700 nm, 490 to 510 nm, and 467 to 475 nm best approximate unique red, green, and blue, respectively (see Box).

THE COLOR GAMUT OF THE CRT

The color range of a device can be observed by plotting its primaries in a CIE diagram. The color range (or gamut) of a CRT is less than that visible to the eye and forms a triangular shape when plotted on the CIE diagram (see Figure 2.11).

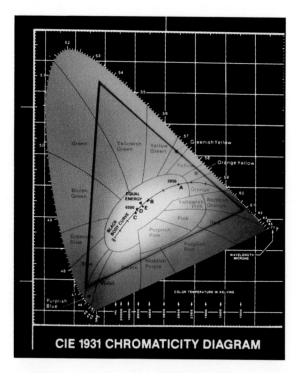

CIE 1931 CHROMATICITY DIAGRAM

Figure 2.11 *Color Gamut of a CRT* The triangle superimposed on the chromaticity diagram shows the range of color generated by a CRT compared to all visible colors. Vertices of the triangle show the chromaticity coordinates of a color display. The triangle only covers part of the diagram, demonstrating its color production limits. (*Adapted from Minolta.*)

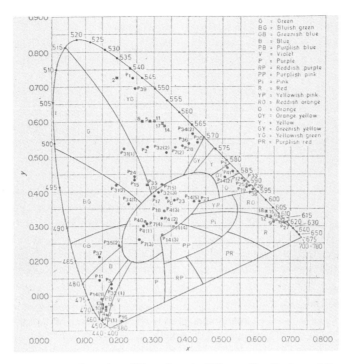

Figure 2.12 *Location of Phosphors in Different Hue Regions of the CIE Diagram* Red, green, and blue phosphors whose dominant wavelengths are 700 nm, 490–500 nm, 467–475 nm, respectively, approximate unique red, green, and blue. Most CRT phosphors are in desaturated regions of this geometric color representation (see Box). (*By permission of Butterworth Scientific Ltd., 1982.*)

However, few phosphor hues are unique (see Figure 2.12). Most green phosphors appear yellow-green rather than saturated green and even red CRT phosphors appear reddish-orange. Several blue phosphors are similar in appearance to unique blue and appear more saturated than other CRT colors. However, since the light intensity output of blue phosphors is low, they typically result in insufficient brightness contrast for good legibility or for visibility of small or fine-line blue images particularly on a black background.

VOLTAGE AND LUMINANCE CORRECTION   The luminances of the three primary CRT colors and drive voltage of the display electron guns are not linearly related (see Figure 2.13). Increasing drive voltage does not produce a linear increase in luminance or brightness perception. An engineering technique called *gamma correction* transforms the relationship between the display drive voltage and luminance into a linear function (see Box).

GAMMA CORRECTION

In general, intensity of the display light is a power function of drive voltage or

$I = \text{constant } (V)^\gamma$

The voltage necessary to obtain a particular intensity (k) is

$$V_k = \left(\frac{I_k}{\text{constant}}\right)^{1/\gamma}$$

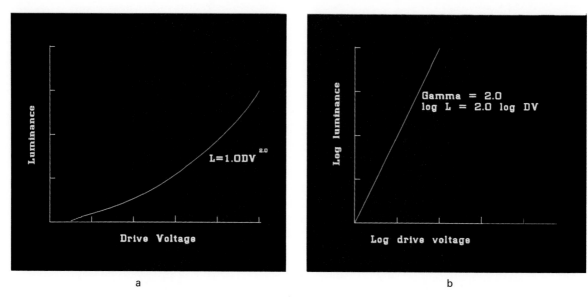

a   b

Figure 2.13 *Relationship between Luminance and Drive Voltage* a) Plot of luminance as a function of drive voltage shows their non-linear relationship. b) Plot of the same data on a log-log coordinate system linearizing their relationship.

Gamma correction is an important tool for displays requiring precise color control. The display gamma, represented on a log-log coordinate system, is the slope of its intensity to its voltage. Since the output of each electron gun has a different slope, a color produced by combining the primary colors at one voltage changes in hue appearance when combined at another voltage. Thus, white (the result of combining the red, green, and blue phosphors) generated at 17 volts may appear bluish at seven volts (see Figure 2.14).

The goal of gamma correction is to determine the degree of contrast of the display image (its gamma) and a constant for each color gun. After making photometric measurements, the calibrated values are stored in the computer system color look-up table (see Chapter 10). The corrected values can then be used for manipulating color spaces (see Chapters 9 and 10). Some color spaces (for example, CIE XYZ) require that the display

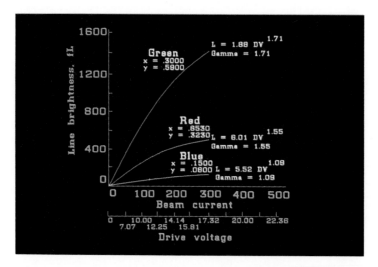

Figure 2.14 *Relationship between Drive Voltage, Beam Current, and Light Output* The same voltage applied to the three CRT guns results in different luminance values and thus different brightness values. (*Adapted from Silverstein and Merrifield, 1985.*)

be gamma corrected. In general, gamma correction is necessary for the precise color control required for realistic scene computation.

Since the gamma of displays varies, measurements should be made on each display. Moreover, since display brightness decreases over time, its gamma should be evaluated periodically.

REFRESHING CRT IMAGES   Sustaining lighted images requires continual movement of the electron beams across phosphor pixels from the top to the bottom of the screen. This movement pattern is called *raster scanning* and each line drawn by this process is called a *raster line*. The result is an electronic painting of images. If this refreshing process does not occur, the glow of the phosphors will soon decay and no longer emit light.

To create an image that appears stable, the electron beam must relight (or refresh) the individual phosphors at least 60 times each second. The frequency at which the images are relighted is called the *refresh rate*. During this process, the computer is controlling the electrical (on and off) signals to the electron beams which cause the phosphors to emit or not emit light.

PHOSPHOR DECAY AND FLICKER   When the electron beam reaches the bottom of the CRT screen, the glow of the phosphors at the top of the screen begins to fade. By the time the beam reaches the top, the phosphors at the bottom of the screen begin to lose their brightness. This is called *phosphor decay*. As the beam resweeps the screen, the phosphors are restimulated. Ideally, phosphor decay should not be visible. However, if relighting the phosphors does not occur at a sufficient rate, a flashing sensation called *flicker* occurs.

In some displays, the scan process is *interlaced*: The beams scan even and then the odd lines of phosphors 30 times each second. The refresh rate of the entire screen is thus 60 times each second. This refresh rate may also produce flicker.

Intensity and flicker.   Sensitivity to the perception of flicker depends on several hardware and visual factors (see Chapter 8). A primary hardware factor is the intensity of the electron beam. As the intensity of the luminance increases regardless of its color, flicker becomes more visible. In most color CRTs, the phosphors comprising the color triads are different intensities. Since mixing CRT color primaries makes the resultant colors brighter, primary color mixes result in more flicker perception.

GHOST IMAGES   Changing some of the hardware features of CRTs can reduce or eliminate flicker. Special long persistence phosphors are available which retain their glow longer than other phosphors. A major disadvantage of these phosphors is the trails of light (*ghost images*) that remain momentarily after the electron beam moves from the area and the phosphors begin to decay.

Solutions to flicker.   Since high brightness increases flicker perception, one solution to eliminate flicker is to lower the brightness of illuminated areas. However, reducing brightness reduces image contrast and resolution (see Chapter 8). Illuminating images also results in less flicker than illuminating the background.

The solution that best eliminates flicker but retains image quality is increasing the refresh rate. Increasing the refresh rate raises the relighting of the image to the level at which people will begin to perceive flicker. However, this is a more expensive process and requires a substantial increase in circuit complexity. Interlacing reduces flicker, but it causes the unintended perception of *jitter* (appearance of movement of lighted pixels).

ACCEPTABILITY OF CRTS   Despite all the limitations of CRTs, they are widely used and accepted. CRT phosphors produce colors that are familiar to and accepted by people with color televisions. The reason both these are acceptable is that the visual system does not match colors in an absolute manner: The eye cannot measure wavelengths or remember absolute values of colors. Thus, CRTs' lack of ability to perfectly match the colors of real objects is typically not noticed. (Colors that look the same even though they have different spectral distributions are known as *metameric* colors. They contribute to the acceptance of CRT colors.)

Flat Panel Displays (FPDs)

Despite CRTs' acceptance, their disadvantages have led to an increase in development of alternative technologies such as the *flat panel display* (FPD). As the quality and range of FPD colors improve they are beginning to compete with CRTs in computer business applications (for example, text processing and graphics). The principal difference between a standard CRT (there are also flat panel CRTs) and a typical FPD is the method of image production (Figure 2.15). As previously described, a CRT produces an image by scanning an electron beam one line at a time across the face of a phosphor-coated screen. Modulating the beam during the scan causes the phosphors to emit light at an intensity proportional to the beam current. By contrast, most FPD images are created by activating gases, or crystals, at the cross-points of horizontal and vertical electrodes. This causes light, or a modulation of reflected light, to appear at their junction. Thus, FPDs are either *active* (emitting light) or *passive* (reflecting light). As in CRTs, the activated area (pixel) creates a contrast to the surrounding area and produces an image.

FPD ADVANTAGES AND DISADVANTAGES   The primary advantages of FPDs vary with different technologies. The conventional CRT requires a comparatively long tube for the projection and deflection of the electron beam. In contrast, the horizontal (x plane) and vertical (y plane) addressing of the FPD requires very little spacing between the x and y electrodes (see Figure 2.15). The flat panel display therefore requires much less depth to produce images. In general, they are small, lightweight, portable, have high resolution, are flicker-free, and require less power consumption.

Disadvantages also vary between FPDs, but include limited range of hues and intensities, high cost, limited addressability, low contrast (luminous efficiency), and specular reflections.

There are a number of FPD technologies. Those most typically used for computer

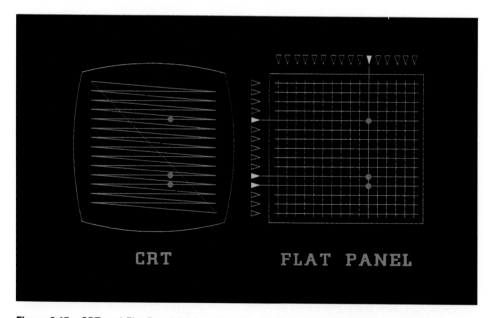

Figure 2.15 *CRT and Flat Panel Addressing* Comparison of creation of images by CRT raster scanning technique (left) and FPD direct addressing (right).

Figure 2.16 *Liquid Crystal Display* LCD colors have a more pastel (desaturated) appearance than CRT colors. (*Courtesy of Hewlett-Packard.*)

applications include liquid crystal displays (LCDs), electroluminescent displays (ELDs), plasma panels displays (PPDs), and light emitting diode displays (LEDs). (Other FPD technologies are electrochromic and electrophoretic.)

Liquid Crystal Displays (LCDs) Currently, the only flat panel technology commercially available with full color capability is the *liquid crystal display* (LCD) (see Figure 2.16). Until recently, its primary use has been for watches, calculators, and miniature televisions.

LCD image and color production. Liquid crystals are similar to fluids but, over certain temperature ranges, exhibit optical characteristics similar to crystals. LCDs operate in a similar fashion to shutters: They either dynamically scatter or reflect light or they pass or block light. An LCD creates an image when an electric field is applied across a material having both liquid and crystalline properties. LCDs polarize light which passes through crystal cells. The cells are sandwiched between a reflecting surface and a polarizing filter so that only ambient light falling on the front of the display is modulated by the polarization of the cell.

In more common types of LCDs, the molecules of the crystals change alignment when charged by an electric field and change the cell's optical properties. When a field is generated, the liquid becomes transparent and reflects light. When the electric field is not present, the liquid becomes stabilized and the crystal becomes transparent, eliminating its ability to reflect light. Color is obtained by adding dyes to the liquid crystal material or by using fixed filter arrays. Since LCDs only modulate reflected light, the brightness of the colors of images and their background depends on the amount of incident light falling on its screen surface.

LCD limitations. LCDs have some unresolved technical problems that can negatively affect color quality and recognition. One is the *specular* (or mirror like) *reflections* visible from the front glass surface. Any bright sources of light (emitted or reflected in the environment) within the range of the screen surface can be reflected. The reflections not only compete visually with images generated by the LCD but can reduce their apparent contrast. These reflections also reduce the saturated appearance of colors. Since LCD colors typically have a desaturated appearance, further reduction of saturation due to reflections significantly affects perceived color quality. Thus, although high ambient illumination enhances image contrast on an LCD, it reduces color appearance.

In addition, off-axis viewing of images and colors on an LCD is limited. The images may thus be difficult to see unless the screen is perpendicular to the line of sight. This severely reduces the viewer's ability to identify and discriminate colors when the screen is moved away from this position. Recent advances in color LCDs reduce both these problems.

ELECTROLUMINESCENT DISPLAYS (ELDs)

ELD image production.   Images are created on an electroluminescent display by applying an electric field across a thin layer (film) of a polycrystalline phosphor (or zinc-sulfide). This stimulates the phosphor and causes it to emit light.

Adding impurities to the zinc sulfide produces colors. Also, superimposing transparent film layers produces thin film ELDs available in a wide range of colors. Colors are due to single or blended phosphor characteristics and phosphors with photoluminescent dyes or overlays.

ELD advantages and disadvantages.   One of the advantages of an ELD compared to a CRT is that color appearance does not change when its voltage is reduced. However, some color shift occurs at different frequencies. Also, unlike CRTs, color production does not reduce image resolution (see Figure 2.17). A major disadvantage of ELDs is their high power consumption. In general, ELDs are most appropriate for low ambient conditions and backlit panel graphics.

PLASMA PANEL DISPLAYS (PPDs)

PPD image and color production.   Plasma panel displays create a lighted image when an electric field is applied to two active electrodes which, when they reach a specific voltage level, causes a gas (neon) located at their junction to ionize and emit light. The neon continues to emit light until another electrical field is applied. The process is similar to that which causes the aurora borealis, or northern lights.

Almost all plasma panel displays currently in use for computer applications are orange (see Figure 2.18). Using different gas mixtures to excite different colored phosphors contained in the pixel cells produces different colors. Significantly altering voltage and using different filter enhancements can produce colors like red and brown.

PPD advantages and disadvantages.   Plasma panels have a high addressing capability and are thus useful for office applications like presentation graphics and text processing. However, they have high power requirements.

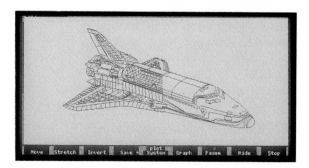 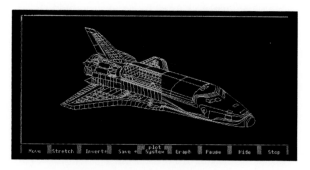

Figure 2.17 *Electroluminescent Displays*   The yellow ELDs show their high resolution in both positive and negative video. The jagged appearance of the diagonal elements of the images is almost invisible. (*Courtesy of Hewlett-Packard.*)

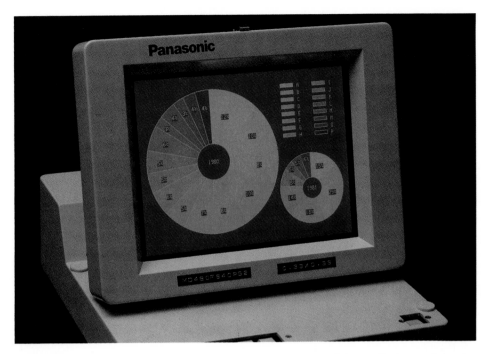

Figure 2.18 *Plasma Panel Display* The sixteen gray scale state-of-the-art display produces the appearance of 16 lightness shades. (*Courtesy of Panasonic Matsushita.*)

Light Emitting Diode Displays (LEDs)

LED image and color production. A LED is a semiconductor device consisting of a single crystal that emits light when stimulated by an electrical current. Most LEDs have low power requirements, high efficiency and high reliability. Although LEDs are available in many colors (see Figure 2.19), blue LEDs are not commonly used for computer displays because they have high power requirements, low efficiency, and poor visibility in high ambient light levels. Although the exclusion of blue limits full color production, combining red, yellow, and green LEDs can produce different colors (for example, brown and orange).

Figure 2.19 *Light Emitting Diode Displays* Individual LEDs can be combined to produce area-fill images. Many LEDs are not visible in high illumination like sunlight. (*Courtesy of Hewlett-Packard.*)

Display Technologies

There are two types of flat panel LEDs. One is a hybrid type, which is used in large screen displays; the LED chips are arranged in a matrix on a ceramic substrate. The other is a monolithic type used in miniature display screens in which chips are arranged in a matrix on a crystal substrate.

LED advantages and disadvantages. Because they appear to be more saturated than other display colors, LEDs should be able to produce faster visual responses. Theoretically, this should be possible because the eye responds most quickly to saturated colors (for example, narrow spectral bandwidths). LEDs produce the most narrow bandwidth of all display lights.

The low luminous efficiency of LEDs is a major disadvantage. LED displays require more power than other display light sources to produce the same light output. In addition, the high power requirements seriously limit their use for high resolution displays.

Ratings of the characteristics that affect color production and appearance for different display technologies are shown in Table 2.1.

Interactive Devices to Control Color

The color on displays is controlled by both hardware and software (see Chapter 10). However, the most common method for color selection and alteration or drawing is by an input device. Typically, a user moves the device while watching the resulting movements of a *cursor* or tracking symbol on the display screen.

The input device allows the user to specify a horizontal and vertical (x,y) screen location and to select an object or command on the screen. The resulting screen appearance depends on the interpretation of the activity by the application program. For example, an input signal could cause the system to draw a line, select a menu item, or invoke a command.

The most common input devices are keyboards, mice, light pens, digitizing tablets, thumbwheels, and trackballs. Keyboards are usually sufficient for creation of simple graphics. In general, creations and manipulations of complex color images (like engineering drawings) require more specialized interactive devices like a mouse or a digitizing tablet.

The speed and accuracy of color selection and manipulation are highly dependent on the appropriateness of the interactive device for a specific task.

TABLE 2.1

Ratings of Display Characteristics That Can Affect Color Perception

	CRT	LCD	ELD	PPD	LED
All Colors	good	good	fair	fair	good
Color Quality	good	poor	fair	poor	fair
Purity	fair	poor	good	good	good
Brightness	good	fair*	good	fair	good
Gray Scale Levels	good	fair	poor	fair	good
Power Consumption /Energy Emissions	fair	good	fair	poor	good
Resolution	good	fair	good	good	good
Contrast	good	poor	good	good	fair
Flicker	poor	good	fair	good	good
Glare/Reflections**	poor	poor	poor	poor	good
Viewing Range	good	poor	good	fair	good
Size	poor	good	good	fair	good
Weight	poor	good	good	fair	good

* Depends on ambient illumination
** Untreated screen

Figure 2.20 *Keyboard* The four cursor keys marked with arrows (up, down, left, and right) control the cursor's vertical and horizontal movements. Continuous depression results in continued movement of the cursor. (*Courtesy of Hewlett-Packard.*)

Keyboards

Keyboards are less convenient than other input devices for manipulation of display color. The keyboard allows a user to type information which is then displayed on the screen. Function keys used for specific commands reduce the number of keystrokes required for a command. Keyboards do not allow easy pointing or drawing. For example, moving a cursor to a specific color on a screen requires more time with a keyboard than with a mouse or stylus. Most keyboards have control keys which allow the user to move the screen cursor in an x or y direction (see Figure 2.20).

However, since the cursor control keys are integrated into the alphanumeric keyboard (usually the right side), it does not require much extra tabletop space.

Keyboards that can record continued depression of a key are similar to a continuous positioning control of vertical or horizontal movements. The continued depression of the keys, converting the keyboard into a continuous control, allows color values to be easily scaled. The numeric keys can define the values of a specific color, which is a major advantage for color control.

Mice

A *mouse* is a rectangular or round device (see Figure 2.21) that fits under the hand and contains a potentiometer. Its movement controls the location of the screen cursor. Moving the cursor to a specific color on the screen and depressing one of the buttons on the top or front of the mouse can cause the color to be selected for manipulation. The mouse can be used for discrete or continuous color selection by depressing its buttons or by moving the cursor across a color palette. For example, depressing one of the buttons can vary the values (hue, saturation, or brightness) of colors.

Because it fits under a user's hand, and can be used by either hand, a mouse permits easy and efficient selection and manipulation of display color. However, use of a mouse does require more tabletop space than does a keyboard.

Figure 2.21 *Mouse* The rounded shape of the top of the mouse fits easily into the palm of the hand and allows easy use and reach of the control buttons. (*Courtesy of Hewlett-Packard.*)

Digitizing Tablet-Pen/Stylus Systems and Pucks

A *digitizing tablet* resembles a small drafting board. It is useful for drawing or tracing images on its surface, and is mainly used for the creation and manipulation of color images for CAD/CAM applications. A tablet is most like traditional forms of drawing. To review the correctness of the drawing, however, it must be previewed on the screen. A tablet requires more workspace than other devices and is more expensive than other input devices. It provides an interaction with the cursor and images on the computer screen by a specially designed *pen stylus* or a *puck* (see Figure 2.22).

Styluses are generally pen shaped and pucks are similar in appearance to mice. Both send electronic signals to the display via the tablet. A software program converts the movements of the stylus to electronic signals which control the images on the screen. Pushing down on the microswitch located in the stylus tip or the buttons on the puck

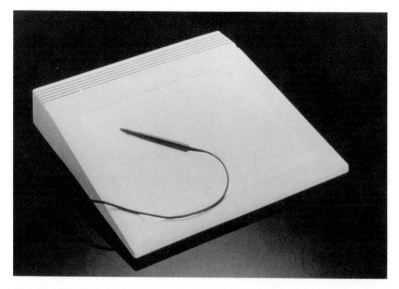

Figure 2.22 *Tablet and Stylus* The stylus controls the movements of the cursor on the screen. Images can be drawn on the tablet and simultaneously viewed on the display. (*Courtesy of Hewlett-Packard.*)

activates commands. The location and thus movements of the cursor on the screen relate directly to the location and movements of the stylus or puck on the tablet. There are few functional differences between the ability to select items from the screen with a puck or a stylus system. The major advantages of a stylus are its functional familiarity (which is similar to a pen), comfortable shape, size, and ease and accuracy of manipulation and control.

Buttons are integrated into pucks which send input signals interpreted by the application software. Common interpretations are

- Item selection of a function shown on a template overlay on the tablet
- Selection of a screen object in the applications database
- Specification of an x,y position for digitizing

Thumbwheels

A thumbwheel is a dial which, when rotated, controls a potentiometer that controls the position of the cursor on the screen. A thumbwheel is a one-dimensional continuous positioning device. Two thumbwheels are necessary to control the vertical and horizontal positions of the cursor. In addition, a key called a pick, located close to the wheel, is necessary for selecting images on the screen or confirming x,y locations of the cursor or sending a command.

Manipulating images and color by a thumbwheel is similar to a mouse and tablet stylus in that it is a two-step operation: one step to move the cursor via the wheel and a second step to make a selection via the pick. Thumbwheels are more efficient for creating continuous color changes because their mechanics optimize continuous actions. They also require less precise hand movement to control horizontal and vertical (x and y) cursor movements.

Thumbwheels are often integrated into the keyboard and therefore do not require extra space on the work surface. They are typically located on the right side of the keyboard and are thus inconvenient for left-handed users.

Trackballs

A trackball (see Figure 2.23) is similar in operation to a thumbwheel but rotates in any direction to control the position of a screen cursor. It only requires manipulation of one physical device for drawing and movement. The trackball shares the disadvantage of

Figure 2.23 *Trackball* The trackball allows unrestricted placement of the cursor on the screen. Its location allows easy access to the fingers. (*Courtesy of Hewlett-Packard.*)

TABLE 2.2

Input Device Color Usability Comparison

Feature	Mouse	Tablet	Thumbwheel	Keyboard	Trackball
Discrete color selection	X	X		X	
Continuous color selection	X	X	X	X	X
Drawing ability	X	X			
Tracing ability		X			
Good for simple graphics (such as pie charts)	X	X	X	X	X
Good for complicated graphics (such as integrated circuit designs)	X	X			
Requires extra work surface	X	X			X
Accuracy	X	X	X	X	X
Right or left hand use	X	X			X
Fast pointing speed	X	X			X

the mouse and thumbwheel in that it requires a button, or pick, to signal selection of a screen item or position.

Input devices which best accommodate requirements for selecting and manipulating color are listed in Table 2.2.

Useful Facts

Display Image Production	Displays produce images by emitting or reflecting light.
CRT Image Production	Images are produced on the CRT when an electron beam strikes spots of phosphorescent material coating the screen causing them to emit light.
Image Composition	Pixels are the smallest spot that can be illuminated on a screen and compose a display image.
Brightness and Saturation	A change in brightness usually changes saturation appearance.
Color Disadvantages of CRTs	Color resolution and light generation are not optimized.
Beam Alignment	If the electron beams are misaligned, color fringes can result.
Flicker	The relighting of the phosphors causes the perception of flicker if its frequency is insufficient.
	The perception of flicker increases with brightness.
	Reducing flicker can be accomplished by a number of methods including decreasing the illumination of the screen images or background, using long persistence phosphors, or increasing the refresh rate.

Color Range of CRT	The range of colors generated by a display is less than that visible.
CRT Color Mixing	Simultaneously illuminating different pixels results in increased brightness (additive color mixing).
Increasing the Number of CRT Colors	Although CRTs generate three primary colors, the number of colors can be increased by varying the number and proportions of the primaries that are energized and the intensities of the electron beams.
Advantages of FPDs	Flat panel displays provide a technology that offers some advantages not available with CRTs: better resolution and they are smaller, lighter, and therefore more portable. Flat panels providing colors are LCDs, ELDs, PPDs, and LEDs.
Flat Panel Displays	The most common FPDs are LCDs, ELDs, PPDs, and LEDs. Currently, LCDs have the largest color range but have problems producing and maintaining a saturated color appearance.
Manipulating Color	Interactive devices like mice, tablets, thumbwheels, or keyboards manipulate color on a display screen.
Appropriate Input Devices	The most appropriate interactive device for manipulating color depends on the application.
Fastest Input Devices	Mice and tablets are the fastest devices for color selection and manipulation.

REFERENCES

Allen, D., "Flat Panels: Beyond the CRT," *Computer Graphics World*, February 1986, pp. 21–24.

"Display Devices for Developing New Markets and High Value-added Products," *JEE*, September 1986, pp. 28–31.

"Display Devices Moving Toward Multicolors and Large Size," *JEE*, September 1986, pp. 78–114.

Foley, J. D. and A. Van Dam. *Fundamentals of Interactive Computer Graphics* (Menlo Park, CA: Addison-Wesley Pub., 1982).

Godman, A. *Barnes & Noble Thesaurus of Science* (New York: Barnes & Noble Books, 1981).

Goede, W. F., "Display Technology Overview," *SID*, 1986, pp. 2.1-2–2.1-24.

Human Factors Consideration for the Use of Colour in Display Systems, Snodd Scientific and Technical Reports, Jan. 1975, #NAST-TN X-72196, T.R., 1986.

Judd, D. B. and G. Wyszecki. *Color in Business, Science and Industry* (New York: John Wiley and Sons, 1975).

Kinney, J. S., "Brightness of Colored Self-luminous Displays," *Color Research and Application*, 8(2), 1983, 82–89.

Laycock, J., "Selected Colours for Use on Colour Cathode Ray Tubes," *Displays*, 1984, pp. 3–14.

Meyer, F., "Picture Brightness for Flat-panel Displays," *High Technology*, March/April 1982, pp. 33–40.

Murch, G., "Effective Use of Color: Cognitive Principles," *TEKniques*, 8(2), 1984, 25–31.

Murch, G., M. Cranford, and P. McManus, "Brightness and Color Contrast of Information Displays," *Society of Information Display*, 14, 1983, 186–189.

Nassau, K. *Color* (New York: John Wiley and Sons, 1982).

Niina, T., "Extended Applications of the LED with the Development of High Brightness Technology," *JEE*, September 1986, pp. 43–46.

Schanda, J., "On the Evaluation of Display Brightness" (Budapest, Hungary: Research Institute for Technical Physics, Hungarian Academy of Sciences, 1984).

Schmidt, V. P., *A Selective Review of Relevant Aspects of Colour Perception for the Application of Colour to Displays*. Royal Aircraft Establishment Technical Memorandum FS 114, Farnborough, Hants, 1977.

Sherr, S. *Display System Design* (New York: Wiley-Interscience, 1970).

Silverstein, L. D. and R. M. Merrifield, "The Development and Evaluation of Color Systems for Airborn Applications," U.S. Dept. of Transportation, FAA, Patusent River, MD, 1985.

Snyder, H. S., *Human Visual Performance and Flat Panel Display Image Quality*, Virginia Polytechnic Institute, HFL—80-1/ONR-80-1, July 1980.

Tannus. *Flat Panel Displays and CRTs* (New York: Van Nostrand, 1985).

Wyszecki, G. and W. S. Stiles. *Color Science*, 2nd ed. (New York: Wiley and Sons, 1982).

3

Transferring Color to Hard Copy

Merely think, here is a little square of blue, here an oblong of pink, here a streak of yellow, and paint it just as it looks to you, the exact color and shape until it gives . . . [the] impression of the scene before you.

Claude Monet

Soft Copy to Hard Copy

Creating effective color images is not easy. It is necessary to know the factors that affect color perception, the colors that are most appropriate for particular applications, and the limitations of the hardware. Transferring images between different display technologies and from displays to hard copy media further complicates this task. An understanding of hard copy color production is useful for control and prediction of the appearance of colored images reproduced from displays (see Figure 3.1).

Figure 3.1 *Hard Copy Technologies* The color images created on an interactive display are being transferred to hard copy media. (*Courtesy of Hewlett-Packard.*)

The computer devices that transfer display color onto hard copy media include plotters, printers, and camera systems. Plotters transfer display images to paper and plastic transparencies, printers transfer images to paper, and camera systems transfer images to 35 mm slides and instant prints. Their particular technologies and the characteristics of their output media affect color appearance in different ways.

Differences in soft copy and hard copy technologies and the way their media generate light (emission or reflection) cause the same color values to look different. Exact color reproduction requires a hardcopy device with a range of colors, lightness controls, and color mixture capabilities matching those of a display. However, hardcopy devices do not have the same color-producing technologies and light-mixing processes as displays (see Box). Even if they did have identical color production capabilities, colors on media like transparencies and slides change their appearance during projection. In addition, ambient light and magnification of the image affect the appearance of color. The closest match between display and hard copy color is on 35 mm color slides produced by computer-controlled camera systems like film recorders.

MIXING HARD COPY COLOR INKS

Color paints and dyes mix according to the principles of subtractive color mixture: Mixing them produces a color which reflects less light and a darker color than the original (primary) colors. This process is similar to passing light through a colored filter (see Figure 3.2). The pigments in a colored ink act like small filters, trapping (or absorbing) some wavelengths and reflecting others. Thus, an ink surface appears yellow if its pigments absorb short (for example, blue) wavelengths and reflect the remaining colors of the spectrum (for example, green and red). An ink will appear

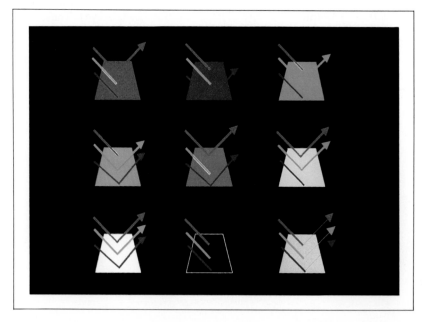

Figure 3.2 *The Principle of Subtractive Light Mixture* Nine color samples of paint or ink pigments are shown. Rays entering to the left represent the red, blue, and green components of a white light impinging on the sample. Rays exiting to the right represent the RGB components not absorbed or transmitted and hence are reflected into the viewer's eyes. (*Adapted from Osborne, 1980.*)

(continued)

black if all the wavelengths of a source light are absorbed by it. Thus, combining red and green inks produces dark yellow or brown; red, green, and blue inks combine to produce black because all wavelengths are effectively subtracted from the incident light.

Many inks and dyes can produce unpredictable results due to their dye concentration, light scattering properties, and surface absorption. Unlike additive mixture, the mathematical laws of subtractive mixture are complex. Artists' techniques of color ink mixing (for example, mixing yellow with blue to create green) are predictable because their pigments are specially selected. Manufacturers of hard copy devices select inks and dyes that minimize the loss of lightness and saturation to produce high reliability in their color reproduction process.

Matching Color Hard Copy to Display Colors

Regardless of whether color is created with additive or subtractive light mixture, its appearance depends upon the light entering the viewer's eyes. The differences in the range of brightness values produced by soft copy and hard copy technologies will cause colors to appear different even though the wavelengths may be measurably equal and the hues perceptually identical (see Figure 3.3). Thus, a bright green on a display will appear brighter than the same hue value plotted onto paper because more light is entering the viewer's eyes from the display.

In addition to the difficulty in matching hues, it is also difficult to match the saturations between display and hard copy. Mixing hard copy inks not only results in less light being reflected than emitted from the display, but it also results in less purity. This occurs because a broader spectrum is being reflected into the viewer's eyes. Thus, subtractive color mixing puts an upper bound on the purity and, hence, the saturation of hard copy primary colors.

a b

Figure 3.3 *Appearance of Display and Hard Copy Color* Photographs of display and hard copy demonstrate the recent advances in transfer fidelity possible between these devices. (*Courtesy of Fuji Film, USA.*)

Pen Plotters

The plotter was the first computer hard copy device to reproduce display images in color. The plotter most similar to manual writing or drawing is the *pen plotter*. It draws images by mechanically moving pens across paper or a plastic sheet called a transparency (see Figure 3.4). In one type of plotting technique, a carriage selects a pen from a carousel, presses it onto the media, and moves in a lateral direction drawing lines or dots.

There are two methods of paper input to plotters: flatbed and drum (see Figure 3.5). Both can move paper along a perpendicular axis to the movement of the pen carriage. With a *flatbed plotter*, the pen carriage moves in one of two directions (x or y) and the paper is moved along the y axis. With a *drum plotter*, the pen carriage moves in the x direction and a rotating drum moves the paper in a y direction. Flatbed plotters create images on single sheets of paper or transparencies. Drum plotters hold a continuous paper roll producing drawings of any length. Business graphics are typically created on flatbed plotters; and most engineering drawings are created on drum plotters.

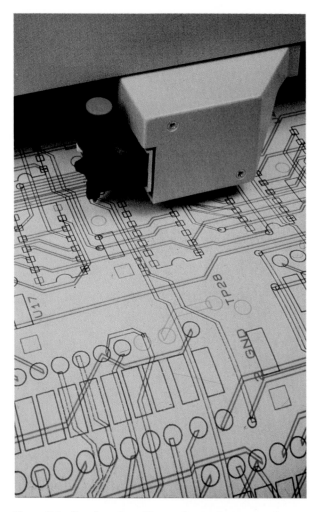

Figure 3.4 *Pen Drawing* The carriage selects a pen from a carousel, mechanically lowers it onto the paper, and moves in a lateral direction. The paper moves orthogonally to the lateral movement of the carriage.
(*Courtesy of Hewlett-Packard.*)

Figure 3.5 *Pen Plotters and Plotting* The drum plotter (back) draws on rolled paper producing large-size engineering drawings. The flatbed plotters (foreground) draw on single sheets which move across a flat surface. (*Courtesy of Hewlett-Packard.*)

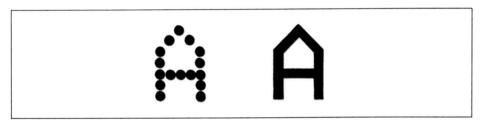

Figure 3.6 *Raster versus Vector Imaging* The "A" (left) is a result of a raster drawing device that creates images by dot formations. The "A" on the right is a result of a vector drawing. These images are compositions of consecutive straight lines or vectors. (*Courtesy of Hewlett-Packard.*)

Image Production

Plotters create images by using pens to draw lines, or *vectors* (see Figure 3.6), and are thus known as vector-driven devices. One of the primary advantages of creating color images with vectors instead of raster technologies is that the edges of vector images are sharper and thus have better resolution than the series of dots of the raster method.

Plotter Advantages and Disadvantages

Pen plotters have many advantages over other hard copy technologies. The major advantage is the ability to create high quality overhead transparencies and the ability to plot on a wide range of media sizes (from standard paper to engineering D size drawings). Moreover, plotter inks produce highly saturated colors. The major disadvantage of pen plotters is the plotting time required for area-fill graphics. (Since plotters are vector-driven devices, area-fills must be made with many adjacent vectors.)

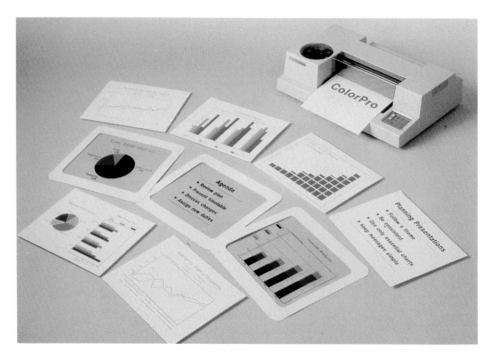

Figure 3.7 *Color Appearance on Plotting Media* Plotters draw color images on plastic transparencies and paper. Large block graphics preserve saturation appearance from the desaturating effects of light projection through transparencies. (*Courtesy of Hewlett-Packard.*)

Plotter Pens

Plotter pens may be *fibertip*, *ball-point* or *liquid ink* type. Fibertip pens are used for both paper and transparencies; ball-point pens are best for paper; liquid ink pens are appropriate for either transparencies or paper. Pens are available in a number of colors and line widths. For plotting colored text with good visibility, color recognition, and legibility, fine lines are best for paper, and thick lines are best for transparencies (see Figure 3.7).

Inks

Plotter pens use either water or solvent base inks. Solvent-based inks are used in liquid ink and roller ball pens. Solvent-based inks adhere to plastic surfaces and thus do not absorb into a medium. If used on paper, solvent-based color images may appear darker than colors of water-based inks. Water-based inks are used for plotting images onto both paper and transparencies; they partially absorb into these media. Applying an ink to a medium for which it was not designed causes a change in its appearance. In addition, it may not dry properly.

Plotter inks are available in several colors (see Figure 3.8). The visibility and discrimination of the colors depends on the media onto which they are transferred, the size of the area-fill, and the image.

Paper and Plotter Color Appearance

Saturated appearance of plotter inks depends on the types of inks used and media. For example, most plotter inks have a more highly saturated appearance on glossy paper than on standard bond paper (see Figure 3.9). This is because the gloss (caused by a clay

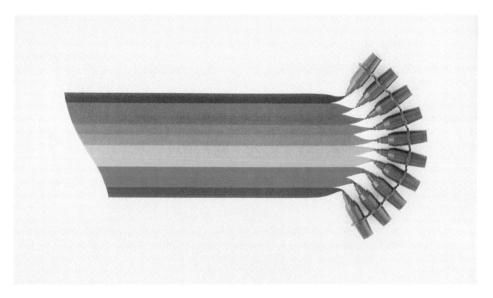

Figure 3.8 *Plotter Ink Color Palette* Ink colors of different plotter pens. (*Courtesy of Hewlett-Packard.*)

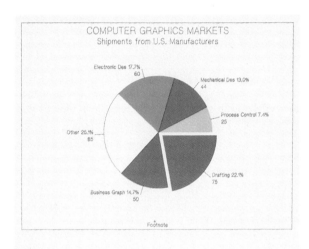

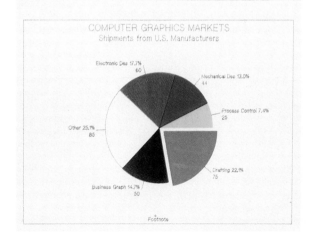

Figure 3.9 *Plotter Ink Appearance on Different Types of Paper* The ink on the standard bond paper (top) is desaturated and has printed through the paper; the ink on the glossy paper (bottom) appears more saturated. (*Courtesy of Hewlett-Packard.*)

coating) produces a very white surface with *specular* (rather than *diffuse*) reflections. In addition, the coating of glossy paper retains the dye of the ink near the surface instead of allowing it to absorb. Both the surface coating of the paper and the ink thus affect saturation. Use of standard bond paper will result in a less saturated appearance because some of the ink absorbs into the paper and reflects less light. Also, the ink can penetrate through the paper (print through) which further reduces saturation. Using paper specially designed for a particular ink optimizes color quality and image resolution.

Evaluating Color Match

Plotter pen colors are now available that more closely match colors produced by a display. However, it is easier to match the colors on a display to inks. Colors like yellow that have good visibility on a dark background display have less contrast, and hence visibility, on paper. Adjusting the display background to white helps to evaluate the degree of color match because it shows more closely how the colors will appear on paper.

The colors of plotter inks often need to be discriminated at different distances—particularly on transparencies which are often viewed at far distances such as in lecture halls.

Projection and Viewing Distance

The projection of light through hard copy media like plotter transparencies (or 35 mm slides) also affects the appearance of ink saturation. The higher the intensity of the light, the greater the reduction in saturation. Lighter colors such as yellow and green are particularly vulnerable to this effect. In addition, discrimination of similar hues such as orange and red or blue and green can be difficult, especially when the images are fine-lines or small shapes (see Chapters 7 and 11).

Desaturation effects become even more apparent as viewing distance increases because as the apparent size of the image decreases colors become more difficult to identify and discriminate. Viewing alphanumeric characters or fine-line images on transparencies from distances farther than 60 cm often results in poor visibility of desaturated colors like cyan, yellow, and green. Even with area-fill images, such as pie and bar charts, discrimination of saturated colors like blue, red, and brown may be difficult (see Figure 3.10). Area-fill graphics on transparencies should be relatively large, and fonts should be bold type to ensure color discrimination, particularly for far viewing distances.

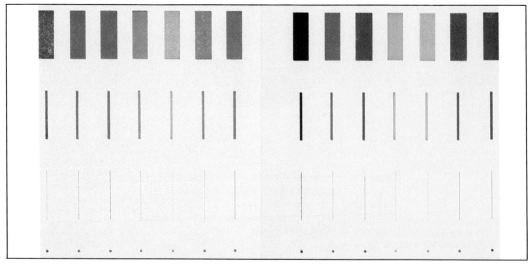

Figure 3.10 *Visibility of Plotter Colors* The plotter inks appear less saturated on the transparency (left) than on the paper (right). Plotter colors of the larger areas (thick lines and rectangles) are easier to see than the dots and thin lines.

Printers

Color printers are another way of transferring color screen images onto paper. Unlike plotters, but similar to CRTs, printers use a raster technology to transpose images to paper. In one type of printer technology, a printhead moves in a left-to-right direction and transfers images to paper by depositing one or more ink spots on the paper with each pass. The resulting images are dots deposited in an array of rows and columns. In some printers, the printhead is stationary and prints lines the width of a page. The paper advances and the process repeats until it completes an image. Another type of print technology uses a laser beam to transfer images to paper.

Elements of Printing Color: Deposition, Paper, and Ink

PRINT DEPOSITION The technique of depositing ink (or *toner* in laser printers) on paper determines the number of colors. The simplest printing technique, *dot-on-dot* or *binary printing*, produces images by the presence or absence of dots. Binary color printers superimpose three inks (for example, cyan, magenta, and yellow) to produce additional colors. The resulting colors depend upon the order of dot deposit. The combination of all three primaries produces black, but can cause excessive ink deposit. To solve this problem, some printers have a separate black ink. Thus, some printers use four inks (three primary colors and black) instead of three to produce colors.

PAPER AND PRINTER COLOR QUALITY Special paper that has a smooth, glossy surface best replicates the appearance and saturation of colors on CRT displays because it reduces diffuse reflections of incident light that desaturate colors (see Box). In addition, glossy white paper allows a wider range of printer color because its high light reflections optimize the range of brightness values. The reflective properties of glossy paper are especially important for some printing technologies (for example, dot-matrix and ink-jet ink) which do not produce highly reflective colors. The gamut of color produced by the printer is thus effectively increased by this type of paper.

IMPROVING COLOR APPEARANCE WITH GLOSSY PAPER

High quality magazines and art books are printed on smooth, glossy paper. The gloss produces a very white surface with specular (rather than diffuse) reflections. In specular reflection, the light reflected is highly directional. Rough surfaces induce diffuse reflection in which the reflected light rays from a given area contain wavelength components from adjacent areas. This scattering dilutes the color from any given spot.

In addition, the coating of glossy paper retains the dye of the ink near the surface instead of absorbing it. This allows the colored ink (and not the white paper) to make a greater contribution to the wavelengths in the reflected light.

Glossy paper improves both printer and plotter colors. Laminating materials for presentation graphics or placing them in a glossy plastic folder will improve their appearance.

Some printers can produce relatively good quality colors on standard paper stock. However, since paper surfaces vary in smoothness and whiteness, using plain paper stocks for printing produces highly variable results. Plain paper stock is best for applications where the color fidelity is not critical. If this type of paper is not available, laminating a plastic film to the paper or placing it in a clear plastic folder produces a glossy appearance. The color saturation appears significantly better because light diffusion of the rough surface of the newsprint is eliminated by the smooth, reflective surface of the glass or plastic.

PRINT QUALITY   The best hard copy color raster printing is comparable to the high quality of color photography and lithography. In fact, a high-resolution, halftone raster print on smooth, glossy paper is almost indistinguishable from a color photograph or commercial lithography such as those found in *National Geographic Magazine*.

One of the limitations of different printing technologies is the restriction of the types of color materials used in inks and toners. Another limitation is the range of colors available. In addition, the ink mixtures that produce black (for example, cyan, magenta, and yellow dots) do not usually balance well and cause it to appear like purple or brown. Also, if ink dots fail to overlap properly, color fringing may occur at the edges of images. This is particularly apparent in thin lines and text. If the spread of ink causes the dot size to increase when three basic colors combine in one pixel, the small open areas in characters like ''a,'' ''e,'' ''m,'' and ''w'' will appear closed. This causes the letters to lose their distinguishing characteristics and reduces legibility. Printers which have the capability to deposit black ink in addition to cyan, magenta, and yellow avoid these problems and produce high quality black images. In addition, single-pass printing increases print speed and reduces the amount of color inks consumed.

The quality of print color also depends on the technique of ink (or toner) deposit. The two basic techniques of ink deposit are impact and nonimpact printing.

Impact Printers

PRINTING TECHNOLOGIES   Impact printers are similar to typewriters in that they use hammers with an embossed surface to press a character stamp through an inked ribbon onto paper. Like an electronic typewriter, the hammer of an impact printer is electro-mechanically driven.

Other impact printers use a flat hammer located behind the paper to press the paper and ribbon together against a moving drum or band containing embossed characters. The hammer strikes the paper when the desired character stamp moves into position.

The number of separate color ribbons or color bands on a single ribbon determines the number of colors producible by an impact printer. Three- or four-color ribbons are commercially available. The quality of the strike and the resulting resolution of the printed image is generally independent of paper because of the number and the speed of the printhead passes which combine ink.

ADVANTAGES AND DISADVANTAGES   There are a number of advantages of impact printers. These include the ability to use common paper stocks without special coatings that have either a smooth or raised fiber surface.

Although *impact printers* have existed longer than other technologies that transfer display images onto paper, they have only recently been able to produce these images in color. However, the quality (resolution, color, and print speed) of impact printers is inferior to other technologies.

Nonimpact Printers

Nonimpact printers do not use mechanical components to create images on paper. They produce fast, high quality color hard copy and include ink-jet, thermal transfer, electrostatic, and electrophotographic technologies.

INK-JET PRINTING   The most common form of nonimpact computer color printing is ink-jet technology of which there are two types (see Box). An ink-jet printer forms pixels with droplets of liquid ink that are ejected at high velocity from a printhead onto paper (see Figure 3.11). The printhead does not touch the paper as in other technologies (such as thermal transfer).

INK-JET TECHNOLOGIES

There are two types of ink-jet printing: *continuous* and *drop-on-demand* (see Figure 3.12). In *continuous* ink-jet printing, a thin jet of ink is produced by forcing the ink at high static pressure through a small nozzle or array of nozzles. A high-frequency pressure signal is superimposed on the ejection pressure. This causes the jet to become unstable and breaks up the ink into a series of small regularly spaced droplets. The drop generation rate can exceed 100,000 drops per second, and each droplet must be sensed and either allowed to hit the paper or be caught in a receptacle. An electrostatic charge is placed on each drop; the drop is then directed into a receptable as it passes between high voltage plates of opposite polarity. Uncharged drops pass undisturbed to the paper. Usually 75 percent of the drops pass into the receptacle, resulting in an effective ink rate of 25,000 drops per second. Continuous ink-jet printers have dot resolutions up to 1000 dots per inch, although 240 to 400 dpi is more common.

Drop-on-demand printers are much simpler than continuous ink-jet printers because every dot generated hits the paper. This eliminates ink recycling and the necessity for a drop selection system. A droplet of ink is ejected with a repeatable velocity and volume when a pressure pulse is produced behind the nozzle.

Most drop-on-demand printers generate about 8000 drops per second and have a resolution of about 80 to 300 dpi. Although drop-on-demand is a simpler technology than continuous printing, it is slower and has inferior resolution.

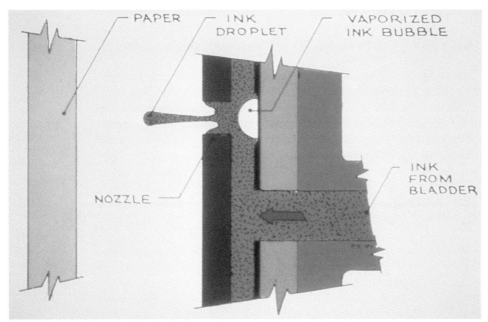

PAPER   INK DROPLET   VAPORIZED INK BUBBLE

NOZZLE

INK FROM BLADDER

Figure 3.11 *Ink-Jet Color Deposit* Process of ejecting ink onto paper. (*Courtesy of Hewlett-Packard.*)

Figure 3.12 *Ink-Jet Color Print* These high quality ink-jet colors were printed on semi-gloss paper. (*Courtesy of Hewlett-Packard.*)

The quality of ink-jet printing varies with the optical density, color, size, and shape of the ink-jet printed dot. The dye and liquid of ink-jet printers are absorbed into paper. Common paper stock has a range of surface characteristics that affect penetration and spread of ink. On rough paper, fibers spread or "feather" the ink, causing blurring of the edges of dots. In addition, some paper contains chemicals that change the appearance of the colors over time.

Some ink-jet printers are specially designed for plain paper in that they use inks that minimize the effects of paper on color appearance. In spite of this, the color quality on some types of plain paper is better than on others. Since plain paper surfaces vary in texture and whiteness, the quality and appearance of color will vary accordingly. The highest color quality (even with plain-paper ink printers) requires the use of special paper (see Figure 3.12). Plain paper color printing is primarily useful for business and technical graphics where exact replication of the displayed image color is not critical.

THERMAL TRANSFER   One of the more recent types of nonimpact print technologies is *thermal transfer*. Thermal printers transfer images by pressing a printhead containing an array of small electrical heaters against a ribbon with a waxy ink onto paper. The heaters liquify the ink allowing it to transfer onto paper. With a scanning-type printhead, the array of heaters prints one color per scan in a character high pass. The color inks are pressed one after another in sequential segments on a ribbon. Some printers make as many as four scans before the paper is advanced. Because the color is on the ribbon, the same set of heaters can be used for all colors. Unlike ink penetration from ink-jet printers, thermal transfer binds ink onto the surface of paper. The primary advantages of thermal printers include their ability to print on plain smooth paper and the resistance of their colors to fading.

Thermal transfer generally produces highly saturated primary colors (cyan, magenta, and yellow). Their high saturation can give a brash or cartoon-like appearance to lines and area-fills. Special arrangements of color spots improve image quality and expand the color palette by producing different saturations (Figure 3.13). Special types of thermal transfer printers (such as sublimation printers) exist which do not produce a cartoon-

Figure 3.13 *Thermal Printer Output* The ability of thermal printers to produce a saturated appearance enhances realism. (*Courtesy of Seiko Instruments, U.S.A.*)

like color appearance. These printers can vary the amount of each color deposited on a particular spot.

The only paper requirement of thermal transfer printers is a smooth surface because the inks used do not easily flow into the voids between raised fibers of common bond paper.

The primary colors of thermal printers are opaque. Thus, the top layer of dye becomes the dominant color of ink deposit. One of the problems with colors resulting from thermal ink combination is that mixtures resulting from combinations of the subtractive primaries (red, green, and blue) have a high gray content. Three-color blacks usually contain undesirable hues and for this reason a separate black printer is often used. In addition, the ink of thermal processes remains soft and does not penetrate the paper to any significant degree. The surface is thus susceptible to damage by abrasion. Also, each new scan must use an unused portion of ribbon. At present, most thermal transfer printers have single-use ribbons because transferring ink from a spot on the ribbon makes that spot unusable. Therefore, for each color printed, the area of ribbon used per page is equal to the page area.

ELECTROSTATIC AND ELECTROPHOTOGRAPHIC PRINTING   Electrostatic and electrophotographic printing are other types of nonimpact printing technologies. The primary advantage of these printing technologies is speed; the major disadvantages are color quality and range of colors.

Electrostatic printers produce images on paper by negatively charging the area of electrically sensitive (dielectric) paper to be imaged and allowing the charged area to attract a positively charged toner (a special form of ink). There are two methods of electrostatic color printing: multi-pass and single-pass. In the multi-pass method, the paper passes through the electrostatic charging station several times. The number of passes depends on the number of primary colors used. The paper passes under the printing stylus which charges the paper each time a different color is printed. In the single-pass printing

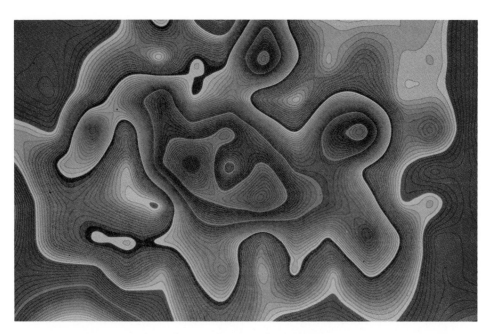

Figure 3.14 *Electrostatic Color Output* Spacing of color lines on contour map gives the impression of shading and enhances the appearance of contour depth and color range. (*Courtesy of Versatec.*)

method, the paper only passes through the toner station once because there is a different stylus for each color and all the styluses print at one time.

Color quality of electrostatic printers depends on the toner chromaticity, opacity, and registration, and the gap between the stylus and the paper surface (see Figure 3.14).

Electrophotographic printers use a laser beam to scan and discharge an image area on a rotating drum. Dry toner is then transferred electrostatically to a positively charged area on paper. The paper then passes through a fuser station where the toner is heat-bonded to the paper. To produce color, the process repeats for each color. The photoconductive drum rotates one revolution for each color. Methods which allow two- and three-color toner deposits in one drum revolution reduce the time required for color printing.

Electrophotographic color quality is a result of toner chromaticity, opacity of the toner, effectiveness of toner combination, color registration, toner fusing, and paper surface (see Figure 3.15).

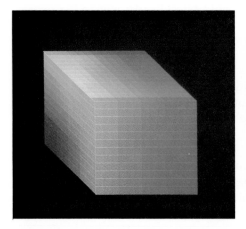 

Figure 3.15 *Electrophotographic Color Output* The block on the right is an electrophotographic reproduction of the slide on the left. The colors of the electrophotograph print are less saturated than those of the 35 mm slide.

Practical Concerns for Printers

Each of the printing technologies has advantages for different applications. Generally, thermal transfer is best for low cost and lower performance applications; electrostatic or electrophotographic technologies are most useful for high quality and speed, but are the most expensive. Ink-jet is a medium speed, high quality print technology and less expensive than electrostatic and electrophotographic printing. In general, the present state-of-the-art color quality of printers is not comparable to that commonly available from a standard commercial process used for magazines or books. The hard copy technology with the best color fidelity is photography.

Expanding the Appearance and Number of Colors

There are several techniques available for increasing the number of hues and saturations on color hard copy. Some of these (such as halftoning) have been used for several decades in the printing industry. Others (such as overplotting, cross-plotting, and density plotting) are only just beginning to be used.

Expanding Plotter Saturations

Technical plotter pen inks have a choice of opaque or transparent saturations of colors. However, the most common plotter pen sets provide a limited number of basic hues and no saturations or shades of the hues. These basic hues are sufficient for most business and technical graphics, but a wider range of plotter colors is often required for complex graphics or artistic purposes.

When technical pens are not available, there are several techniques available to create a different saturation appearance. One of these is *overplotting* which superimposes colors and creates a darker shade with each over-plot (see Figure 3.16). The color shading associated with three-dimensional perspective can be created or enhanced by applying a darker value of a color (overplot) to the side of a rectangle or bar in a graph.

Figure 3.16 *Overplotting* Dark shades are created by superimposing inks. (*Courtesy of Hewlett-Packard.*)

Figure 3.17 *Creating a Scale of Saturation by Area-Fill* Increasing the texture (pattern) density produces an impression of higher saturation. This illusion can be produced with different types of patterns, such as cross-hatches and diagonal lines.

Another way to produce the impression of a variety of saturations is by *cross-plotting* (using different densities of area-fill patterns such as cross-hatchings, diagonals, and dots) (see Figure 3.17). This technique is useful for aesthetic purposes and is not commonly seen in business graphics. Highly saturated color appearance results from dense area-fill patterns; desaturated color appearance results from less dense patterns. This technique produces the best results on small area-fill images which will be viewed at a sufficient distance for the eye to blend the white background and colored inks together.

Expanding Plotter Hues

Colors can be combined in repetitive patterns to expand the number of basic hues beyond those provided in the plotter set. Two colors alternating in a series of diagonal lines or superimposed at right angles to each other can create the impression of a third hue. The eye integrates, or blends, the two colors, and a different hue than each individual color is apparent. This technique is most effective when the viewing distance is sufficiently far so the individual colors of the pattern cannot be seen (see Figure 3.18).

Like the technique previously described for enhancing the number of saturations, the method to enhance the number of hues is useful for aesthetic purposes. These techniques are not widely used in business graphics.

The major advantage of these techniques is that they do not typically require programming. However, they are time consuming (for example, overplotting requires duplicate pen passes). These techniques also require that the registration of the plotter be accurate. In general, the cross-plotting and overplotting techniques are most efficient with area-fill graphics (like scenes, bar charts, and block diagrams).

Figure 3.18 *Expanding the Number of Colors Using Textures* When diagonal lines of the two colors are superimposed at right angles, an intermediate color appears to be produced. This technique can enhance the number of available colors. The image on the top is a magnification of part of the bottom image. *(Courtesy of Susan Brown, Hewlett-Packard.)*

Expanding Printer Colors

EXPANDING PRINTER SATURATIONS: SATURATION SCALING Varying the ratio of ink dots of the same hue to white areas on paper produces different saturations or gray scale levels. As with plotters, saturation varies with different densities of area-fill patterns. Dense textures result in a saturated appearance; less dense patterns result in a desaturated color appearance. This technique also results in a blended appearance of the colored inks and white background.

EXPANDING PRINTER HUES: DITHERING A number of color enhancement techniques also exists for printers. For a simple binary printer, the dots that compose an image are one size and combine to produce a standard set of eight colors: cyan, magenta, yellow,

Figure 3.19 *Halftoning* The different colors are produced by combining various sizes of color dots. (*Courtesy of Hewlett-Packard.*)

red, blue, green, black, and white (the lack of dot deposit). Additional colors are possible by a technique known as dithering. *Dithering* is the variation in arrangement of dots (pixels) of a fixed size. Different arrangements of black, white, and colored pixels can produce a large color palette.

Like cross-plotting, dithering capitalizes on the spatial averaging ability of the eye. However, the resolution of a dithered picture is usually poor. For example, a 240 dot per inch binary printer using a 2 x 2 dithered matrix will only print 120 picture elements per inch. High quality images with a large color palette can be made with 3 x 3 and 4 x 2 dithered cells by increasing the dot resolution.

Expanding Printer Hues and Saturations: Halftoning   Another technique available to increase the number of colors on printers is halftoning. It is used in newspapers, magazines, and books to expand saturation levels. *Halftoning* occurs when a printer deposits ink dots of different sizes arranged within the pixel boundary. A large dot will produce a black area; small dots appear as a light gray area. Halftoning is efficient because it provides a larger color palette without decreasing the printer's dot resolution.

With halftoning, the number of different dot sizes determines the number of available saturations and hues (see Figure 3.19). A single dot size produces two-level or binary printing, two dot sizes produce three-level printing, and so on. When only a limited number of tone levels (for example, between four and eight) are available, combining halftone dots in a 2 x 2 superpixel can produce a larger color palette.

Camera Systems

Camera systems reproduce computer display images onto 35 mm slides, prints, or microfiche. There are two methods of photographing images from display screens: manual and automatic film recording. The first method is the common photographic technique: manually taking a photograph of the display screen. The second method, *automatic film*

Figure 3.20 *Automatic Screen Photography* Film recorder and instant print and 35 mm output. (*Courtesy of Hewlett-Packard.*)

recording, electronically transfers a digitized version of images to a separate CRT and then to an automatic camera system (see Figure 3.20).

Manual Screen Photography

Manual photography of a display screen is relatively simple, inexpensive, and easily available (see Box). However, this method often results in poor quality reproduction and exaggerated screen distortions (see Figure 3.21). In addition, the pixels of low resolution displays which cause a stair step appearance (*jaggies*) along diagonal lines and edges are typically obvious in manual photographs.

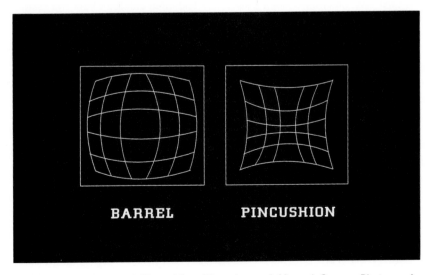

Figure 3.21 *Barrel and Pincushion Distortions of Manual Screen Photography* (Right) Pincushioning causes distorted expansion of screen center. (Left) Barreling causes distorted contraction of screen center.

Camera Systems

Also, the effects of anti-glare filters are often apparent in a manual photograph (see Chapter 8). These distortions include line dispersion caused by etched screens, texture of woven filters, or reduction of image brightness from tinted coatings.

MANUALLY PHOTOGRAPHING SCREEN IMAGES

A number of techniques are available that will minimize the problems associated with manually photographed screen images. These include

- Using high speed (for example, 400 ASA) color slide film
- Photographing screens in a dark room or under a black cloth
- Using a telephoto lens to eliminate barrelling (a lens distortion in which straight lines curve increasingly as the lines approach the lens periphery)
- Removing any accessory glare shield that might reduce the brightness of the display
- Calibrating the convergence of the display before photographing (see Chapter 2)

Film Recorders

Film recorders can omit most of the problems of manual photography because they receive input directly from computer memory. There are two techniques for transferring images to film: video signal transfer and laser imaging. Video signal transfer reproduces images from a CRT color display to 35 mm slides by transferring video signals to a small, monochrome CRT contained in the camera system. The monochrome CRT projects light sequentially through one of three (red, blue, or green) filters which expose the film. By combining these three filters, other colors are exposed onto the film by additive color mixing. The amount of time of light exposure and the intensity of the light as it passes through each filter determines color saturation. The three colored filters and various time exposures can produce thousands of colors. Laser imaging exposes the film to different lasers and draws on the film much as a plotter draws an image on paper.

Film recorders eliminate the physical distortions apparent in manual photography because they photograph images based upon electric rather than optical screen output. In addition, film recorders can achieve much better resolution than a display screen. This is especially apparent in film recorders that use vector technology because the dots produced from the raster technology that cause jaggies do not exist.

Film recorders are relatively easy to use (they do not require a sophisticated knowledge of photography), more convenient, and less susceptible to photographic errors. In addition, some have an automatic color balance for different types of film. Film recorders also allow multiple images to be placed on the same film frame by using multiple exposures. Thus, it is possible to place different pictures in different quadrants of the frame and apply a variety of resolutions to them for special effects. Some film recorders offer special software that allows production of color separations. This can reduce the cost of separations by professional printers.

Film recorders are very useful in applications where a wide range of colors and quick processing time is required. For example, very detailed cartography images can require five to ten times more production time with a plotter than with an automatic camera system. These images can be photographed by a film recorder in five to 15 minutes. Film recorders are especially useful for applications requiring the transfer of detailed images of multiple colors and area-fill images such as those used in mineral and petroleum exploration, remote sensing, and environmental monitoring.

Choosing Film: Speed versus Quality

As previously stated, the quality of 35 mm slides produced by film recorders is superior to the image appearance on most displays. However, the type of film used also affects the quality of images created with film recorders. If high quality slides including a number of colors and gray scales are required, a film with a low speed (for example, ASA 64 or 100) is appropriate. The resulting image will have a less grainy appearance than high speed film (for example, ASA 400). However, reproducing images with slow speed film will take more time due to the long exposure time necessary. For vector-driven film recorders, the time required to expose the image depends on several other factors including the number of vectors required to draw the image and the number of colors in the image.

Hard Copy Quality Comparisons

While this chapter has been primarily concerned with the color quality of different hard copy devices, other aspects of these devices are also important in considering the system most appropriate for an application. Comparisons of these devices can be made with respect to

- Resolution
- Number of colors available
- Speed
- Cost of the device
- Cost per copy

One way of comparing color quality is to evaluate the color range or gamut of the various color technologies. Color ranges for thermal transfer, impact printing, and color displays can be compared by plotting them on chromaticity diagrams (see Chapter 9). In general, the larger the area representing the color production of a device, the more colors it produces (see Figure 3.22). None of these computer devices fills the chromaticity diagram, demonstrating their inability to produce all the colors that people can see. However, color film produces the most colors; color CRTs produce fewer colors than film but more than printers; thermal nonimpact printers produce more colors than impact printers.

Plotters produce high resolution output and can be relatively inexpensive. Their disadvantages are chiefly in speed: As drawing becomes more complex and requires more lines, drawing time increases. Another problem is device compatibility: Plotters are inherently vector devices, whereas most displays use raster technologies. The interface between a raster display and a plotter is thus more complex than that between a raster display and a raster printer.

A primary advantage of impact printers is their low cost and the high letter-quality print (at least for fixed-character printers). However, impact printers are usually more noisy and produce inferior quality color compared to nonimpact printers. With the exception of thermal transfer, nonimpact printers are faster but are more expensive than impact printers.

Camera systems provide the advantage of being able to produce a wide range of colors in a relatively short time. Moreover, 35 mm slide film has better spatial resolution—

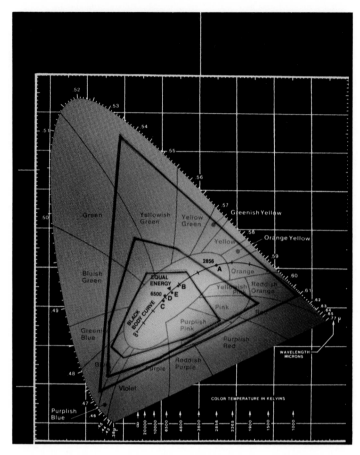

Figure 3.22 *Color Gamuts of Color Reproduction* The typical color gamuts for impact printing (inside polygon), thermal transfer (middle outline), and color TV (triangle) demonstrate their limited range of color production. (*Modification of diagram supplied by Photo Research.*)

4,000 lines—than common color CRTs—512 lines. However, cameras and particularly film recorders can be expensive.

Comparison of the color quality of plotters, impact and nonimpact printers, and photographed media (slides and prints) demonstrates that slides from film recorders are best in terms of color contrast, color saturation, and color fidelity. Table 3.1 summarizes the color quality, resolution, and reproduction speed of the devices.

TABLE 3.1

Hard Copy Technology Comparison

	Color Quality	Resolution	Copy Speed (A size)*
Pen Plotters	good–excellent	~ .001 in.	variable
Printers:			
Ink-Jet	fair–excellent	75–600 dpi	1–5 min.
Thermal Transfer	good	200–480 dpi	60 sec.
Electrophotographic	good	2000–4000 lines/frame	3–8 min.
Electrostatic	fair	200–800 dpi	1 min.
Film Recorders	excellent	16,344 lines	15 min.

* A size = 8½" x 11"

The hard copy technology most suitable for an application depends on its intended use. For example, plotters with very high quality, fine-line resolution may be excellent for creating engineering drawings, but not necessary for reproducing area-fill graphics such as bar or pie charts. If high color quality is a concern, but speed is not, thermal transfer is a good choice. However, if high color quality and speed are concerns, ink-jet printing may be an acceptable color reproducing technology.

The following table can be used to evaluate appropriate hard copy media.

TABLE 3.2

Hard Copy Media Comparisons

	Advantages	Disadvantages
Transparencies	Creation and duplication inexpensive	Limited color visibility and quantity
	Short creation and duplication time	Long time required for area-fill
	Do not need to project to review	Limited to positive background
	Can be projected in lighted rooms	
	Can be used for small to medium size audience	
	Can write on media during presentation	
35 mm slides	Unlimited color	Complex process to reproduce image onto paper
	Best fidelity of display color	
	Positive/negative background	Projection required to preview visibility
	Can be duplicated	
	Small size	Long production time
	Easy to organize	

CREATING EFFECTIVE PRESENTATION GRAPHICS FOR COLOR TRANSPARENCIES AND PAPER

The following suggestions will help ensure that colors of data symbols, curves, text, and lines will be distinct. When using a graphics editor or paint software, match the screen background to the bright white of a transparency or paper. This will allow the selection of colors as they will appear to an audience. (Color appearance can be significantly changed by the hue and brightness of the background, see Chapter 7.)

Use large size and bold type fonts, lines, and data points appropriate for the graphic image. (The ability to distinguish colors depends on the size of the object.) Larger sizes produce colors easier to distinguish (see Chapter 7).

(continued)

Preview visibility of colors of the completed graphic at the light level and at viewing distances matching those of the presentation room.

Use a white display screen background when choosing and assigning colors for transfer to paper and transparency presentations. Colors like yellow which are highly visible on a dark screen have poor contrast and low visibility on most paper and transparencies.

Avoid colors which are low in saturation such as yellow, light green, and cyan or similar in hue like red and orange. (Light projection through transparencies desaturates colors. Desaturated colors are difficult to tell apart from each other. Formulas exist for selecting colors which are easily discriminable—see Chapter 9.)

Useful Facts

Hard Copy Devices	Devices that transfer display images to color hard copy include plotters, printers, and cameras or film recorders.
Hard Copy Media	Hard copy media consist of plastic transparencies, paper, and 35 mm slides.
Color Appearance on Display and Hard Copy	Colors transferred to hard copy appear different than on a screen; their quality depends on the particular hard copy medium used.
Hard Copy Color Mixing	Hard copy colors combine subtractively; the primaries are cyan, yellow, and magenta. They combine to produce a set of secondary colors: red, blue, and green. Combining all three primaries produces black.
Appearance of Hard Copy Mixed Colors	The composites of subtractive primaries are darker and more saturated than the primaries.
	Perfect matching of screen colors and hard copy colors is not possible.
Range of Hard Copy Colors	Hard copy devices have a smaller color gamut than CRTs and human perceptual range.
Hard Copy Color Appearance Factors	The appearance of the color depends on the technology, the way it is deposited, and the surface properties of the medium onto which it is deposited.
Setting Display Background to Review Color on Transparencies	When creating colors on the screen for transparencies, use a white screen background.

Saturation Appearance	Colors appear less saturated on transparencies, more saturated on paper. Avoid using desaturated colors on transparencies.
Colors for Distant Viewing	For far viewing distances, use saturated colors on transparencies and desaturated colors on 35 mm dark background slides. Avoid very thin lines or small images.
Plotting Color	Pen plotters produce colors by drawing on paper or plastic transparency sheets. Pen plotters are best used to reproduce large text representations and graphics.
Ink Saturation	Plotter inks appear most saturated on glossy paper and darkest when solvent-based colors are used. Plotter inks on transparencies become desaturated as the intensity of the projection lamp increases and as viewing distance increases. The appearance of different levels of saturation of plotter colors is possible by using different densities of area-fill patterns.
Expanding the Number of Plotter Colors	The appearance of an expanded number of plotter colors results from superimposing different colors in diagonal and perpendicular lines.
Printer Types	Printers include both impact and nonimpact. Some nonimpact printers are thermal transfer, ink-jet, and electrostatic. Ink-jet printers are either drop-on-demand or continuous depending on the way they deposit ink on paper. The best printer depends on the number of colors needed, speed required, resolution and color quality desired, and cost considerations.
Raster Printing	Raster printing is like imaging on a computer screen because both images are composed of spots of color.
Increasing the Number of Colors	A larger set of different saturations and hues result from techniques like dithering (superpixeling) and halftoning.
Effects of Paper	The appearance of color depends on the quality and type of paper. Use paper recommended by the plotter and printer manufacturer.

	Other printers, like thermal transfer, can produce good quality color on any common stock paper.
Print Quality	While some impact printers can produce more colors than thermal printers, the quality of the saturation is generally inferior.
Gray Scales	Different levels of gray are produced by using different ratios of intermixed light and dark ink dots.
Camera Systems	Computer camera systems produce better quality slides than manual photography.
	Slow speed film produces better quality slides than fast speed film.
	Film recorders producing 35 mm slides ensure the closest match to the colors created on the screen.

REFERENCES

Allen, R., *Review of Color Printer Techniques*, HP Technical Report, 1986.

"Continuous Ink-Jet Produces True Color Halftone Images," *Information Display*, July 1986, pp. 14–15.

Finkel, J. I., "Cutting the Cost of Color Hardcopy," *Computer Aided Engineering*, Jan./Feb. 1984, pp. 34–44.

"Hi-res Color Hardcopy Meeting User Needs and Image Quality," *Information Display*, Oct. 1986, pp. 38–42.

Kenney, T., "A Color Match: Screen to Paper," *Computer Graphics World*, May 1986, pp. 89–94.

Kerlow, I. V. and J. Rosebush. *Computer Graphics for Designers and Artists* (New York: Van Nostrand Reinhold Co., 1986).

Marrs, R., "Graphics Workstation for Color Printing," *Computer Graphics World*, Dec. 1986, pp. 24–26.

McManus, P. and G. Hoffman, "A Method for Matching Hardcopy Color to Display Color," *Society for Information Display*, XVI, 1985, 204–206.

Meilach, D. Z. *Dynamics of Presentation Graphics* (Homewood, IL: Dow Jones-Irwin, 1986).

Murch, G. M., "Perceptual Consideration of Color, Marketing Display and Hardcopy Colors," *Computer Graphics World*, 6(7), July 1983, 32–40.

Osborne, R. *Lights and Pigments* (London: John Murray, 1980).

Porell, G., "The New Color Hard-Copy Market," *Computer Graphics World*, March 1986, pp. 49–68.

Robertson, B., "Film Recorders for All Reasons," *Computer Graphics World*, Feb. 1986, pp. 45–52.

"Smaller Dots Make Better Plots," *Computer Graphics World*, Dec. 1986, pp. 21–22.

Starkweather, G. K. "A Color-Correction Scheme for Color Electronic Printers," *Color Research and Application*, 11, 1986, S67–S72.

Starkweather, G. W., "Electronic Color-Printer Technologies," *Color Research and Application*, 11, 1986, S73–S74.

Thomas, R., "Thermal Transfer Color Technology," *Computer Graphics World*, May 1986, pp. 45–48.

Wandell, B. A., "Color Rendering of Color Camera Data," *Color Research and Application*, 11, 1986, 530–533.

4

Color Coding

What beautiful thoughts can be made out of forms and colors.

Paul Gauguin

Coding Computer Images

Image coding is the use of a visual feature to communicate a meaning or functional property of an image. Types of coding used in computer images include

- Shape
- Blinking
- Reverse video
- Underlining
- Type fonts
- Brightness levels
- Color

Research shows that color is superior to most of these types of coding (see Chapter 1). It can reduce the need for detailed explanations, show relationships and status, segregate, imply physical characteristics, highlight, and aid in learning. For example, red, yellow, and green can be used to color code program messages. Error messages can be color coded in red, caution messages in yellow, and user-generated messages (inputs) in green. Different color values can also show relationships between data or features. For example, long wavelengths (such as red and orange) can represent high stress areas in a computer-rendered mechanical design, and short wavelengths (such as blue and green) can represent low stress points. Color can also show the active status of screen windows by coding the borders of active windows and those of inactive windows.

There are a variety of images used to represent different types of computer data. These include natural scenes, pictures, symbols, icons, graphs, and alphanumerics. Color coding can be applied to all of them. In addition, color can enhance their visual impact and that of other forms of coding. However, the arbitrary use of color can degrade these effects, visual processing, and thus operator performance.

Also, some of these codes can enhance or degrade the perception of color. For example, excessively fast blink rates or sparse area-fill patterns can reduce the perception of color (see Chapter 7).

The way in which colors are assigned for coding purposes depends upon the application and the intended effect. For example, the use of highly contrasting colors (such as blue and yellow) attract attention. Low contrast colors (such as yellow and white) subdue image appearance. Similar hues (such as red and orange) are more likely to be associated with each other and to have similar meanings than extremely different hues (such as red and cyan).

To ensure correct interpretation of a color code, a user must understand the meaning assigned to a color. When color codes do not conform to obvious conventions (such as red for a dangerous condition or green for safe), color coding schemes should be accompanied by a color legend.

Coding to Enhance Performance

Colors chosen for coding should accommodate the visual and cognitive activities required in the task. Color coding can improve the time and efficiency required to make decisions by increasing the visibility of images. For example, proofreading can be simplified by color coding punctuation, checking program code can be made easier by color coding segments of mathematical expressions, and checking inventory listings can be enhanced by color coding supply levels.

Choice of colors for coding purposes also depends on the intended effect such as emphasizing a category of items, showing common pathways in flow diagrams, or associating wave forms to data (see Figure 4.1).

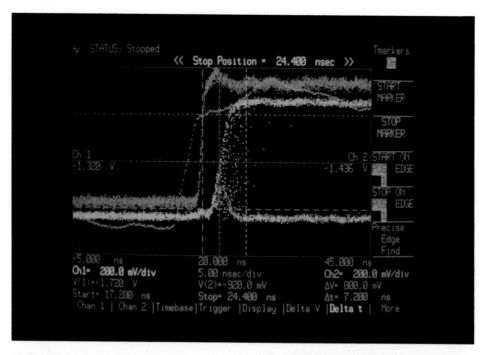

Figure 4.1 *Color Coding for Association* Color distinguishes different wave forms. Parameters associated with a given wave form (such as channel and sampled voltage) share the same color code. Thus, use of color coding both facilitates distinguishing the different wave forms (different hues) and locating the information related to the wave forms with the same hue. (*Courtesy of Hewlett-Packard.*)

Color Coding Compatibility

Color selection for coding purposes should be based on how easily the colors can be discriminated and their meanings interpreted. Color codes should be designed to accommodate the worst case conditions (such as smallest image size or lowest contrasts) in which color recognition will be required. In addition, the effects of brightness of the surround color on the appearance of the image color should be considered. Color coding should be compatible with either dark or light backgrounds (negative or positive polarity). Because colors of very small images (like data points in a scattergram) are difficult to discriminate, it may be more appropriate to color code the background than an image (see Chapters 7, 8, and 11).

Coding Concrete and Abstract Meanings

Color can be assigned to images in either a concrete or abstract way. Concrete assignment occurs when colors are chosen on the basis of their similarity to colors of objects. For example, showing the quantity of lemon and lime exports in yellow and green bars on a histogram increases the speed of association of the data with its representation (see Figure 4.2). Concrete use of color is thus relatively straightforward.

Abstract or symbolic assignment of color occurs when it represents a less obvious functional property of an object. Abstract and symbolic use of color ranges from assignments of stereotyped meanings (like red for hot) to less obvious meanings (like red for a selected command).

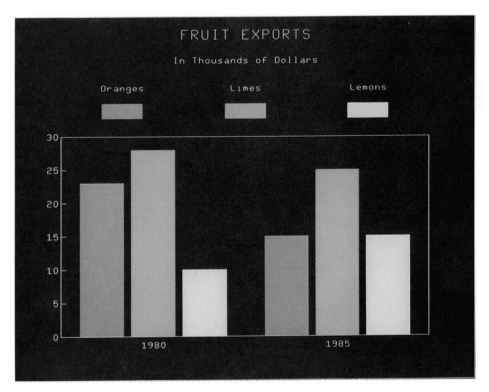

Figure 4.2 *Concrete Association with Color* Bars representing exports of oranges, lemons, and limes are easy to interpret because they are the color of the fruit.

Showing Logical Relations

Logical relations emphasize similarity, dissimilarity, temporal sequence, or common functions. Careful use of color coding enhances the logical relations between images by directly mapping the properties of color perception (hue, saturation, and lightness) onto images. Thus, the identity, association, and ordering of a concept to an object can be made more obvious if the concept is coded in discrete or continuous values.

Identity

The simplest form of color coding is matching the colors of the object they represent. For example, a bar graph showing differences in reproduction of a natural resource can be color coded in the color of the resource. If the purpose of a graph shows lumber production, using different shades of browns would more closely approximate the natural appearance than other colors.

Discrete and Continuous Variables

Color enhances or codes the discrete or continuous features of data. Extremes in hue are most effective in emphasizing different categories of data. However, spectral arrangements of hues are less likely to imply order than linear arrangements of saturation and lightness levels. Hue is therefore an appropriate perceptual property of color to code discrete or mutually exclusive information.

Since scales of saturation and lightness values are graded variations of a particular hue, they are appropriate for indicating the continuous properties of data (for example, temperature values, stress, time, or pollution amounts) (see Figure 4.3). However, hues can represent continuous features if their differences are sufficiently small to appear to vary smoothly (for example, gradual changes from blue to green to yellow). Combining saturation and lightness values with hues is also appropriate in many applications.

Complementary colors maximize a discrete appearance. Complementary colors (for example, blue and gold) emphasize differences (for example, research versus manufacturing facilities), more than similar colors (for example, yellow and gold). For these

Figure 4.3 *Coding Continuous Variables* Land height is shown by graduation along the visible spectrum. Blue indicates lowest land forms, red shows highest. (*Courtesy of UNIRAS.*)

purposes, there should be sufficient differences in colors to ensure obvious discrimination and different appearance.

Opposites

Complementary colors can code and emphasize extreme differences like opposites (such as night-day, partner-competitor, profit-loss, logic components like and/nand gates or or/nor gates). Since using color complements to code opposites represents the most dramatic differences of all color combinations, it best indicates extremes. Opposites will appear more different if color coded in complements like blue-yellow, red-cyan, and green-magenta combinations than if coded in similar colors like red-magenta, blue-cyan, and yellow-green combinations.

Complementary colors can match the colors associated with opposite concepts (such as dark blue to represent data collected at night and yellow for data collected during the day). Although complementary colors (like red and cyan) can be used for abstract variables like profit and loss, other color associations for these variables may already exist (such as black for profit and red for loss). These known associations are typically better to use unless a color legend is provided describing the meaning of the colors.

Common Axis Data

Color codes are useful to clarify data plotted in a Cartesian coordinate graph with two ordinates. Data and their corresponding ordinate can be visually related without the need for descriptive labels and legends. This technique can also be used with histograms.

Cause and Effect Relationships

Color coding is also useful to show the relations between causes and effects. For example, it can enhance the visibility of images that vary as a result of a process change (see Figure 4.4) or values that result from iterative calculations (see Figures 1.3 and 5.24). In addition, in electronic spreadsheets, the values that result from new calculations will be obvious if presented in colors that are a high contrast hue (such as magenta) to the original values (such as green) (see Figure 5.4).

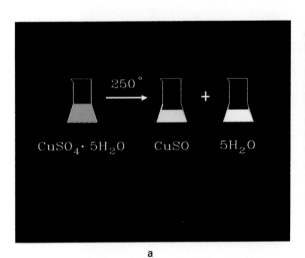
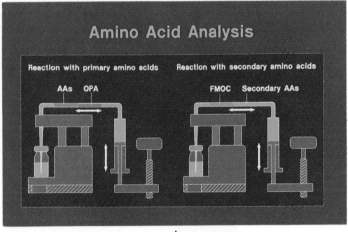

a   b

Figure 4.4 *Color Coding of Processes* a) Color shows the effects of heating on a chemical mixture. As the mixture of yellow copper sulfate and water ($CuSO \, 5 \, H_4 \, O_2$) is heated to 250 degrees, it separates into copper sulfide ($CuSO$) and water (H_2O). The colors represent the colors of the chemical compounds. b) Reactions to different amino acids are coded in different colors. (*Courtesy of Hewlett-Packard.*)

In CAD/CAM applications, the results of changes in stress loadings on solid objects can be shown by the same technique. Slight changes can be made obvious by small changes in hues or brightness. For example, as the stress load increases, its color can change from orange to red or become brighter. The critical element in this technique is that the change in color is obvious. In addition, displaying the original image on the screen (in a different window) is useful for comparison purposes.

Sets and Structure

Logical relations are more visually obvious when related data are grouped together. Color coding these images can enhance their common meanings and associations. Different and similar relations between sets and structures can be shown by hues and saturations. Levels of hierarchy can be shown by changing saturation from light to dark or by continuously varying hue from short to long wavelengths.

Typical sets and structures like organization charts and process flow diagrams are good candidates for color coding. For example, a corporate organization chart might show executive officers in saturated colors and divisions that report to them in desaturated values of the color assigned to each executive (see Figure 4.5). Process flow diagrams can be similarly color coded. For example, the beginning of the process can be coded in saturated colors with each stage becoming less saturated. Operations occurring simultaneously can also be coded by different hues.

Duplicating Codes (Redundant Coding)

Color coding affects the visibility and interpretation of other codes such as blinking, underline, reverse video, shape, texture, and type font. In general, combining colors with other codes emphasizes their appearance. (In addition, using other codes with color allows

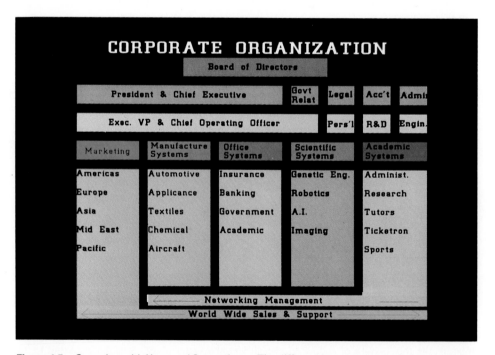

Figure 4.5 *Grouping with Hues and Saturations* The different hues represent the main product groupings across the corporate structure; the reduced saturations represent the division levels within the product groups.

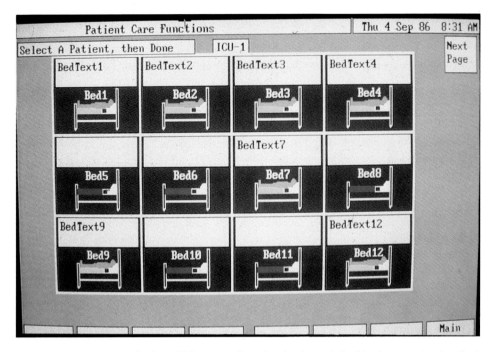

Figure 4.6 *Redundant Coding* This screen is redundantly coded with shape and color. Bed occupancy is shown by either the icon of a patient or by yellow. Lack of a patient icon and the use of blue represents an empty bed. (*Courtesy of Hewlett-Packard.*)

the code to be interpreted by individuals who cannot perceive color differences. (See Chapter 6.)

Using color with another code when the color and the code convey the same meaning is known as *redundant coding* (see Figure 4.6). Examples include a red and blinking light (both signifying an error) or magenta and italic font (both signifying important words in a paragraph). Redundant coding is especially useful for color vision deficient people, in variable light conditions or with media (such as transparencies) where colors can be difficult to perceive or discriminate.

The skillful use of redundant color coding requires a thorough understanding of the properties of the images as well as the properties of color. It is essential that the viewer understand the coding scheme either through an explicit legend or an implicit use of commonly understood connotations of color.

For example, if a sparse texture pattern (such as dots) indicates low population density on a demographic map, blue is probably not appropriate because of the inability of the visual system to identify extremely small blue images (see Chapter 7). Green may therefore be more appropriate.

Nonredundant Color Coding

Simultaneous use of two codes (in the same image) that have different meanings is *nonredundant coding*. An example of nonredundant coding is when the color (such as red) signifies unprotected files and blinking means the system is compiling data.

Nonredundant codes should be chosen with care because they can be easily confused or their meanings may not be easily apparent. For example, the meaning of brightness as a code may not be obvious because the visual system has difficulty comparing the relative brightness values of colors. Thus, if yellow and brown were used to code the bank accounts of two different customers (A and B), and high brightness coded assets and low brightness coded debits, customer A's debits (dark yellow) could look like customer B's assets (light brown).

Color Coding Shapes

Color affects the recognition and discrimination of different shapes, especially small shapes such as data points on scatter diagrams or superimposed on line graphs. Since contrast is the determining factor for edge detection, colors can enhance the visibility of image details. For example, small yellow squares in a scatter diagram may appear as yellow circles. Changing the color to magenta will enhance the visibility of the corners of the square. (Magenta is darker than yellow, producing a higher brightness contrast against a light background, and thus produces sharper edges.) Assigning a bright color (like yellow) to a shape with less detail (like a circle) will not significantly degrade its appearance.

Colors can optimize shape recognition and image details if they provide maximum contrast. Color combinations that cause blur (see Chapter 7) are not appropriate for shapes with a lot of detail. For example, assigning a dark saturated color (like red) to a shape with a lot of edge detail (like a star) produces better visibility of its points than a lighter color like yellow or cyan. Assigning a light, desaturated color (like yellow or cyan) to an image with few edge details (like a circle) does not significantly reduce its resolution (see Figure 4.7).

Enhancing Icon Recognition and Association

Color enhances the recognition of shapes, symbols, and icons if they are sufficiently large and if their color is meaningfully related to the application. Colors should not interfere with icon recognition particularly when the color coding scheme has an assigned meaning. Color interferes with icon recognition when it is inconsistent with expectations (see Figure 4.8). For example, coding a caution icon (circle with a diagonal line through it) in green will produce a less immediate response than coding it in red. Coding a normal temperature condition in blue and an abnormal condition in green would result in slower interpretation than using red for the abnormal condition.

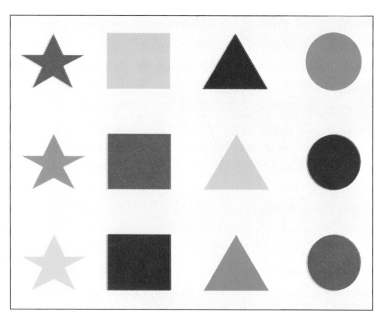

Figure 4.7 *Color Coding Shapes* (top row) Lightness and hue assignment are balanced to optimize legibility: Darkest colors are assigned to areas with most details (such as star and triangle) and lighter colors are assigned to shapes with least details (such as square and circle). (bottom row) Lightness and hue assignment are not balanced.

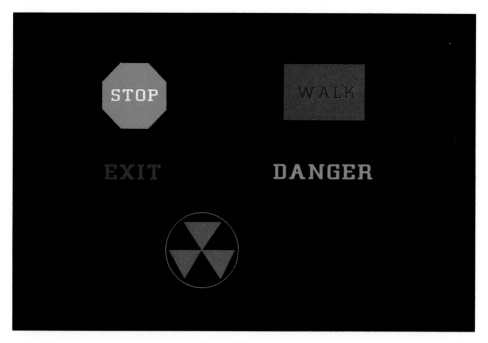

Figure 4.8 *Incorrectly Coded Icons* The colors assigned to these icons are not those commonly associated with their meaning. The inappropriate color assignment causes confusion and more time for interpretation.

Assigning Colors to Patterns

Colors can also code different patterns or textures. These include solid, broken, dotted diagonal lines, and cross-hatch patterns. Color coding patterns is particularly useful for cartographic and solid modeling applications. However, since desaturated colors (such as yellow and cyan) appear more desaturated when viewed on paper or transparencies (see Chapter 3), assigning these colors to dense patterns will enhance their saturation and their recognition.

The assignment of colors to patterns also affects the aesthetics of the image. Designers often consider the visual weight or balance of colors in a composition. Color offsets the appearance of line thickness and pattern densities. To balance this appearance, dense line and area-fill patterns should be color coded in light, desaturated colors. Less dense lines and area-fills should be coded in dark and more saturated colors (see Figure 4.9).

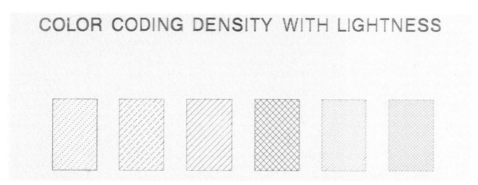

Figure 4.9 *Coding Density with Lightness* The assignment of these colors to the patterns results in a balanced saturation and lightness of appearance. The lower density of the darker colors blends with the white background to produce a lower saturation, and the higher density of the lighter colors blends to produce a more saturated appearance.

Another area where color coding is useful is in the assignment of colors to single color (monochrome) line and area-fill patterns. In most computer applications, colors are randomly assigned to these patterns. This situation most often occurs when graphs to be reproduced to hard copy are created from monochrome screens. The random assignment causes problems in color identification and discrimination because some colors will not be able to be identified when used for certain patterns. For example, saturated blue data points in a scatter diagram or a blue dotted line in a line graph may not appear different than other images of the same form in brown or black (see Chapter 3).

Coding to Emphasize Images

Some applications (such as decision support systems like process control and radar tracking) require that color codes produce a fast response from display operators. Other applications require a lot of information presented at one time and that critical or important information be more obvious than less important information. Some colors and their combinations are better than others for these purposes.

Creating Maximum Attraction

Brightness contrast is the primary factor in the speed of seeing an object (see Chapter 6). Regardless of color, high contrast colors attract attention before low contrast colors and reach the visual processing area of the brain first. In addition, reaction time to saturated colors is faster than to desaturated colors and faster to brighter colors than darker colors. Saturated, high contrast colors, like complements, optimize rapid response (see Figure 4.10).

For displays with eight colors, optimal colors for rapid response for images on a dark background (black or dark gray) are usually primary hues and bright colors like green, yellow, or cyan. For a white background, the best color to maximize attention is red.

Another way to attract attention to specific areas is to use color contrast to subdue unimportant information which, in effect, highlights images that are important (see Figure 4.11). Color contrast is particularly useful in enhancing or subduing foreground and background graphics, such as text on pictures or graphs.

Figure 4.10 *Attracting Attention* Example of colors which maximize contrasts. The red and green are color complements used to emphasize the differences between beer consumption in the different regions. (*Courtesy of Hewlett-Packard.*)

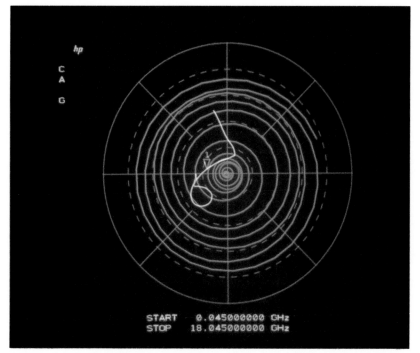

START 0.045000000 GHz
STOP   18.045000000 GHz

Figure 4.11 *Contrasting Superimposed Images* Visibility of plot of a frequency sweep (yellow) on a polar coordinate graph is enhanced by using its complementary color (blue) for the background grid and black for the general background. It thus uses both color and lightness contrast to emphasize foreground and background colors. Using blue and green for the polar grid subdues its visibility and thus enhances the visibility of the frequency sweep. (*Courtesy of Hewlett-Packard.*)

Colors that produce a high contrast with respect to their background (such as yellow on black) are useful for foreground images. Conversely, low contrast color combinations (such as blue on black) are useful for background images. Low contrast colors are useful for themes and high contrast combinations are best for messages or information of primary importance (see Figure 4.11). This technique can be very useful for educational or tutorial purposes where the conceptual model is in the background, and the salient points are highlighted by dominant (more visible) colors.

Low contrast colors produce subtle effects; very low contrasts and images of equal brightness values camouflage images. Equally bright foreground and background colors decrease visibility of unimportant information or inactive screen areas. Camouflaging information with subtle contrasts diverts attention to more important or current information coded in high contrasts. It is also useful for subduing information for security purposes and the protection of classified information (see Figure 4.12). For example, some pre-

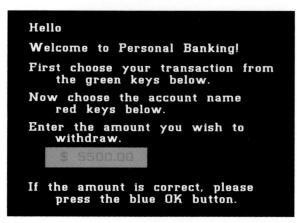

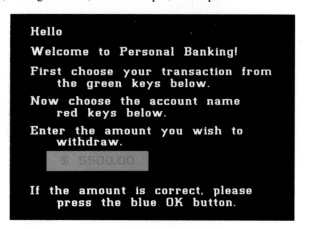

Figure 4.12 *Camouflaging Information with Color* Low color and brightness contrast are used to reduce the visibility of the amount of money displayed on the automatic bank teller display. Low contrast makes it difficult to see the amount unless you are directly in front of the display. The screen on the right shows how the display would appear to the next person in the queue at a distance of five feet.

Figure 4.13 *Making Visual Tasks Difficult* From left to right, the panels show progressively decreasing lightness contrast between targets and background color.

cautions exist in sidewalk bank teller systems for maintaining privacy between the display teller and the customer. These include side walls and anti-glare treatments that prevent off-axis viewing. However, these precautions do not eliminate the visibility of the displayed information to the person standing behind the customer. Displaying the images in low contrast colors will reduce their visibility, particularly at far viewing distances. The color contrast of the transaction can be sufficiently high to allow visibility by the customer, but not enough for recognition by a more distant observer.

Other applications for low contrast combinations and camouflaging include video games and flight simulators. Decreasing the contrast between targets and background increases the difficulty of seeing the targets (see Figure 4.13). Players can increase their eye-hand reflex coordination with practice much more easily than increasing visual responses to low contrast color combinations.

Useful Facts

Factors in Color Choice	The color(s) appropriate for a particular application depend on several factors including the task, meaning intended, contrast of the image and background necessary, and placement in the visual field.
Color Coding	Well-designed redundant color coding enhances interpretation.
	Color can show logical relationships such as identity, discreteness or continuity of variables, similarity and opposites, cause and effect, interactions, and sets and structures.

	Color can replace or be used in combination with different types of highlighting.
Translating Monochrome to Color Codes	Monochrome patterns can be color coded by their assignment to specific lightness and saturation values.
Coding Shapes	Shapes can be color coded by assigning high contrast values to shapes with the most complex features.
Highlighting or Subduing Images	High brightness contrasts attract attention first; low brightness contrasts subdue information. Likewise, high contrast images are good for immediate action items.

REFERENCES

Chute, A. G., "AECT/RTA Young Researchers Paper: Effect of Color and Monochrome Versions of a Film on Incidental and Task-relevant Learning," *ECTJ*, 28(1), 1980, 10–18.

Dreilling, L., "Fractal Art," *Computer Graphics World*, July 1986, pp. 91–92.

Dwyer, F. M., "Color as an Instructional Variable," *AVCR*, 19(4), 1971, 399–416.

Elio, R E. and D. B. Reutener, "Color Context as a Factor in Encoding and as an Organization Device for Retrieval of Word Lists," *J. of General Psychology*, 99, 1978, 223–232.

Farley, F. H. and A. P. Grant, "Arousal and Cognition: Memory for Color versus Black and White Multimedia Presentation," *J. of Psychology*, 94, 1976, 147–150.

Hopkin, V. D., R. E. Carswell, and N. Z. Hilton, "The Separation of Characters by Colour instead of Spacing," *International Conference on Colour in Information Technology and Visual Displays*, IERE Pub. #61, 1985, pp. 39–45.

Katzman, N. and J. Nyenhuis, "Color vs. Black-and-White Effects on Learning, Opinion and Attention," *AVCR*, 20(1), 1972, 16–28.

Lipman, A., W. Bender, G. Soloman, and M. Saito, "Color Word Processing," *Computer Graphics World*, 5(6), June 1985, 41–46.

Otto, W. and E. Askov, "The Role of Color in Learning and Instruction," *J. of Special Education*, 2, 1968, 155–165.

Reising, J. M. and T. J. Emerson, "Color in Quantitative and Qualitative Display Formats: Does Color Help?" *International Conference on Colour in Information Technology and Visual Displays*, IERE Pub. #61, 1985, pp. 1–5.

Saito, M. and W. Bender, "A Color-based Text Editor," *Society for Information Display*, 1985, pp. 24–27.

Tolliver, D. L., "Color Function in Information Perception and Retention," *Information Storage and Retrieval*, 1973, 257–265.

Waller, R., P. Lefere, and M. MacDonald-Ross, "Do You Need That Second Color?" *IEEE Transactions*, PC25 (2), June 1982, 80–85.

5

Computer Color Applications

The eye should not be fixed on one point, but should take in everything while observing the reflections which the colors produce on their surroundings.

Camille Pissarro

The Demand for Computer Color

When color is available at a reasonable cost, there is an overwhelming trend, regardless of the media, for color. This phenomenon is observed in printing, photography, cinema, television, and engineering design terminals. It is evident in the rapid growth of satellite photography and medical imaging, newspapers, colorizing of old black and white movies, and in personal computers. Marketing projections show that within the next few years, 65 percent of the computer screens in business, industry, government, and education will be displaying color images just as color TVs now outnumber black and white sets (see Figure 5.1).

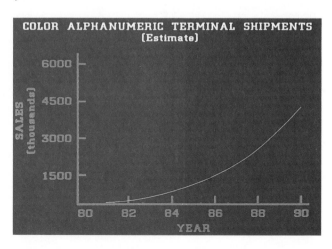

Figure 5.1 *Projected Shipments of Color Displays* Forecasts of the numbers of color displays that will be shipped by 1991. (*Adapted from* Dataquest, *1983.*)

Multiple markets thus drive the demand for color media. In the business sector, color is an important presentation tool. In education, it is an effective teaching aid. In the entertainment industry, color is a requirement for high quality image production. In desktop publishing, color adds a realistic dimension to the graphics which accompany text. The increasing demand for color displays has resulted in an increasing demand for devices which reproduce color images onto hard copy. These include plotters, printers, film recorders.

The Expansion of Color Applications

The use of color is becoming more common in applications that in the past were the domain of monochrome displays (such as text processing and spreadsheets). Color images are now integrated into almost every application for which computers are used, including presentation graphics, process control, technical illustration, mechanical modeling, signal analysis, molecular biology, satellite and medical imaging (see Figure 5.2), production control, and radar tracking (see Chapter 1). More recently, color is being used creatively for computer-aided instructional purposes in schools, control and monitoring of commercial aircraft, and automated mapping systems in automobiles.

Color computer image applications are thus expanding in the fields of business, industry, medicine, astronomy, scientific research, and education. Some of its uses include

- As an aid in on-line interactive management tool
- As a part of photorealism in animated three-dimensional graphics
- As an enhancer of images in medicine, astronomy, and cartography

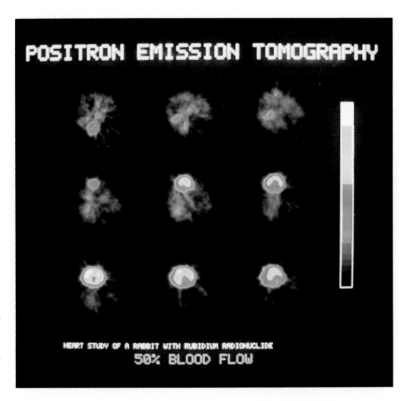

Figure 5.2 *Computer Use in Medical Analysis* A positron emission tomograph (PET) of a rabbit's heart. Different colors show different radiation energy levels. (*Courtesy of 3M Comtal.*)

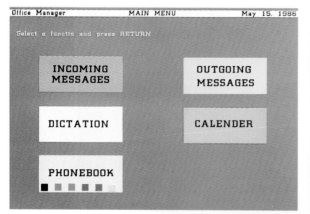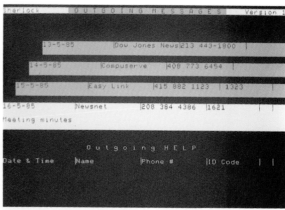

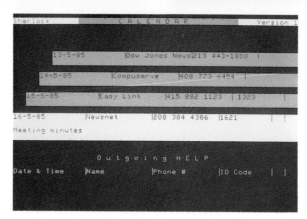

Figure 5.3 *Integrated Desktop System* Each different color set of bands represents different office functions in a desk management program. (*Courtesy of Hewlett-Packard.*)

Color Use with Window Managers

Color is useful as an identifier for menus and screen environments. It is particularly useful with multiple screen environments displayed as tiled and layered windows. (Tiled windows are adjacent to each other; layered windows overlap.) For example, colors segregate different environments or, conversely, group similar environments (see Figure 5.3). Specific color values can create depth effects (see Chapter 8) to enhance the appearance of active windows and the overlapping appearance of layered windows. Saturation levels can indicate the depth of active menus within a particular environment.

Planning and Data Analysis

In business graphics and simulations, color often shows the relationships between cause and effects. For example, it highlights check points and potential bottlenecks of time schedule charts and state diagrams. By visually highlighting critical stages of a project, it helps the viewer quickly make decisions. Timely and critical decisions are often based on the way information and its related flow appear to affect cost and profit. Color enhances the ability to perceive the flow of related information.

In spreadsheet programs, color also assists in viewing the global effect of a change in one data point (cell) upon all related data. The results of a change in a single value become apparent when the colors of all affected data change (such as subtotals and totals). Thus, changes are immediately shown (see Figure 5.4).

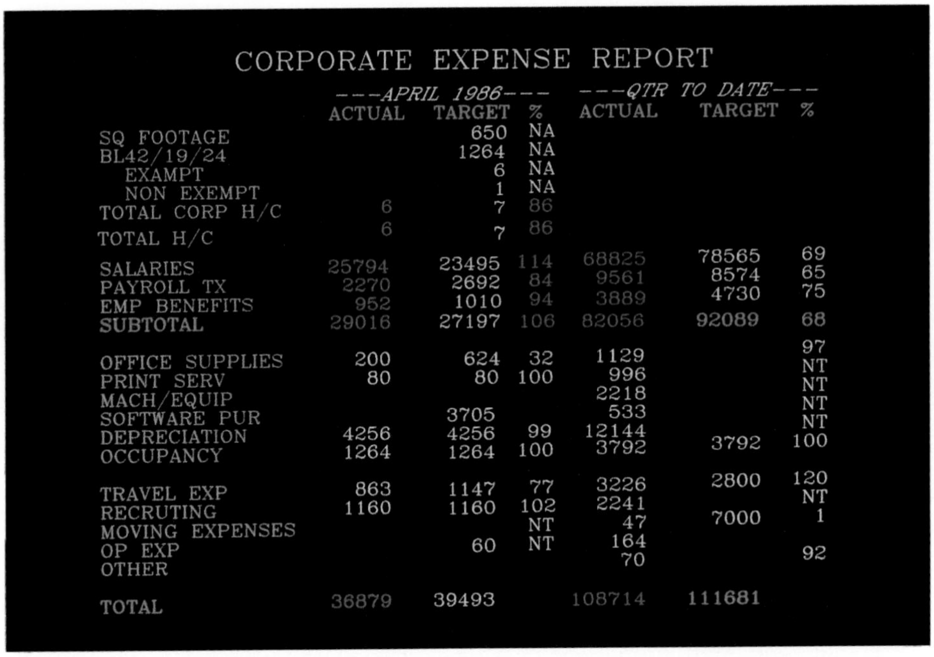

```
                    CORPORATE EXPENSE REPORT
                 ---APRIL 1986---     ---QTR TO DATE---
                 ACTUAL  TARGET  %    ACTUAL   TARGET   %
SQ FOOTAGE                 650   NA
BL42/19/24                1264   NA
  EXAMPT                     6   NA
  NON EXEMPT                 1   NA
TOTAL CORP H/C      6        7   86
TOTAL H/C           6        7   86

SALARIES        25794    23495  114   68825    78565    69
PAYROLL TX       2270     2692   84    9561     8574    65
EMP BENEFITS      952     1010   94    3889     4730    75
SUBTOTAL        29016    27197  106   82056    92089    68

OFFICE SUPPLIES   200      624   32    1129              97
PRINT SERV         80       80  100     996              NT
MACH/EQUIP                             2218              NT
SOFTWARE PUR             3705            533              NT
DEPRECIATION     4256     4256   99   12144              NT
OCCUPANCY        1264     1264  100    3792     3792    100

TRAVEL EXP        863     1147   77    3226     2800    120
RECRUTING        1160     1160  102    2241              NT
MOVING EXPENSES                 NT       47     7000      1
OP EXP                     60   NT      164
OTHER                                    70              92

TOTAL           36879    39493        108714   111681
```

Figure 5.4 *Color Use in Spreadsheets* The change in color to magenta indicates the effects of changing an allocation (in this case the addition of one more person) within the matrix.

In more recent business application programs (such as HP's New Wave), color establishes links across related data. If a value in a spreadsheet which is used in a pie chart is changed, the color of all related data will change in both the table and the pie chart.

Presentation Graphics and Text

Presentation graphics use color to highlight and group complex information. Traditional single color presentations identified relationships by grouping similar information. Color allows the identification of related items even if the items are positioned in very different areas on media.

Guidelines for the use of color in text applications have a different emphasis than those for color graphics. In graphic applications, color mainly differentiates graphic forms to add realism to a scene.

Technical Writing and Desktop Publishing

In technical writing, color formats, segregates, and associates categories of information. For example, highlighting keywords and their definitions in two different colors distinguishes them from the rest of the text. This technique is also useful to create a glossary and index for technical documents and books. Color coded keywords and definitions embedded in text can be easily located for later compilation into a glossary or index (see Figure 5.5). Color also codes related subjects in indexes, mailing lists, and reference lists.

Color can identify later editions of a document by highlighting new material. This aids location of material from earlier versions that may require adjustment or deletion. Color also highlights important points on standard forms of letters, legal briefs, insurance billings, and inventories (see Figure 5.6).

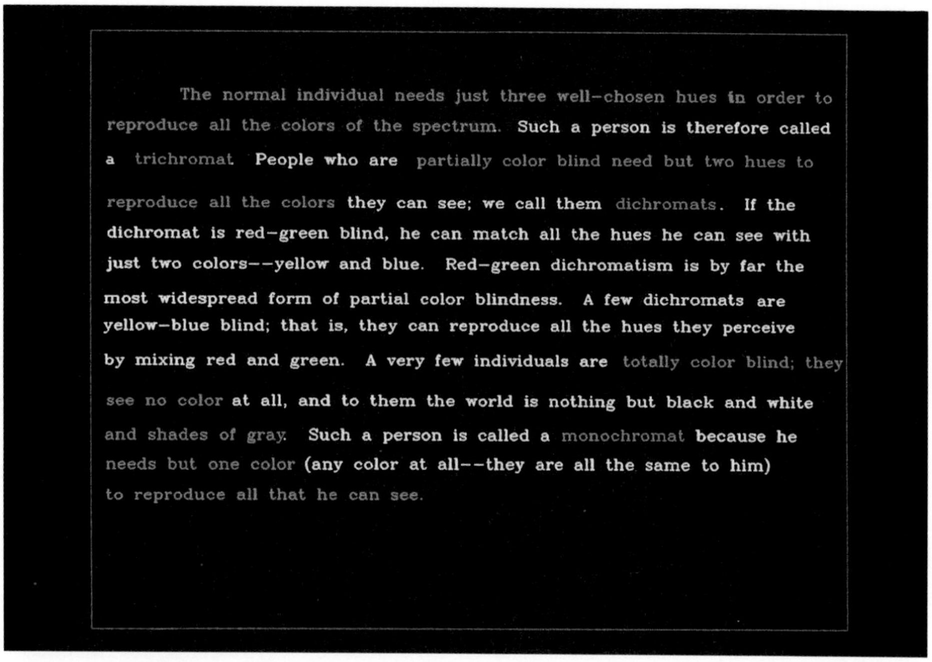

The normal individual needs just three well-chosen hues in order to reproduce all the colors of the spectrum. Such a person is therefore called a trichromat. People who are partially color blind need but two hues to reproduce all the colors they can see; we call them dichromats. If the dichromat is red–green blind, he can match all the hues he can see with just two colors––yellow and blue. Red–green dichromatism is by far the most widespread form of partial color blindness. A few dichromats are yellow–blue blind; that is, they can reproduce all the hues they perceive by mixing red and green. A very few individuals are totally color blind; they see no color at all, and to them the world is nothing but black and white and shades of gray. Such a person is called a monochromat because he needs but one color (any color at all––they are all the same to him) to reproduce all that he can see.

Figure 5.5 *Highlighting Keywords and Definitions* Keywords and their definitions are highlighted by being color coded in orange and cyan.

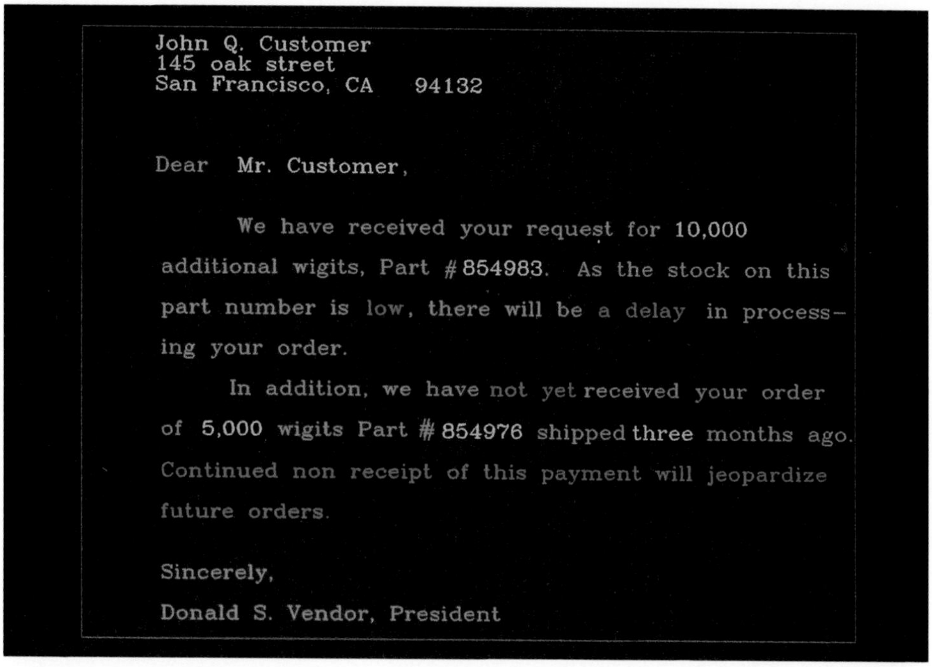

John Q. Customer
145 oak street
San Francisco, CA   94132

Dear   Mr. Customer,

We have received your request for 10,000 additional wigits, Part #854983. As the stock on this part number is low, there will be a delay in processing your order.

In addition, we have not yet received your order of 5,000 wigits Part #854976 shipped three months ago. Continued non receipt of this payment will jeopardize future orders.

Sincerely,

Donald S. Vendor, President

Figure 5.6 *Coding Different Types of Information in a Form Letter* Standard text is coded in cyan, text that changes in each letter is coded in yellow, and critical information unique to a specific customer is coded in magenta.

Creating and printing text with color graphics from a computer terminal system increases the potential of desktop publishing. Even those with little knowledge of the perceptual effects of color can produce documents with a professional appearance.

Desktop publishing places very high demands on color printers. The existing color lithographic technology in the publishing industry offers image resolutions on the order of 1000 dots per inch and millions of colors. This kind of high quality color output from computer-based printers has been difficult to achieve (see Chapter 3). However, color ink-jet printers are rapidly approaching high quality magazine photographs with the recent development of plastic inks. The new color printing technology allows 240 x 240 dots per inch and over 25,000 color shades.

Administration

Administrative applications use color coding for sorting and editing to show the status of projects, floor plan organizations, and grouping and highlighting records processing information. In medical environments, historical or critical data on patient status sheets or the occupancy status of hospital rooms can be effectively color coded to enhance their analysis (see Figure 5.7). Medical applications can make use of a variety of color coding schemes depending on the type of information displayed.

Computer-Aided Manufacturing and Design

Computer-aided manufacturing (CAM) and *computer-aided design* (CAD) are engineering disciplines that rely increasingly on the use of color. The dense information of engineering drawings (for example, integrated circuits and geological survey maps) requires displays with higher resolution than those used for office applications like text processing and business graphics. With a 19-inch, high resolution display, a user can easily see the details in simulated models.

CAD and CAM systems allow user interaction at several stages of a product life cycle: from development (for example, designing a mask on a silicon wafer) to manufacturing (for example, mechanical design of the devices which manufacture silicon chips), to monitoring of manufacturing processes like etching and diffusion (see Figure 5.8).

SICU104 Jones, Robert S. 123-45-6789-xx Dr. Cameron						Thu 4 Sep 86 8:31 AM		

Vital			Wed Jul 3				Thu Jul 4		
Signs	FLOWSHEET	8PM	9PM	10PM	11PM	12 M	1AM	2AM	3AM
I&O	HR	100	95	110	100	100	110	124	132	
	Resp Rate	20	20	20	18	16	18	16	16	
	Temp	39.8	39.2	38.8	38.6	38.3	38.1	38.1	38.0	
Meds	ABP Systol	125	130	130	120	120	120 *	92	125	
	ABP Diast	75	75	70	75	70	75	56	70	
Resp.	D5W .25	50	50	50	50	50	50	50	50	
	Saline							150	150	
	Whole Blood									
Labs	Hyperal	100	100	100	100	100	100	100	100	
Treat-	Wound Care									
ments	Drsg Change		[BEP]					[FSN]		
	Chest PT		[BEP]					[FSN]		
Events	C,T,&DB		[BEP]					[FSN]		
	I + S			[BEP]		+			*[FSN]	

⏪	⬅ earlier	later ➡	⏩

Chem I results available.

Figure 5.7 *Coding of Patient's Medical Status* Red is used to highlight the current day's reading for a patient's physical responses. Yellow is used as a neutral value to help separate rows. Cyan indicates information areas regarding patient's vital signs. (*Courtesy of Hewlett-Packard.*)

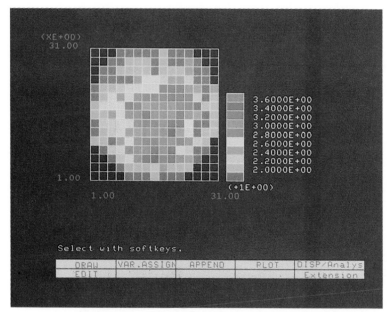

Figure 5.8 *Color as a Manufacturing Inspection Tool* The different colors indicate different levels of chip quality on a silicon wafer. (*Courtesy of Hewlett-Packard.*)

Color Use in CAE

Color in *computer-aided engineering* (CAE) applications enhances the segregation and dimensions of components and provides realistic appearance of images by replicating their colors (see Figure 5.9). CAE workstations use color to

- signify temporary drawing aids such as grids, rubber-band lines, and triangulation points
- identify multiple layers of a complex electrical circuit diagram
- distinguish labels from drawn objects
- produce realistic color shading in solids modeling
- distinguish or associate distinct categories of data objects (for example, NAND gates from NOR gates or labels of wires from circuits)

Figure 5.9 *Color as an Engineering Aid* Most CAE systems use a menu design like the one on the right of the screen. The top right corner displays the entire image. The main working area of the screen displays an enlarged section of the image. (*Courtesy of Hewlett-Packard.*)

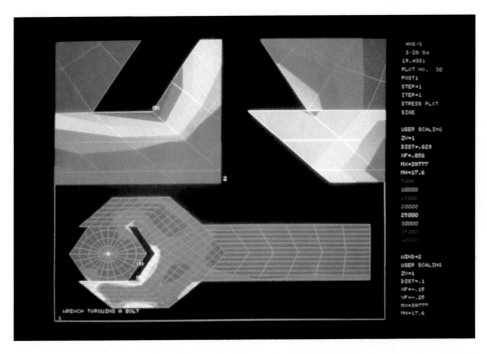

Figure 5.10 *Stress Points of Two Interacting Forces* Color highlights areas on a wrench that show maximum stress points when tightening a bolt. (*Courtesy of Hewlett-Packard.*)

Color in Mechanical Stress Simulations

In mechanical simulations, color shows the ability of structures to withstand stress forces such as vibration, weight, torque, pressure, and acceleration (see Figure 5.10). This helps the designer visualize those areas of the object that require redesign. It also shows the designer which areas are not susceptible to stress points and do not need to be considered for redesign.

Enhancing Inspection and Monitoring

In CAD/CAM applications, color helps the visual inspection of alignments of parts like connectors. For example, if a connector is coded blue and its plug is red on a display screen, errors in positioning are easy to see by superimposing the components. The correct superimposition of blue and red can be shown in magenta (their additive mixture—see Chapter 2) and the misalignments will remain in either red and blue.

The on-line monitoring of manufacturing processes by computers is not novel. However, the use of color on computer screens to enhance these activities is relatively recent. Showing the changes in processes by very different hues enhances the perception of changes in their state. For example, a manufacturing operator may use color as a tool to monitor changes in a metal alloy during its exposure to high temperatures. High temperatures decrease the rigidity of metal alloys. At specific temperatures, the molecular structure of a metal alloy can change beyond the desired state. Computer graphics display the stability of the alloy by real-time tests as the metal heats. Color coding can show state changes and critical or ''out-of-spec'' conditions.

Scheduling

Another application that benefits from the utilization of computer color is the monitoring of part flow and inventory. Simulations are available that model a manufacturing floor and warehouse layout. Color coded flow diagrams of icons show where parts are needed or where they are in surplus. This information is then incorporated into scheduling normal and overtime shift loads.

Material Design and Appearance

Textile industries, architects, and fashion deigners are increasing their use of computer color in their creations. The on-line capability to alter color and observe the effects is resulting in an increase in production, the number of unique styles, and color combinations of materials.

One of these areas that shows significant benefits of computer color is carpet manufacturing (see Figure 5.11). For centuries, creators of rugs have been using the depth effects of colors to produce three-dimensional illusions. They have also used the effects of assimilation (see Chapter 7) to create the appearance of colors beyond those available by combining threads of different colors. CAD systems now allow designers to view these effects during design of a new rug pattern before it is woven.

Designers are using computer color graphics to view the effects of the environment on the appearance of their products. For example, rug designers can simulate the effects of different ambient light conditions on the appearance of the colors and dimensions of rugs. Architects, interior designers, and engineers use these same techniques to preview the appearance of structures in different lighting conditions (see Figure 5.12.)

Simulation and the Cinema

The motion picture industry is using color CAD systems to create animated and semi-animated films (see Figure 5.13). The popularity of films like *Star Wars*, *Tron*, *Star Trek*, and *Short Circuit* is partially due to the sophistication of computer color graphics. The use of color to create illusions and moods is especially noticeable in these films. *Star Wars* in black and white would have lacked all the excitement and emotional impact of the brightly colored laser beams, rockets, and flight patterns of the Jedi knights.

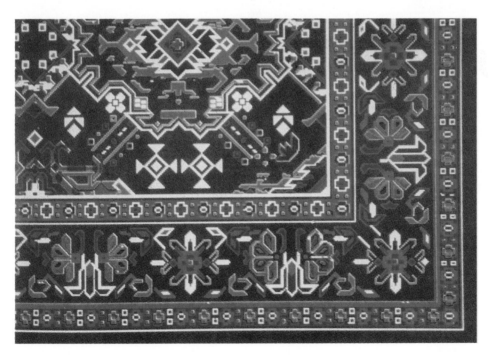

Figure 5.11 *Textile CAD* Carpet design simulated on a computer display. One of the advantages of CAD systems is the possibility of modeling products (like this carpet) or processes without the expense of building prototypes. (*Permission from Adage, Inc.*)

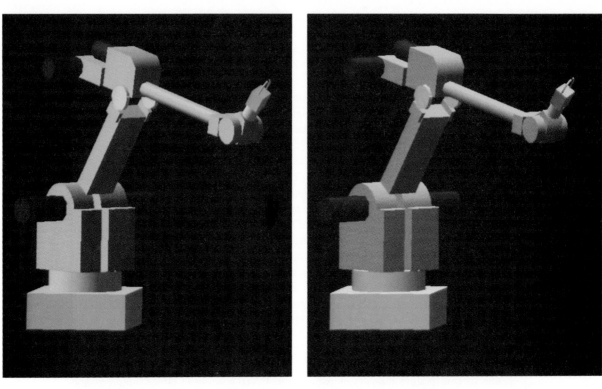

Figure 5.12 *Solids Model with Repositional Light Source* The two versions of the robot show its appearance as a light is moved around it. (*Courtesy of Hewlett-Packard.*)

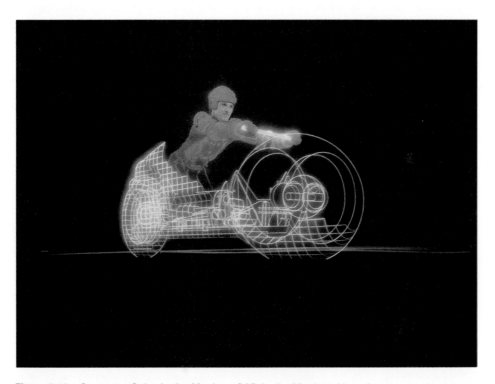

Figure 5.13 *Computer Color in the Movies CAD in the Movies* Use of computer graphics to create a realistic impression of the Light Cycle game in the movie *Tron*. The higher perceived brightness of yellow (compared to the other colors in the picture) highlights Tron's vehicle control bar and his vehicle. (Courtesy and © The Walt Disney Company.)

Colorizing Black and White Movies

Colorizing is the transformation of black and white movies into color. The process is conducted with a color display system that adds color to frames of a duplicate of the master film onto video tape. A technician separates the film into scene categories which are series of frames with common images between the scenes. Technicians select colors to add to elements in the key frame and apply them by using a mouse to trace the borders of images. The computer fills in color in the image area. The images in the key frames and their assigned colors are stored in computer memory. The computer then automatically transfers the colors of the key frame to those with the same images. The process is repeated for all the key frames in the film.

Different color values of colors are determined by the luminance values in the original movie. A more sophisticated, but time consuming technique digitizes colors and manipulates each pixel in each frame. An advantage of this technique is that the computer detects black and white pixels which do not require color assignment. In addition, once the technician has assigned a hue, the program can interpolate to assign different shades to a luminance gradient.

Programming

Software design productivity partially depends on the speed and accuracy to detect a programming error and fix (debug) it. This is often a difficult and time consuming process, one that does not need the extra effort of visual sorting through dense screen information (such as long file listings and program code). Color can help this process by coding various aspects of program codes and associated information. For example, color can aid the programming task by identifying syntactic errors like unclosed parentheses in a complex nested programming statement. Typically, the pairs of statements must be compared to find an odd parentheses. If the nesting is complex, this process can take a lot of time. However, color can code pairs of parentheses in a line. The routine can stop when all parentheses are counted. The odd parenthesis is then apparent (see Figure 5.14).

```
IF ((Y2-YO)*DY.LT.-.001.OR.    (Y2-YO)*DX.LT.-.001)RETURN
KRAN=IFIX (FLOAT) IRAN)/DL+0.4999))
IDZ+ITAB2(NCOIT)- ITAB1(NCOIT)
IF (STHET.LT.STHETX) FOR=FLOAT(IXMAX)ABS(COS(THETA))
SLPE=FLOT/(FDX+1./ (2*FRQ*.03122))

ERROR IS UNCLOSED PARENTHESES IN LINE 2


IF  ((Y2-YO) *DY.LT.-.001.OR.    (Y2-YO)*DX.LT-.001)  RETURN
KRAN=IFIX (FLOAT) IRAN)/DL+0.4999))
IDZ+ITAB2 (NCOIT)-  ITAB1(NCOIT)
IF (STHET.LT.STHETX)  FOR=FLOAT(IMAX) ABS(COS (THETA))
SLPE=FLOT/(FDX+1./ (2*FRQ*.03122))
```

Figure 5.14 *Finding Syntactic Errors* In the top Fortran statement, an error (omission of a parenthesis) exists. The error is difficult to find because all the elements are white. In the bottom color coded version, it is easier to check parentheses placement because they are a different color than the main coding statement and their nested groups are a different color.

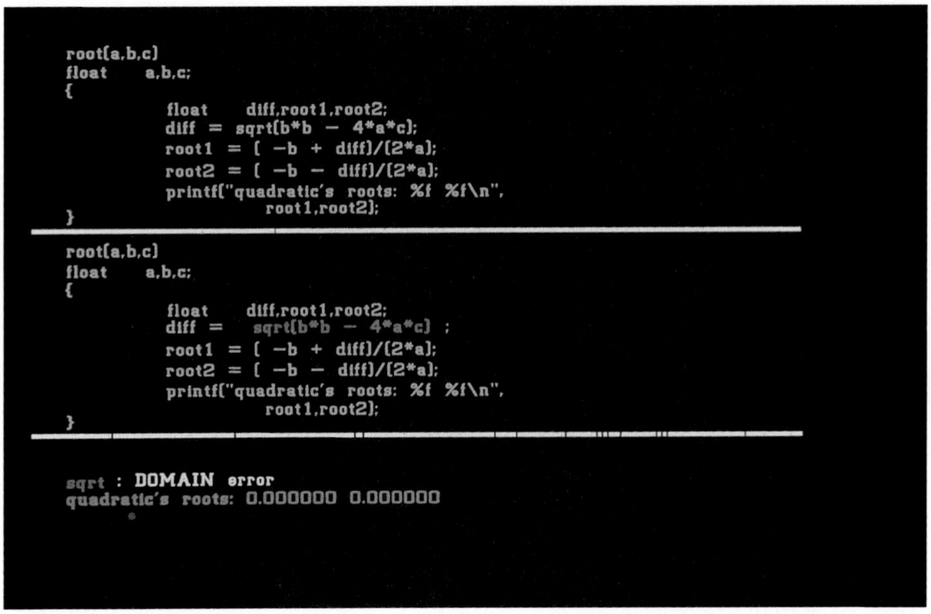

Figure 5.15 *Fatal Bug and Corresponding Code* Programming C statement in which the original statement is in green, its duplication with the error in magenta, the error description in yellow, and the error as it appears in output in cyan.

Color can also highlight routines or source lines where a fatal or near-fatal bug has been detected (see Figure 5.15).

Color coding system status messages has existed for some time. Most computer manufacturers offering alpanumeric color displays have adopted conventions for assigning colors to these messages. These conventions are based on well-known associations.

Cartography

With the increase in power, reduction in cost, and use of color in computer devices, cartography is now more than the drawing of geographic maps. It also includes the assembly of geographic, topographic, demographic, socioeconomic, and political data onto maps and related graphics.

However, much of the data now mapped by cartographers begin as numbers. These quantifiable data (such as demographic and economic trends, air quality, political boundaries, birth rates, and literacy) are assembled and stored in a database that is later converted to geographic representations.

Depending on their details, map representations can be the most complicated form of visual imagery. Many different forms of images exist in maps including lines of different thickness and spacing, area-fills, textures, pictures, icons, type fonts, colors, and shadings.

These images combined with the dense formats of typical maps are a major challenge for the computer color industry. Likewise, the effective use of computer color to show salient features, similarities, and associations of the images is a major challenge for cartographers.

Cartographers follow several conventions for color use. In traditional mapping systems, colors duplicate the appearance of natural features (such as blue for lakes, green for forests, and brown for mountains). In topographical maps (where heights of land masses are geometrically represented), colors replicate the perceived appearance of the environment (for example, green for lower, dense vegetation areas and brown for higher, sparse vegetation areas). In simulated weather maps, colors replicate concepts associated

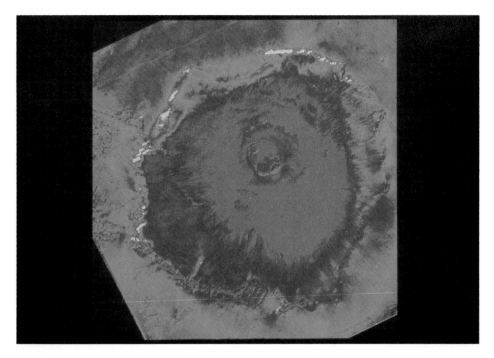

Figure 5.16 *Showing Unusual Land Forms* Close-up false colored image of the largest volcano on Mars. The color represents different temperatures: Magenta represents the highest land levels and therefore is the volcano, yellow represents low rises in elevation, and blue represents flat land surfaces. (*Courtesy of Mike Carr, U.S. Geological Survey.*)

with mental models of temperature (for example, red, orange, and yellow associated with warm weather fronts and blue and purple for cold fronts).

With the advent of computer color and the ability to quickly create and change map representations, many novel colors and their applications are now in use. Cartographers use false colors to show unusual and dramatic land forms in colors that enhance their appearance (see Figure 5.16). They can also convert data that are invisible to the eye but measurable by scientific instruments (like infrared radiation) into a visible form.

Many modern mapping systems (such as for environmental impact and reconnaissance analysis) require users to create maps very quickly and accurately. They must be able to quickly identify and discriminate visual images and make life-sustaining decisions based on their perceptions of these images. Applications like these include head-down displays in aircraft, aircraft monitoring displays, and computer maps in automobiles.

Medical Imaging

The advent of computer color and, in particular, advanced image processing, has significantly improved the reliability of medical dignoses (see Figure 5.17).

Image processing techniques like pseudocoloring and density slicing (see Chapter 10) enhance the perception of images on X rays, thermographs, sonograms, and CAT scans. These image enhancing techniques make visible the structures that are not visible in standard X rays.

Imaging processing techniques convert information to gray shades but there are several advantages to using color. First, saturated colors immediately attract attention (see Chapters 6 and 7). A medical pathology barely visible on an X ray recoded in color allows it to be more apparent so that the location and spatial extent of the diseased area can be diagnosed (see Figure 5.18). Color images assist doctors to segregate specific areas for analysis. Surrounding structures, irrelevant to the medical analysis, can be assigned low

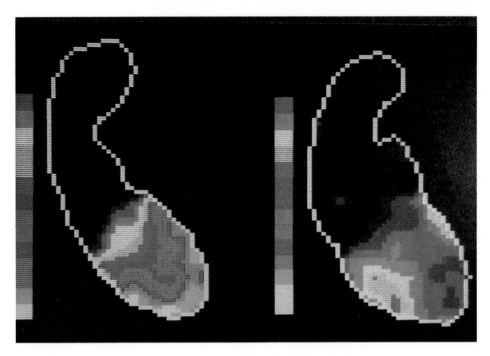

Figure 5.17 *Heart Before and After Stress* Digitized image of heart muscle tissue suffering from severe coronary artery disease. Left image is the heart at rest; right image is the heart after stress. The yellow end of the color scale represents the efficient performance of the myocardium, the green end shows its inefficient performance. (*By permission from Polaroid.*)

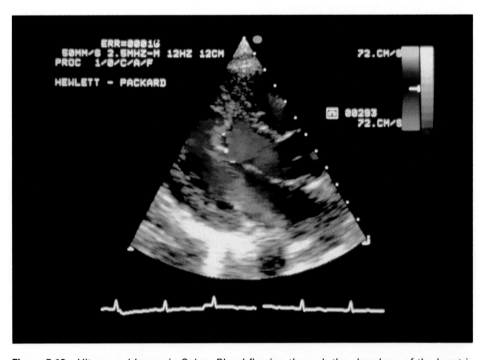

Figure 5.18 *Ultrasound Image in Color* Blood flowing through the chambers of the heart is color coded as to its direction and velocity, which helps diagnose heart disease. Blood flowing toward the instrument transducer is coded in red, and blood flowing away is coded in blue. (Courtesy of Hewlett-Packard.)

contrast colors which reduce their visual attraction and interference with the analysis. For example, blood clots (thrombosis) inhibit circulation which causes the temperature of the affected area to decrease. A thermogram is sensitive to heat and can thus show changes in the temperature of different parts of the body. Such an infrared image can be converted to color for the doctor's review. The thrombosis condition observed on a thermogram will appear in blue or green, depending on the severity of the loss in circulation. After surgery to repair the blood clot, the same area appears in red or yellow indicating a normal, healthy condition.

There are several advantages to medical imaging in color. Besides making latent objects visible, they include

- Three-dimensional imaging
- Reduction of noise interference of surrounding structures
- Complex arrays of biochemical functions
- Imaging through solid structures like bones (not possible with X rays)
- More accurate diagnosis of the diseases
- Modeling of surgical procedures
- Better presurgery planning
- Reducing the number of radiation exposures and chemicals required

Education

Color can enhance learning. Until recently, the high cost of color reproduction has prohibited its liberal use as an instructional element in computer media and textbooks. With increasing availability of color displays and desktop publishing and the decreasing costs of color printers, the visually exciting dimensions of color are opening up to the on-line learner.

System Tutorials

Color can guide the order of sequential operations in system tutorials. It can also guide users of an application program through a menu hierarchy or a file system. All the menus within an application program can be color coded a specific hue. As long as the user stays within this level of the system, all the screens remain the same hue. However, when the user either intentionally or accidentally selects a different environment, the color of the screen changes and alerts the user.

Learning the Sciences

Students learning new subjects often have difficulty understanding relationships between variables and the effects of their changes. Demonstrations of these effects are easy with color simulations on computer screens. For example, the interaction of different phenomena in physics, chemistry, and biology are more obvious when they are presented in color (see Figure 5.19). The color graphic representation of the interactive components of a DNA molecule is a good example of the educational advantages of color.

Industrial trainers can use color to show the results of varying the components in a manufacturing or monitoring process. Interactive software tutorials are safer and more economical than experiments with physical elements and actual processes.

Geometry, algebra, and calculus can also be taught by color schemes instead of confusing letter codes. Learning geometry proofs by examining the diagrams is a relatively difficult task. It involves understanding the mathematical concept and identifying the small

Figure 5.19 *Using Color in Science* The different colors show the differences and relationship between atoms in a section of a protein chain for a scorpion venom neuro-toxin. Each color corresponds to a different type of atom: Hydrogen is white, carbon is red, nitrogen is blue, oxygen is green, and sulfur is magenta. (Courtesy of Hewlett-Packard.)

letters associated with portions of the figure (like polygon abcd) which represent variables in the mathematical concept (see Figure 5.20). This process and its meaning could be greatly enhanced by using color codes to connect parts of the diagram with its associated text.

Color can also be used to parse mathematical statements, revealing discrete units by hue and related operations by saturation. In this manner, color can guide and clarify nested mathematical expressions.

Visual Mathematics: Fractals

Computer color aids the visualization of the iterations of complicated equations, representing shapes derived from recursive equations called *fractals*. The fractal is a term coined by Benoit Mandelbrot to identify objects usually generated by infinite iterations of a random process.

Fractals are being used to aid in the description of shapes seemingly of random natural structures like coastlines and cloud formations. The fractal images have the remarkable property of having intricately detailed shapes regardless of the scale at which they are examined. In addition, any part of the object is actually a scaled-down version of the whole.

Different colors are used to show the state of iteration. For example, reds and oranges may be used to represent the limits of the equation inside the boundary. Different saturations of green could represent the speed at which the iteration will approach infinity outside the boundary. Saturated greens could represent those iterations that approach infinity first (see Figure 5.21).

Constantly iterating formulas like

$$Z_n = Z_{n-1}^2 + C$$

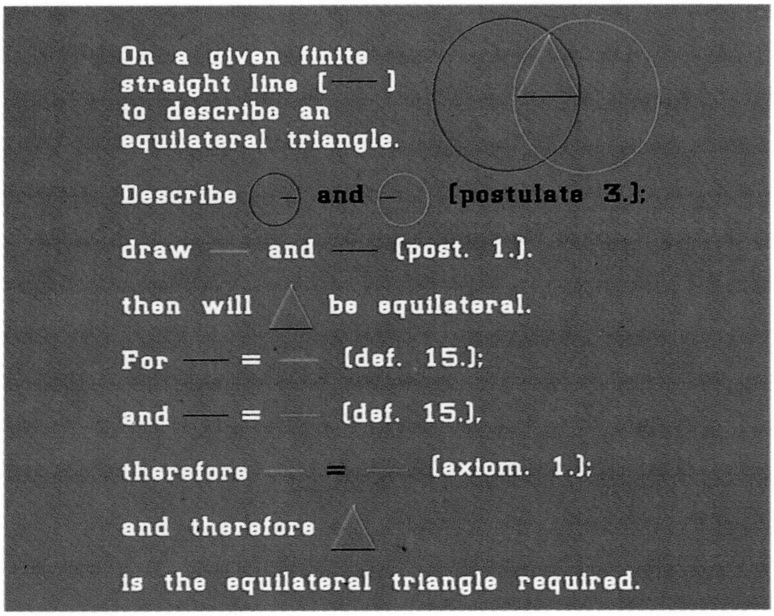

On a given finite
straight line [—]
to describe an
equilateral triangle.

Describe (— and — [postulate 3.];

draw — and — [post. 1.].

then will △ be equilateral.

For — = — [def. 15.];

and — = — [def. 15.],

therefore — = — [axiom. 1.];

and therefore △

is the equilateral triangle required.

Figure 5.20 *Color in Geometry* Color is used to explain a geometric proof. This example is adapted from a 19th century British geometry textbook, *The Ten Elements of Euclid.*

and then replacing them by geometric representations will result in a fractal. Iterating a formula like the one just shown produces a fractal boundary which separates the image into two areas. Outside of the boundary, the iteration will eventually go to infinity; while inside the boundary, the iteration will lead to some finite limit or limits. The speed at which a fractal boundary will approach infinity is determined by the number of iterations needed to reach a specified large number (see Figure 5.21).

Figure 5.21 *Fractal Representations* Red represents the finite points or limits of the equation inside its boundary. The different saturations of blue indicate the speed at which the iteration will approach infinity outside its boundary. (*Courtesy of Nic Lyons, Hewlett-Packard.*)

Education

Useful Facts

Identifying Program Environments	Color can indicate different screen environments (applications programs) and levels within these programs.
	Color can enhance the appearance of layered windows.
Modeling Physical Effects	Colors can model physical effects by corresponding hue changes.
Color in Text	Uses of color in text applications include highlighting areas that require attention, grouping, or editing.
	Color is useful for compiling reference lists and glossaries and can assist editing.
Color in CAD	Color adds realism to CAD models.
Enhancing Programming	One of the unique uses for color is improving programming productivity. Color can show when variable bounds exceed their limits, locate syntactic errors, and show fatal bugs and corresponding codes.
Computer Cartography	Computer-generated maps often assign colors to images that are different from the natural image.
Imaging Enhancement	Color image enhancement techniques allow the perception of images that cannot be seen with an unaided eye.

REFERENCES

Castner, H. W., "Printer Color Charts: Some Thoughts on Their Construction and Use in Map Design," *American Congress on Surveys and Mapping*, 1980, pp. 370–378.

Cowen, D. J., "PC CAD Manages Geographic Data," *Computer Graphics World*, July 1986, pp. 38–44.

"Cutting a Rug with Color CAD," *Computer Graphics World*, May 1986, p. 128.

Dataquest, 1987.

Digital Cartographic and Geographic Data, U.S. Geological Survey, Oct. 1985.

Engel, F. L., "Information Selection from Visual Display Units," in *Ergonomics Aspects of Visual Display Terminals*, eds. E. Grandjean and E. Vigliani (London: Taylor and Francis Ltd., 1982), pp. 121–124.

Faintich, M., "The Politics of Geometry," *Computer Graphics World*, May 1986, pp. 101–104.

Farrell, E. J., R. Zappulla, and W. C. Yang, "Color 3-D Imaging of Normal and Pathologic Intracranial Structures," *IEEE CG&A*, Sept. 1984, pp. 5–16.

Franklin, W. R., "Software Aspects of Business Graphics," *Computers and Graphics*, 7(1), 1983, 5–10.

Greene, N. "Environment Mapping and Other Applications of World Projections," *IEEE CG&A*, 1986, pp. 21–29.

Jackson, R. N. and S. R. Turner, "Colour in Visual Display Units," Technical Report, Philips Research Laboratories, 1980.

Jaffe, C. C., "Medical Imaging, Vision and Visual Psychophysics," *Medical Radiography and Photography*, 60(1), July 1984, 1–48.

Kerlow, I. V. and J. Rosebush. *Computer Graphics for Designers & Artists* (New York: Van Nostrand, 1986.

Lerch, I. A., "Medical Images of the Body," *Close-Up*, Polaroid Corp., 13(1), August 1982, 11–15.

Levkowitz, H. and G. T. Herman," Color in Multidimensional Multiparameter Medical Imaging," *Color Research and Application*, 11, Supplement 1986, 515–520.

Samit, M. L., "The Quality Factor," *Computer Graphics World*, July 1986, pp. 28–34.

Sena, M. L., "Computer Mapping for Publication," *Computer Graphics World*, 6(7), July 1983, 68–76.

Spiker, A., S. P. Rogers, and J. Cicinelli, "Selecting Colour Codes for a Computer-Generated Topographic May Be Based on Perception Experiments and Functional Requirements, *Ergonomics*, 29(11), 1986, 1313–1328.

Taylor, R. M., "Color Design in Aviation Cartography," *Displays*, 6(4), Oct. 1985, 187–201.

Taylor, R. M. and G. M. Murch, "The Effective Use of Color in Visual Displays: Text and Graphics Applications," *Color Research and Application*, 11, Sept. 1986, S3–S11.

Topographic Maps, U.S. Dept. of the Interior/Geological Survey 1986, 0–160–430.

6

Color Vision

The rays are not colored.

Isaac Newton

Understanding color vision helps designers build better computer color devices and create more effective color graphics. Understanding color vision requires learning how the visual system converts the physical properties of light into neural signals which are interpreted as color.

Physical and Perceptual Components of Color

The perceptual components of color are closely related to its physical properties (see Chapter 2). When the wavelength composition of a light changes, people usually report a change in hue. When the purity of a light varies, they typically report a variation in its shade or saturation. When the number of photons emitted by a light increases, people usually perceive the light as brighter.

However, the perceptual properties of color are not perfectly correlated with its physical counterparts. Changing the wavelength of a light does not always produce a change in hue. In addition, a change in wavelength may result in a change in lightness as well as hue. Unlike the physical components of color, it is not possible to independently vary its perceptual components. In fact, changing any one of the perceptual dimensions of color usually changes the appearance of the other two components.

The lack of correlation between the perceptual and physical components of light means that color spaces based on CRT primaries (for example, RGB space, see chapter 9) are not intuitively useful. This kind of physical color space is only coarsely representative of the sensory aspects of color perception.

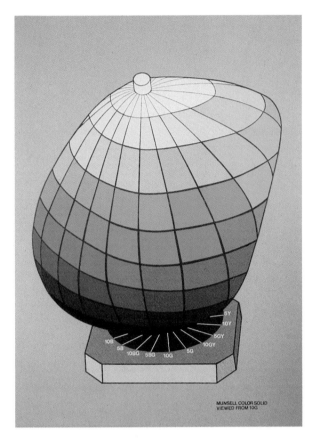

Figure 6.1 *Geometric Color Representation* The shape of this color space represents colors of different hues, saturations, and lightnesses. Hue varies around the perimeter and with radial angle. Saturation varies along the radius, and lightness varies along the vertical axis. (*Courtesy of Munsell.*)

Perceptual Color Space

The interaction of the perceptual components of color can be best shown in a geometric representation known as a *perceptual color space* (see Figure 6.1). In this space, colors are arranged in gradual variations of hue, saturation, and lightness values. Hues vary around the perimeter of the shape (or by radial angle): red blends into orange, which blends into yellow, then to green, blue, violet, and then back to red. Saturations vary across the radius of the sphere, with most saturated values at the perimeter and least saturated values at the center. Lightness values vary along the vertical axis, with extreme values (black and white) at either apex. As colors become lighter they appear more like white and as they become darker they look more like black.

The shape of the perceptual color sphere qualitatively represents the way the visual system filters and transforms the physical properties of light. For example, the taper of the vertical axes represents the restricted range of color perception at extreme lightness values: All colors look white at extreme high lightness values and black at extreme dark values. This limitation is most obvious in dim light (such as twilight) and dark rooms where it is very difficult to identify colors.

Several multi-dimensional color notation schemes have been developed, each with quantified attributes of color serving as axes in the color space (see Box). These systems are useful as references and comparisons for both display and hard copy color.

THE MUNSELL COLOR SYSTEM

The Munsell color notation system, developed in 1905, is widely used and is the basis for the color naming system of the National Bureau of Standards. The numeric values of Munsell colors are a direct result of their arrangement by perceptual color components (that is, hue, saturation, and lightness) into a three-dimensional sphere. It is thus a perceptual color system because it specifies a color by its appearance. Hues are arranged around the perimeter of its sphere, *chroma* (the Munsell expression for saturation) are arranged across its diameter, and *values* (the Munsell term for lightness) are located along the vertical axis (see Figure 6.2).

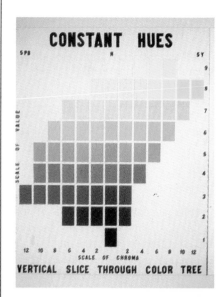

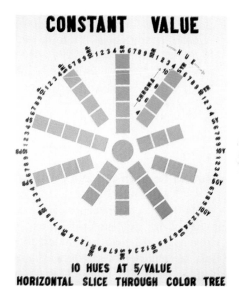

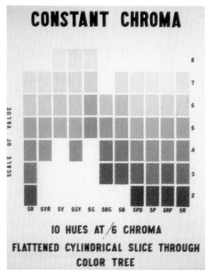

Figure 6.2 *Munsell Color System* Two-dimensional slices of the Munsell space showing hue, value, and chroma. (*Courtesy of Munsell.*)

(continued)

The Munsell sphere reflects many component features of color appearance. For example, some hues (for example, blue) are always seen as more saturated than others (for example, yellow). Thus, the blue portion of the sphere bulges along its horizontal axis. Moreover, the lightness level at which a hue reaches its maximum saturation varies with hue and is apparent in the asymmetrical shape along the vertical axis.

Munsell values are based on equally perceived color differences. The perceptual difference between two adjacent colors (that is, two adjacent chips of different hue, value, or chroma) is not equal to the perceptual difference between two other adjacent colors. However, the perceptual quality of changes in colors along any axis is retained when Munsell color samples are viewed against a neutral gray background and under a standard illuminant.

The Munsell system is useful for describing color because it is almost perceptually uniform: A particular size step in hue, saturation, or lightness appears nearly equal in size to the same size step in another direction. Moreover, the Munsell system can be related to other quantitative color description systems, particularly the CIE system (see Chapter 9).

Computing Color in the Eye and Brain

Color space representations can be models of the perceptual components of color. Their components are more than just useful terms for describing color. They show how the visual system (the eye and the brain) responds to different properties of light. The eye is the beginning of a series of filters through which light information must pass before reaching the brain. Physically, these filters include the optics and a network of neural pathways conveying visual information that is eventually processed in the brain. The physical optics of the eye and the physiological responses of the visual system determine color perception.

Filtering and Focusing Light through the Eye

The two major optical filters of the eye are the *cornea* and *lens*. Light refracts as it passes through these structures and focuses onto the light-sensitive (photoreceptive) area of the *retina* at the back of the eye (see Figure 6.3). The lens of the eye is not color corrected as it is in a high quality camera and as a result, different wavelengths refract and focus at different points in the eye. Simultaneous focus of extreme wavelength lights is thus not possible. This inability has important implications for computer color images. For example, if a wavelength from the middle portion of the visible spectrum (such as green light) is focused on the retina, a short wavelength (such as blue light) will be focused in front of the retina and a long wavelength light (such as red light) will be focused behind the retina. This causes the red and blue lights to have a blurred appearance.

The effect caused by the uncorrected lens of the eye is known as *chromatic aberration*. It is more apparent when changing focus between spectrally extreme wavelengths and particularly with very narrowband light sources (see Figure 6.4). The blue phosphor on a color CRT display produces a relatively narrow band of light. As a result, small text characters (for example, 2.8 mm in height) composed of blue phosphors appear sharp only at short viewing distances (such as 20 to 30 cm). If the viewing distance is significantly greater than 50 cm, blue characters will appear more blurry than characters of other colors.

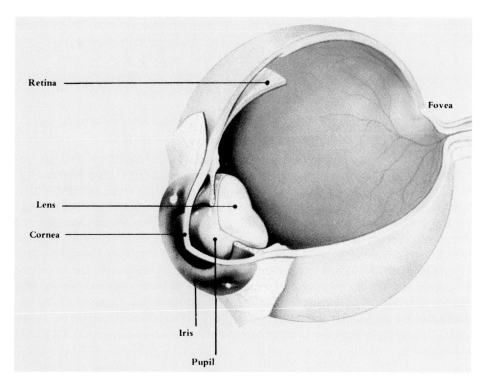

Figure 6.3 *Structure of the Human Eye*   The major structures of the eye: cornea, lens, pupil, iris, retina, fovea, and optic nerve. (*By permission of Marshall Editions, Ltd.*)

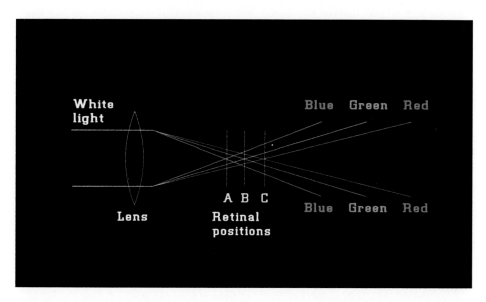

Figure 6.4 *Focusing on Different Colors*   Short wavelengths, shown by blue lines, are naturally focused in front of the retina (position A). Medium wavelengths, shown by green lines, are focused on the retina (position B). Long wavelengths, shown by red lines, are focused in back of the retina (position C).

Refractive Power

The amount of focusing required by the lens is its refractive power and is measured in diopters. One diopter equals the reciprocal of focal length in meters. Thus, one diopter (1 D) is equal to the refraction power required to focus an image at one meter; two diopters

(2 D) is equal to the refraction power necessary to focus an image at one-half meter. Focusing from a red to a green light requires a refractive power change of 0.29 D; focusing from a red to a blue light requires a change of 1.5 D. There is thus a larger refractive power requirement to focus extreme wavelengths (such as red and blue) than spectrally closer wavelengths (such as red and green).

Using Spectral Extremes for Special Effects

In most computer color applications, the blurred effects caused by chromatic aberration are not obvious, although they may have subtle effects on reading performance. Colors which produce these effects should not be used for continuous reading tasks because, as previous described, spectral extreme colors cannot be simultaneously focused. Red alphanumeric characters may appear slightly blurred when reading adjacent blue ones and vice versa. This refocusing may also cause the images to appear to move towards and away from the viewer.

A beneficial use of chromatic aberration is the special effects that can be created for graphic applications. For example, simultaneously displaying extreme wavelengths like red and blue can create a three-dimensional appearance (see Figure 6.5). The appearance of colors at different distances (focal planes) is known as *chromostereopsis*. Its effects are especially useful in creating three-dimensional business graphs, simulations, and animation.

Light Receptors in the Eye

PHOTORECEPTORS: RODS AND CONES   The processing of color begins in light-sensitive cells which compose the photoreceptive area in the retina. There are four types of photoreceptors in the eye: the three types of cone-shaped cells that function in light environments and rod-shaped cells that function in dim light. Cones allow color perception and are more pertinent for computer color applications in light environments.

There are 150,000 cones per square millimeter (mm) in the *fovea* (the area of sharpest focus in the retina) (see Figure 6.6). However, this number represents only four percent of the total number of cones in the eye. The remainder are located in the peripheral areas

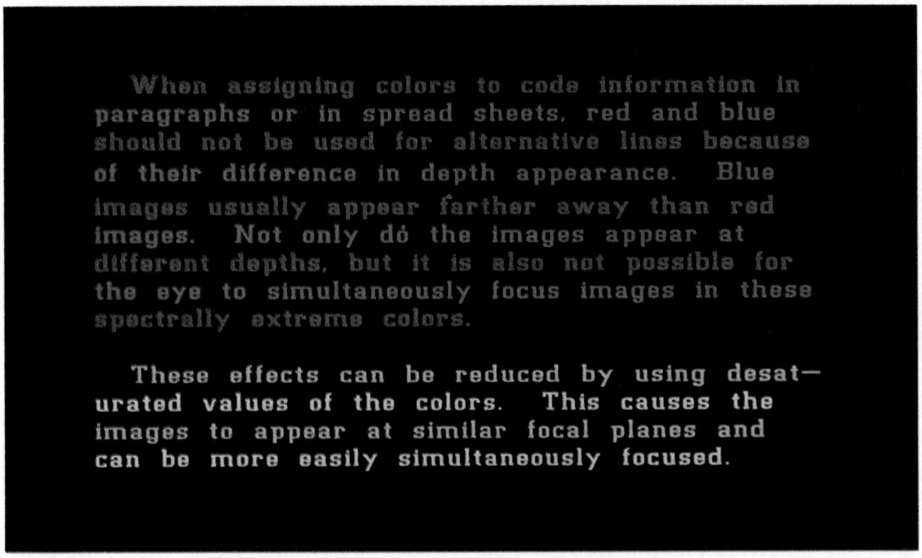

Figure 6.5 *Depth Illusions* Saturated blue and red images often appear to be at different distances from the viewer even though they are on the same plane.

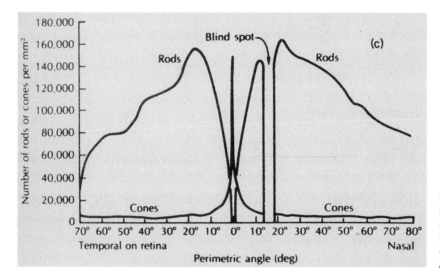

Figure 6.6 *Photoreceptor Distribution across the Retina* Cones are most dense at the fovea (0 degrees); rods are most dense in the periphery (20 degrees from the fovea). *(Courtesy of Academic Press.)*

of the retina. Thus, both the fovea and the peripheral areas of the retina play a role in color vision.

CONE SENSITIVITY Cones can be classified into three groups depending on which area of the visible spectrum they are most sensitive (that is, short, medium, or long wavelengths). Because of these sensitivities, the three cone receptors are often mistakenly labeled "blue," "green," and "red" cells. However, these receptors do not actually send signals to the brain identifying a specific color.

The spectral sensitivity of light sensitive pigments in the cones is relatively broad (see Figure 6.7). The pigments of one type of cone are most sensitive to long wavelength lights and are known as *L* cones; those most sensitive to middle wavelengths are known as *M* cones; those most sensitive to short wavelengths are known as *S* cones. The spectral sensitivity of the L cones is highest (or peaks) in the region of the visible spectrum we perceive as yellow; the spectral sensitivity of the M cones peaks at green; the spectral sensitivity of the S cones peaks at blue.

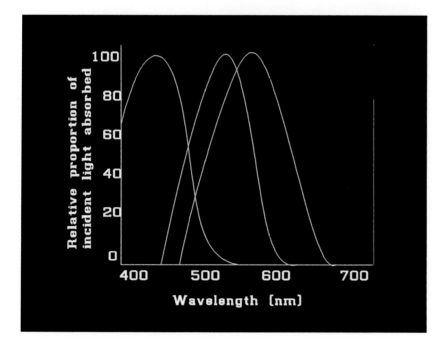

Figure 6.7 *Absorption Spectra of Cones* Because of their relatively broad but selective spectral sensitivity, cones are classified into those wavelengths to which they are sensitive: short (S), medium (M), and long (L). *(Adapted from Wald and Brown, 1966.)*

Computing Color in the Eye and Brain   **109**

Because the spectral sensitivity tuning curves for the three types of cones are so broad, the neural signal from a single type of cone receptor is an ambiguous code for color. For example, the intensity of a medium wavelength light (green) could be adjusted such that an L cone would produce an equal response to that elicited by a red light.

Color Identification

This ambiguity is reduced by neural cells leading to the brain which compare the relative activity rates of the cones. Activated cells suppress (or inhibit) the responses of adjacent cells; inactive cells do not suppress the response of adjacent cells, allowing them to become more stimulated or excited. This process is called *opponency* due to their opponent (suppression versus excitation) activity (see Box).

COLOR OPPONENT CELLS

The electrical activity from a neural cell can be demonstrated by electrode recordings (see Figure 6.8). Each trace is a record of electrical activity (neural spikes) of a color opponent cell as it would appear on an oscilloscope. For example, one type of cell sends out many spikes (excites) in response to a red light, fewer spikes (less response) to orange, and no spikes (no response) to yellow. Moreover, when green and blue lights are shown to the eye, the cell's activity rate is suppressed.

These response characteristics demonstrate the color selectivity of the opponent neural cells. Their responses consist of both increased and suppressed firing. Adjusting the intensities of colored lights cannot produce equal excitation in these cells.

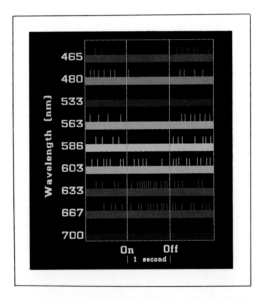

Figure 6.8 *Color Opponency* Diagram of the electrical activity recorded from a single cell in the visual pathway. Each trace shows the cells' responses to a colored light before (first interval), during (middle interval), and after (last interval). Even when there is no light present, the cell emits between one to seven pulses per second. This is a +Red−Green type which emits the greatest number of pulses to a red light (667 nm wavelength) and gives bursts of pulses when a green light (533 nm wavelength) is removed. The firing rate decreases when exposed to short and middle wavelengths of light. (*Adapted from DeValois et al., 1966.*)

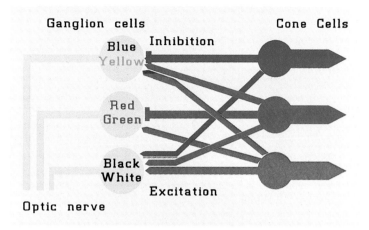

Figure 6.9 *Connections of Cone Cells to Opponent Cells*
Schematic of wiring diagram for a +Yellow−Blue cell,
+Red−Green cell and +White−Black cell. The three classes of
color opponent cells (blue-yellow, red-green, and black-white)
on the left receive input from distinct cone types on the right.
The cones may send excitatory signals (tapered endings) which
connect into the opponent cells. This causes the ganglion cell
to increase its firing rate. The cones may also send inhibitory
signals (blocked endings) which connect into the opponent cells.
This causes the ganglion cell to decrease its firing rate. (*Adapted
from Varley, 1980.*)

Physiological recordings of single cells responding to lights validate the existence
of three distinct classes of color opponent cells by their selective response to specific
regions of the visible spectrum. The class that is excited or inhibited by red and green
lights (red-green opponent mechanism) is typically shown by positive and negative signs
which are labeled $+R-G$ or $+G-R$. The second class (the yellow-blue opponent
mechanism) has a similar response to blue and yellow, with the labels $+Y-B$ or $+B-Y$.
The third class only responds to intensity or lightness (black-white opponent mechanisms)
and are classified as $+B-W$ or $-B+W$.

The responses of the color opponent mechanisms to light show that color perception
is a difference signal (see Box). The neural connections and pathways of electrical signals
of the photoreceptors to the color opponent cells can be shown by diagrams (see Figure
6.9). These diagrams are useful in artificial intelligence to simulate color recognition.

A NEURAL BASIS FOR HUE PERCEPTION

Models of the activities of the color opponent cells are useful to
explain color perception. One model shows how differences in hue are
encoded by the different opponent mechanisms. It shows that if higher
order processing cells exist which compare the outputs of opponent cells
(much like the opponent cells compare the relative activity of the receptor
cells), they could signal unambiguous hue information. Thus, if the
+Red−Green cells were most active, a higher order cell would signal red;
similarly, another cell could signal "yellow" if the +Yellow−Blue cells
were most active.

This model also explains the perception of other hues. For example,
the perception of "orange" occurs if both the +Red−Green and +Yel-
low−Blue cells are equally active and stronger than the other opponent
cell types.

(continued)

This model is also useful to explain two things about the color sphere model of perception. One is that there are specific hue axes in the color sphere: a red-green axis and a blue-yellow axis. Second, if these two axes are orthogonal, all other hues can be represented as a point in the color cone which represents a value of the red-green and of yellow-blue activity of the opponent cells.

The model is also useful for describing the relative activity of the color-opponent and lightness-opponent cells. For example, activating the +Red−Green cells results in signaling a saturated red to the brain. High +Red−Green and +White−Black activity signals a desaturated red or pink signal.

The model explains color perception because of three main factors. First, there is a strong correspondence between the color names people give to different wavelengths and the peak activity regions of the opponent cells. For example, people identify wavelengths between 610 nm and 670 nm as red which are the values where the +Red−Green cells are most active. Similarly, people use the word green to refer to wavelengths where the +Green−Red cells are most active.

Second, a color opponent mechanism helps explain the color after-images (see Chapter 8) observed after staring at a particular color (see Figure 6.10). Color opponent cell activity is apparent because the opponent hue is always the afterimage of the fixated color. Thus, the afterimage of red is green and the afterimage of blue is yellow.

Third, the existence of a special red-green axis is consistent with reports that people do not observe red and green together in a color. They describe colors as yellowish-green and greenish-yellow but never as reddish-greens or greenish-reds.

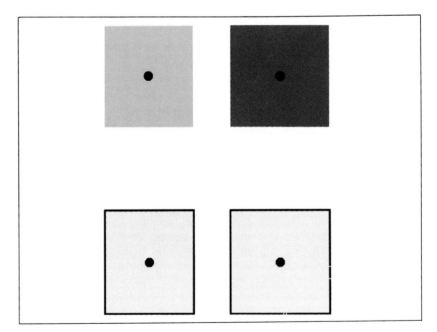

Figure 6.10 *Afterimage Effects* Viewing the colors on the top for about 20 seconds and then shifting the view to the lower blank squares causes an afterimage. The afterimage illusion visible in the bottom square (that is, blue or red) is the opponent or complementary color (that is, yellow or green, respectively) of the top.

Nonlinearity of Color Perception

Computer color applications often require colors to be equally distinguishable. If hues are located at equal distances from one another in a color cone, it implies that they are equally distinguishable. In fact, hues are not equally distinguishable nor is hue discrimination uniform. Thus, using a color cone to model color perception is not accurate. There are, however, alternative color models available for identification of equally distinguishable colors (see Chapter 9).

Detecting Wavelength Changes

As previously stated, a change in the wavelength will not necessarily result in the perception of a change in hue. This is an important consideration in assigning colors for computer devices which produce colors by specification of physical properties. It is also important for tasks where fast and accurate color discriminations are critical.

Determining the amount of change in wavelength necessary to produce a perceived change in color is possible by comparing the perceived differences between constant and varying wavelengths. The amount of wavelength change that produces a perceived difference from a constant wavelength is known as a just noticeable difference (JND) (see Figure 6.11). The JND is a measure useful to describe color detection thresholds and specify minimum difference requirements for color. The size of the JND for hue depends on its location and bandwidth on the visible spectrum.

Detecting Saturation Changes

The ability to see changes in the saturation of a color depends on its wavelength. To see a white light as blue, only a small amount of short wavelength light is necessary (see Figure 6.12). On the other hand, to perceive a white light as yellow, 50 times more middle wavelength light is required.

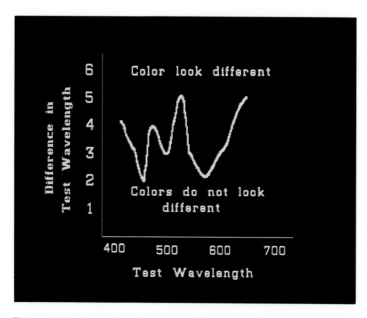

Figure 6.11 *Detecting One Just Noticeable Difference in Wavelength* The height of the curve along different points of the function indicates the size of the wavelength JND to see two lights as different. (*Adapted from Hurvich, 1980.*)

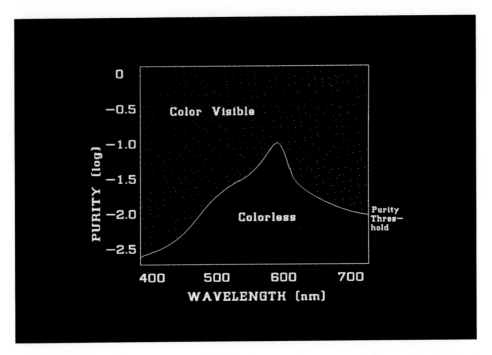

Figure 6.12 *Purity Necessary to See Color* The curve shows the amount of a wavelength added to a white light necessary to see color. (*Adapted from Wright, 1946.*)

For this reason, extremely high intensities cause yellow to lose its hue much more than other colors. When ambient light strikes a display or projection surface, it is like adding white light. Thus, middle wavelengths, and in particular those identified as yellow, are most vulnerable to the effects of desaturation.

Detecting Brightness Changes

In a naturally lighted environment, the eye easily adjusts and can detect lightness differences across a wide range of illumination levels (for example, from the bright light of a sunny day to that of a dim starlit night) (see Figure 6.13). Full color perception occurs best in lighted (naturally or artificially) conditions. In fact, if different levels of ambient illumination are arranged in linear order, color vision occurs only in high orders of light magnitude. Thus, to see computer colors effectively, a certain amount of light must be present.

Any computer application showing shaded imagery requires the detection of small lightness (or brightness) differences. The amount of lightness necessary to detect an image depends on the light level of the background (see Figure 6.14).

Range of Brightness Detection

Although visual perception occurs over a very wide range of luminance levels (ten log units) (see Figure 6.15), the eye does not usually need to respond to luminance changes on the order of ten million to one. (Photographic film covers a two log unit range which is acceptable for normal scene reproduction.)

In interior lighting environments, where most computer color is viewed, the amount of light increment required to see a change in brightness is about one percent. This increment is constant across different illumination levels. Thus, the amount of light necessary to see a change in brightness has to be only one percent of its previous brightness. In environments with illumination levels significantly less than the typical office, less brightness change is needed to detect a difference in brightness.

Perceived Brightness	Luminance (lux)
Bright sunlight	10^5
Cloudy day	10^4
Rainy day	10^3
Office illumination	10^2
Freeway illumination	10
Street lighting	1
Full moon	10^{-1}
New moon	10^{-2}
Clear, moonless night	10^{-3}

Figure 6.13 *Range of Light Visibility* The range luminance sensitivities of the eye to several popular luminance units. The region of color is above 10 cd/19² where the cone receptors of the eye are active.

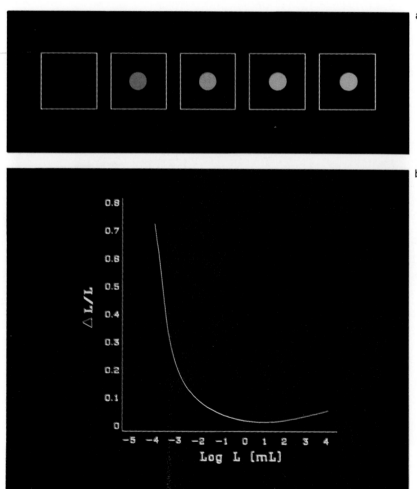

a

b

Figure 6.14 *Detecting One JND in Brightness* a) Each frame shows one JND of brightness reported by the viewer. Thus, the first frame represents one JND of brightness change; b) as brightness increases logarithmically the amount of change necessary for detection in change increases. (*Adapted from Hecht, 1934.*)

Nonlinearity of Color Perception

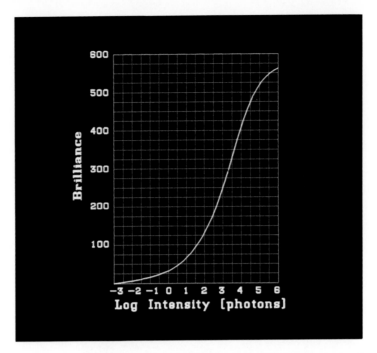

Figure 6.15 *Brightness Range of the Eye* The two log unit range of the slope is used when viewing most scenes. (*Adapted from Bartleson and Grun.*)

Color Blindness

Insufficient sensitivity of cone photoreceptors results in an inability to perceive certain colors. This is important to computer applications where both color identification and discrimination are critical. The term "color blindness" refers to the inability to perceive colors. This term is not an accurate description because there are very few people (less than 0.001 percent) who are unable to see any color (see Figure 6.16).

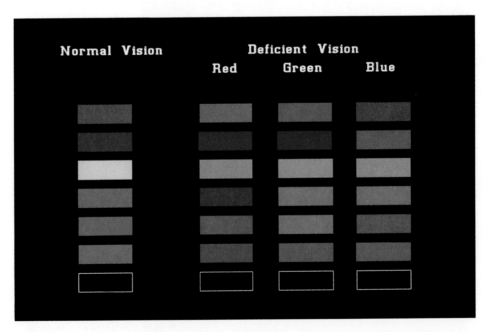

Figure 6.16 *Color Deficiency Table* The left column shows the appearance of colors to an individual with normal color vision. The three columns on the right show the appearance of these colors to individuals with color vision deficiencies for red, green, or blue respectively.

Color vision deficiencies are mostly inherited, and are transmitted by a sex-linked gene. There are more color vision deficient males than females. Between eight and ten percent of all Caucasian males have some form of color vision deficiency. In contrast, only about 0.5 percent of all females are color vision deficient. In addition, only about four percent of non-Caucasian males have this visual characteristic.

People with color vision deficiencies confuse more colors than a person with normal color vision. The most frequently occurring color deficiency is the inability to distinguish red, yellow, and green. Other colors easily confused are cyan with white and blue with purple. These colors are confused whether presented as colored lights on displays or as colored inks on paper. Insuring sufficient brightness differences between colors eliminates confusions between them. Thus, if yellow has a high luminance value, green a medium luminance value, and red a low luminance value, all people should be able to detect differences between them. A number of tests are available to evaluate color perception (see Box).

A less recognized form of color deficiency results from the yellowing of the lens that accompanies aging. This process causes the lens of the eye to act as a filter blocking a certain amount of blue light. Thus, elderly persons are less sensitive to blue and have difficulty distinguishing blue from white, and blue-green from bluish-white lights.

COLOR VISION TESTS

The ability to identify color is evaluated by color vision tests. In a standard color vision test, a series of color samples are matched, ordered, or named. Three common ways to test color vision are the anomoloscope, Pseudo Isochromatic Plates, or the Farnsworth-Munsell 100 Hue Test.

An *anomoloscope* is the most precise and reliable color testing device. It requires an observer to match color samples and is sufficiently precise to identify specific types of color vision deficiencies. However, it is the most expensive method and requires more training to administer than other tests.

A *Pseudo Isochromatic Plate* is a puzzle of colored dots which form one pattern for color vision defectives and another pattern for those with normal color vision. When viewed under standard illumination, the different colored inks provide flat or randomized lightness values so the shapes cannot be distinguished by lightness differences. The plates are quick tests and identify gross, not specific, color deficiencies.

In the *Farnsworth-Munsell 100 Hue Test*, sets of 85 Munsell color chips must be arranged according to their hue order. All members of each set have the same lightness and saturation values. A set is composed of 20 chips to be ordered from red through orange through yellow, a set to be ordered from green through blue-green and blue and so on. The advantage of this test is that the small changes in hue provide a good measure of color discrimination, even for those with normal color vision. The disadvantage is that it requires a significantly longer time than the other two tests.

Enhancing Color Differences

There are several techniques available to enhance the perception of color differences. These include using redundant coding, specific color combinations, and adjacent placement. The best way to ensure perceived differences between images of different color values is by using all the following guidelines:

1. In addition to brightness, use other coding attributes, such as shape, area-fill patterns, or character fonts with color differences.

   This technique is called *redundant coding* (see Chapter 4) and ensures discrimination between differently coded images even if colors are used and viewers are unable to discriminate colors. It also allows differences to be apparent when colored images are transferred to an achromatic technology (for example, black ink plotter, printer, or display).

2. Use color combinations that ensure discrimination by virtually all viewers (such as red and blue, red and cyan, or blue and yellow).

   However, since the contrast of red and blue on dark background CRT displays is not generally sufficient to permit adequate contrast, their combination is not appropriate for many applications.

3. Juxtapose different colors to be compared, particularly similar ones. This allows them to be more easily discriminated than if they are widely spaced.

   Two different colors are easier to distinguish when the color data to be compared are presented in close proximity. The farther apart two marginally different colors appear, the more difficult they usually are to discriminate.

4. Use a color legend showing colors adjacently located with their assigned meanings.

   This is especially useful where different colors represent several variables in a graphic.

Useful Facts

Color Perception	Physical properties of light interacting with physiological properties of the visual system determine color perception.
Color Properties	The physical properties of color are wavelength, purity, and intensity.
	The psychological properties of color perception are hue, saturation, and lightness. Changing one value may change the appearance of others.
	Changes in physical properties do not result in an equal change in color perception.
	For example, equal changes in wavelength do not result in equal changes in color.
Computer Color Properties	Most computer color light is more than one wavelength.
Perceptual and Computer Color	The eye can discriminate more colors than can be produced by most computer devices.
Ambient Light and Color Perception	Ambient illumination most desaturate yellow and green on a CRT display.
Color Perception Deficiencies	More males than females have difficulties discriminating colors. Solutions to this situation include grouping together colors that are similar, using other forms of coding with color, and use of legends.

REFERENCES

Bartleson, J.C. and F. Grum, "Optical Radiation Measurements," Vol. 5, Visual Measurements," Academic Press, San Francisco, CA, 1984.

Bergman, H. and F. Deujhhouwer, "Recognition of VDU Presented Colors by Color Defective Observers," *Proceedings of the Human Factors Society*, October 1980, pp. 611–615.

Billmeyer, F. W., "Optical Aspects of Color," *Optica Spectra*, Jan./Feb. 1968, pp. 43–47.

Boring, E. G., "The Psychophysics of Color Tolerance," *Amer. J. of Psychol.*, S2, 1939, 396.

Boynton, R. M. *Human Color Vision* (New York: Holt, Rinehart & Winston, 1979).

Brou, P., T. R. Sciascia, L. Linden, and T. Y. Lettuin, "The Color of Things," *Scientific American*, Sept. 1986, pp. 84–91.

Campbell, F. W. and R. W. Gubisch, "The Effect of Chromatic Aberration on Visual Acuity," *J. Physiol.*, 192, 1967, 345–358.

Charman, W. N. and J. Tucker, "Accommodation and Color," *J. Opt. Soc. Am.*, 68(4), 1978, 459–471.

Cornsweet, T. N. *Visual Perception* (San Francisco: Academic Press, 1970).

Davson, H., ed., *The Eye* (New York: Academic Press, 1976).

De Valois, R. L., "Processing of Intensity and Wavelength Information by the Visual System," *Investigative Opthalmology*, 11(6), June 1972, 417–426.

De Valois, R. L., I. Abramov, and G. H. Jacobs, "Analysis of Response Patterns of LGN Cells," *J. Opt. Soc. Amer.*, 57, 1966, 966–976.

De Valois, R. L. and K. K. De Valois, "Neural Coding of Color," in *Handbook of Perception*, eds. E. C. Carterette and M. P. Friedman (New York: Academic Press, 1975, Vol. 5, *Seeing*, Ch. 5), pp. 117–166.

Farrell, R. L. and L. M. Booth, *Design Handbook for Imaging Interpretation Equipment*, Boeing Aerospace Company, Seattle, Washington, 1975.

Godman, A. *Barnes & Noble Thesaurus of Science* (New York: Barnes & Noble Books, 1981).

Gregory, R. L. *Eye and Brain* (London: Weindenfield and Nicolson, 1979).

Hecht, S., "Vision II: The Nature of the Photoreceptor Process," *A Handbook of General Experimental Psychology*, ed. C. Murchison (Worcester, MA: Clark University Press, 1934).

Hubel, D. H. *The Brain* (San Francisco: W. H. Freeman and Co., 1979).

Hurvich, L. M. *Color Vision: An Introduction* (Surderland, MA: Sinnauer Assoc., 1980).

Hurvich, L. M. and D. Jameson, "An Opponent-Process Theory of Color Vision," *Psychological Review*, 64, 1957, 384–404.

Hurvich, L. M. and D. Jameson, "Some Quantitative Aspects of an Opponent-Colors Theory. II. Brightness, Saturation and Hue in Normal and Dichromatic Vision," *J. of the Optical Society of America*, 45(8), 1955, 602–616.

Kinney, J. A. S., "Factors Affecting Induced Colour," *Vision Research*, 2, 1962, 503–525.

Kishto, B. N., "The Color Stereoscopic Effect," *Vision Research*, 5, 1965, 313–329.

Kling J. W. and L. A. Riggs, Woodworth and Schlosberg's "Experimental Psychology," 3rd edition (New York: Holt, Rinehart & Winston, 1971).

Lennie, P., "Recent Developments in the Physiology of Color Vision," *Trends in Neuroscience*, 7, 1984, 243–248.

Lu, C. and D. H. Fender, "The Interaction of Color and Luminance in Stereoscopic Vision," *Investigative Opthalmology*, 11(6), 1972, 482–490.

Masland, R. H., "The Functional Architecture of the Retina," *Scientific American*, Dec. 1986, pp. 102–111.

Minnaert, M. *Light and Color* (New York: Dover Publications, Inc., 1954).

Murch, G., "Effective Use of Color in Graphic Displays," *Handshake*, 9(2), 1984–85, 9–16.

Murch, G. M., "Physiological Principles for the Effective Use of Color," *IEEE CG&A*, Nov. 1984, pp. 49–54.

Pirenne, M. H. *Vision and the Eye*, 2nd ed. (London: Associated Book Publishers, 1967).

Ronchi, L. R. and L. Di Frona, "Visual Depth of Focus Measurement for Various Colored Displays," *Color Research and Application*, 11, 1986, S52–S56.

Rushton, W. A. H., D. Powell, and K. D. White, "The Spectral Sensitivity of 'Red' and 'Green' Cones in the Normal Eye," *Vision Research*, 13, 1983, 2003–2015.

Samit, M. L., "The Color Interface: Learning to Use Color Effectively," *Computer Graphics World*, 6(7), July 1983, 42–50.

The Science of Color, Committee on Colorimetry, Optical Society of America (New York: Thomas Crowell Co., 1954).

Thorell, L. G., "Introduction to Color Vision," *IBM Technical Report,* 1982.

Thorell, L. G., "Using Color on Displays: A Biological Perspective," *Proceedings of SPIE*, 386, 1983, pp. 2–5.

Thorton, W. A., "Evidence for the Three Spectral Responses of the Normal Human Visual System," *Color Research and Application*, 11(2), Summer 1986, 160–163.

Ucikawa, H., P. K. Kaiser, and K. Ucikawa, "Color-Discrimination Perimetry," *Color Research and Application*, 7(3), Fall 1982, 264–272.

Varley, H., ed. *Colour* (London: Marshall Editions Ltd., 1980).

Verriest, G., I. Andrew, and A. Uvijla, *Visual Performance on a Multi-color Visual Display Unit of Color-defective and Normal Trichromatic Subjects.* IBM TR #16.241, March 1985.

Wald, G. and P. K. Brown, "Human Color Vision and Color Blindness," *Cold Spring Harbor Symp. Quant. Biol.*, 30, 1966, 345–359.

Wasserman, G. S., "The Physiology of Color Vision," *Color, Research and Application*, 4(2), Sept. 1979, 57–65.

Wright, W. D. *Researches on Normal and Defective Colour Vision* (London: Henry Kimpton, 1946).

Wyszecki, G. and W. S. Stiles. *Color Science*, 2nd ed. (New York: Wiley and Sons, 1982).

7

Color Image Quality

In a figure, always look for the greatest light and the greatest shades.

Edouard Manet

Color perception depends on factors other than the physical components of color (wavelength, purity, and intensity) and their psychological correlates (hue, saturation, and lightness). It also depends on image size, position, length of presentation, motion, background, and adjacent color. There are several ways to characterize these image features to ensure color identification and discrimination.

Color Quality and Context

In general, the quality of image color includes *fidelity* (exactness of color reproduction), *gamut* (color range), and *composition* (combination and arrangement of color images). Another major factor in color quality is the content of a scene. The criteria for judging the quality of color in a landscape is different than that for a page of colored text. Colors in a computer landscape are judged primarily on their color fidelity to landscape images. Colors for text are primarily evaluated by how well they enhance character resolution as well as the meaning of the message.

Spatial Features of Images

The spatial characteristics (that is, size, spacing, and texture) of images also determine color quality and the range of perceptible hue, saturation, and lightness values that can be used to ensure image and color identification. For example, some colors (such as red and cyan) are better for small data points than others (such as violet and blue).

All images have different spatial characteristics whether they are reproductions of natural objects, simulations, graphs, or text. In general, images consist of *global shapes* and *edges*. Global shapes are the general form; edges are the outlines or textures of a shape.

The application of color to images should preserve the visibility of their details.

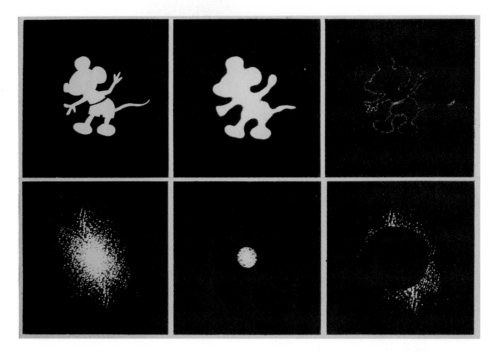

Figure 7.1 *Decomposition of a Simple Image* Top left: area-fill form of Mickey Mouse; center: global shape of Mickey with the borders optically filtered; right: Mickey's edges with his global shape optically filtered. Bottom: optical spectra for each image. (*By permission from Harburn, Taylor and Welberry, 1975.*)

Some color combinations reduce the legibility of text and the resolution of fine-line graphics. However, the important element in resolution, particularly for edge-dominant imagery graphics, is luminance contrast. In addition, excessive use of color generally has a disruptive effect on the intrinsic order of text and tabular data due to interference with their structured appearance.

The effects of global shape and edge features on image recognition are apparent when an image is spatially filtered (see Figure 7.1). Filtering its edges causes it to appear like a fuzzy shape without distinct order; filtering its global features causes it to look like an outline or series of edges. Despite lack of edge or internal details, the identity of shapes is apparent.

Spatial Features of Computer Images

In general, computer-generated images are either global or edge dominant. Global computer graphic images vary from simple forms like pie charts to multi-hued contour maps and complex scene rendering. These images have a number of common features. One is that color is often distributed in large area-fills. Images like natural scenes and solid model simulations include large areas of variations in hue, saturation, and lightness. The details of these images (such as their texture and shading) are actually combinations of small colored edges.

Computer images such as text, tabular data, line graphs, and diagrams are mainly defined by many line strokes, dots, and edges (see Figure 7.2). They require the eye to resolve fine details. However, they also have a global form: Lines of text and rows and columns of data are arranged in groups and in an orderly manner. These organized arrangements and shapes help guide the eye through arrays of information. Thus, both the global form and edges of images in a large table contribute to their interpretation; color contributes further to their order.

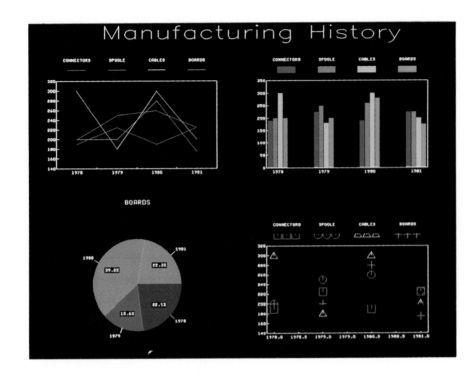

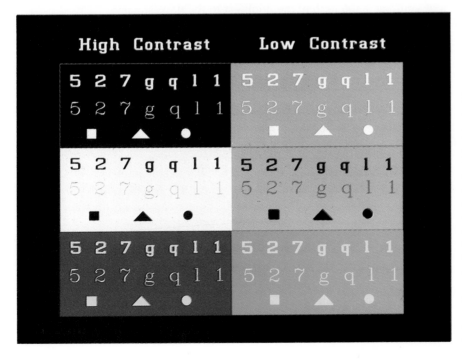

Figure 7.2 *Line and Area-Fill Graphs* These four types of graphs represent forms typically used to show numerical data. Colors of the area-fill graphs (bottom left pie chart and top right bar chart) are more distinct at far viewing distances than those of the line and symbol graphs (top left line graph and bottom right outlines of icons).

Lightness Contrast

The visual system detects shapes and their detail features because of *contrast*: the differences in light levels or hues between images and their surround. Contrast is the most important factor in ensuring recognition of images and their colors (see Figure 7.3). (Those who have left their car lights on during the day can appreciate the importance of contrast.)

Most images are defined by lightness or color contrast (see Box). *Lightness contrast* refers to the difference in the lightness or darkness of an image compared to its background.

Figure 7.3 *Lightness and Color Contrast* The only differences between the blocks of images is their lightness and color contrast. Maximum lightness contrast is shown in the black and white blocks (top two blocks on left). Images on the white block demonstrate that poor legibility (of thin fonts) can occur even if lightness contrast is maximum. On the black background above, the same font is legible. The blue background block shows both maximum lightness and color contrast. The gray blocks show low lightness contrast. The green block shows low lightness and color contrast.

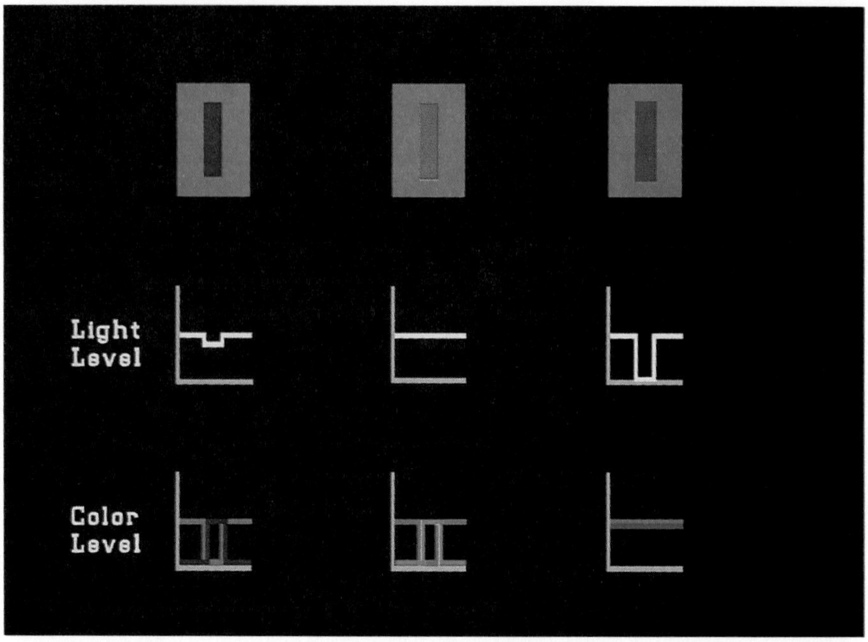

Figure 7.4 *Contrast Profiles* Top row: The left rectangle differs in both lightness and hue from its background; The middle rectangle is the same lightness as its background, but a different hue; the right rectangle differs from its background by lightness only. The second row represents the results of a photometer which measures the amount of light along a horizontal scan across the rectangle. The bottom row shows the corresponding traces for each color component (magenta and green).

Color contrast refers to the difference in hue and saturation of images relative to their background (see Figure 7.4).

CONTRAST

Determining Luminance Contrast

Luminance contrast is the ratio of the brightest to the darkest components within an area.

The formula most used by engineers to measure luminance contrast is *contrast modulation* or

$$C_m = \frac{L_{max} - L_{min}}{L_{max} + L_{min}}$$

where L_{max} is the maximum luminance level of an image (or its background), and L_{min} is the minimum level of its background (or the image).

This formula adjusts any luminance difference for the backgound level and thus represents the relative light level. The luminance contrast of an image to its background must be sufficient to allow image identification or legibility.

Color Contrast

Color contrast can be determined using a color difference formula:

$$\Delta E = [(L^*)^2 + (u^*)^2 + (v^*)^2]^{1/2}$$

where L is luminance and u and v are the color's coordinates in a numerical color space known as UCS (see Chapter 9).

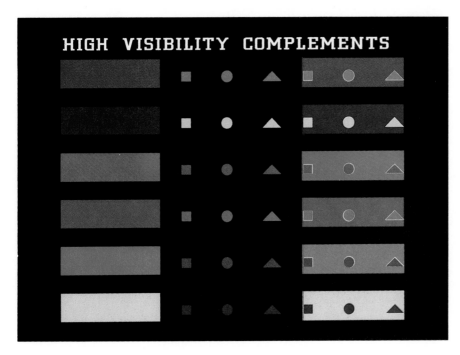

Figure 7.5 *Complements with Good Visibility* The colors of the shapes in the middle are the same as those on the right. The colors of the rectangles are the complements of the colored shapes. When the complementary colors are superimposed, the color contrast is maximum and the saturation of the images is enhanced.

Creating Effects with Contrast

Complements to Enhance Saturation

Color contrast is useful for enhancing color perception and in particular saturation appearance. For example, superimposing an image on its complementary color background enhances its saturation (see Figure 7.5). This technique is useful for enhancing the contrast of text without sacrificing the brightness contrast necessary to produce the appearance of sharp edges. In addition, placing light colored text on its complementary dark background (for example, yellow text on a blue background) typically maximizes the visibility of the text and its color. In general, this technique is most effective for area-fill graphics and when the lightness values between the color and its complementary background are equal. (A thin yellow type font may appear white on a blue background CRT display because of the high brightness value of its yellow; using a bold font increases the perception of its color.) Since complementary colors (such as green and magenta) maximize color contrast, they most enhance color appearance and image perception.

Simultaneous Contrast

Using complements to enhance saturation (*simultaneous contrast*) is particularly useful to enhance the saturation appearance of colors in displays and 35 mm slides. Thus, a red CRT image will appear more saturated on a green background than on any other color (including black or white). Another effect of simultaneous contrast is that gray images may appear like a pastel version of the complement of the background color (see Figure 7.6). Thus, gray on red may have a light green appearance and on blue may have a yellow appearance. The shift from gray to another color depends on the size of the image relative to the background. Simultaneous contrast is most apparent when the background area is significantly larger than the image area and if the luminance of the image is less than its background.

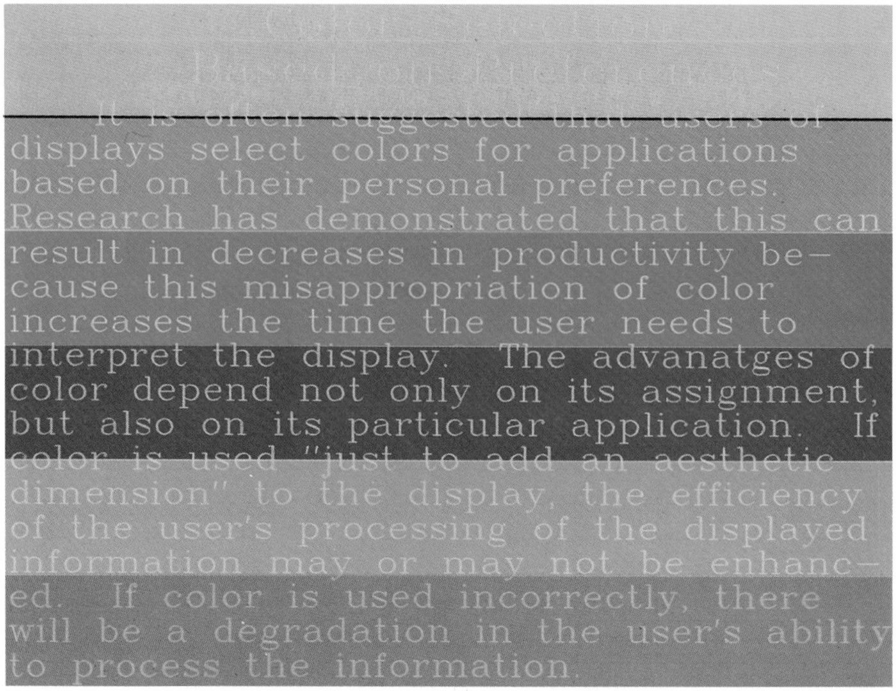

Based on Preferences

It is often suggested that users of
displays select colors for applications
based on their personal preferences.
Research has demonstrated that this can
result in decreases in productivity because this misappropriation of color
increases the time the user needs to
interpret the display. The advanatges of
color depend not only on its assignment,
but also on its particular application. If
color is used "just to add an aesthetic
dimension" to the display, the efficiency
of the user's processing of the displayed
information may or may not be enhanced. If color is used incorrectly, there
will be a degradation in the user's ability
to process the information.

Figure 7.6 *Simultaneous Contrast* The colors of the gray characters look like a desaturated value of the complement of their background color (for example, gray text on blue appears yellowish, red appears greenish, and yellow looks slightly blue).

Low Contrast Effects

The opposite of simultaneous contrast (*color assimilation*) occurs when a foreground color looks like a lighter shade of its background color (see Figure 7.7). Edge-dominant imagery, like thin lines and text, is particularly susceptible to this effect. Assimilation is important because it reduces the perceived contrast between images and their background colors. This significantly reduces image resolution and color discrimination.

Figure 7.7 *Effects of Background Color on Neutral Images* All the color values of the text are identical. The characters look like lighter versions of their background colors. The effect depends on the character brightness, ratio of the image size to background, and area.

Color assimilation is most obvious when the foreground and background colors are approximately equal in area. Thus, a dense screen of thin line gray type fonts will appear light blue on a blue background, light green on a green background, and pink on a red background. Assimilation effects can be reduced by avoiding gray thin fonts, and using bold or white fonts with saturated color backgrounds.

Contrast and Image Quality

The contrast of an image thus affects its perceived resolution and color quality.

Fuzzy Edges

If edge sharpness of an image is important, both brightness and color contrast should be maximized. If images are similar in hue to that of the background (such as orange text on a red background or blue text on a green background) and identical in brightness, their contrast will not be sufficient to ensure good legibility. As a result, the edges formed by these images, as well as the overall shape, may appear fuzzy (see Figure 7.8).

In addition, some color combinations (like those that selectively stimulate the blue-yellow opponent cells in the eye—see Chapter 6) may appear fuzzy. This effect occurs even on high resolution (more than 1,000 raster lines) displays. Color combinations that produce fuzzy borders have low contrast and similar saturation values. Examples include blue and green, cyan and yellow, white and yellow, and green and white.

Sharpening Edges

Color and lightness contrast can be enhanced and edges sharpened by a thin dark line (border) around light colors or a thin white border around dark colors (see Figure 7.9). This technique creates a brightness contrast at the border of an image and makes its edges appear more distinct. It is best for area-fill graphics because the stroke width of edge-dominated graphics (like alphanumeric characters and lines) is too narrow to be practical. Contrast bordering is thus most useful for adjacent area-fill images such as pie charts and maps.

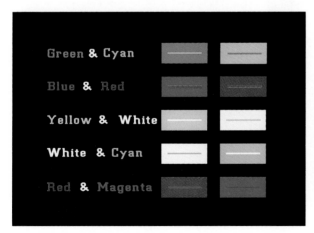

a

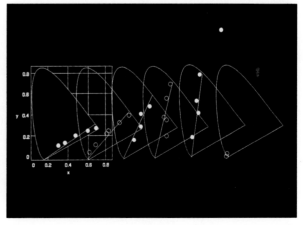

b

Figure 7.8 *Combinations Making Fuzzy Borders* a) Color combinations that can produce blurry edges are shown on the left. Increasing the lightness contrast, as on the right, reduces edge blur and increases sharpness. b) When no brightness differences are present, an edge whose colors are defined by chromaticity coordinates which lie on any one of the lines shown on CIE space produces a fuzzy border. (*Adapted from Valberg and Tansley, 1977.*)

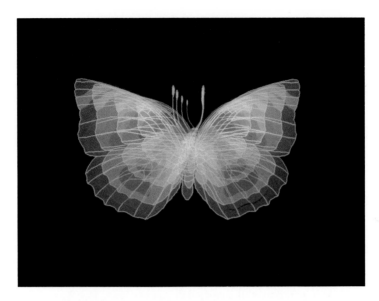

Figure 7.9 *Effect of Neutral Borders on Edges* The white border around each of the different colors of the butterfly's wings enhances the resolution of their borders. Without these borders, the point at which the colors (with the same or very similar lightness values) change will appear blurry.
(*Courtesy of Hewlett-Packard.*)

Mach Bands

A border of low lightness contrast often produces an optical illusion interfering with lightness and hue discrimination. One of these illusions, called *Mach bands*, is the lightness difference that appears along the borders of adjacent colors of equal and uniform intensity (see Figure 7.10). An illusory brighter band appears on the bright side and an illusory darker band appears along the dark side. Mach bands can interfere with image resolution.

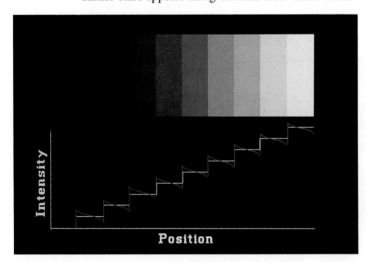

a

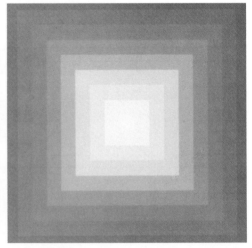

b

Figure 7.10 *Mach Bands* a) A series of gray shades (top) and their photometric luminance profile distribution (bottom) in white and perceived brightness distribution in red. Although each gray level is uniformly bright, bright and dark borders (Mach bands) appear at each edge transition. (Adapted from Hurvich, 1980.) b) The computer adaptation of a "Vasarely square" shows how Mach bands create the illusion of brightness highlights along the diagonals of the superimposed squares. As in the gray levels in part a, the brightness of each Vasarely square is uniform.

The visual system produces Mach bands to sharpen borders of gradual or diffuse intensity differences (see Box). Therefore, increasing the lightness of one of the bordering colors can reduce or eliminate Mach bands because they are not visible at high contrast borders.

Minimizing Mach bands is especially important where the discrimination of different lightness values is critical. X-ray image visibility is reduced by the existence of Mach bands (which may be present due to adjacent, gradual changes in brightness). Image enhancement can be used to minimize the Mach bands while preserving the X ray's integrity.

NEURAL RESPONSE TO MACH BANDS

Mach bands are produced by lateral inhibition, an inter-neuron effect common throughout the nervous system. Adjacent neurons are interconnected, and when one is stimulated, the resulting activity can have inhibitory effects on neighboring neurons. That is, the strongly stimulated neuron's activity reduces the spike rate in surrounding neurons. When this occurs in retinal photoreceptors as a result of stimulation by a light/dark border, the contrast at the border is enhanced.

Impacting Response Speed

The color of an object affects how quickly we perceive it. However, under most circumstances, it is the differences in lightness and not hue, which determine visual reaction time in locating an object. Different color items of equal lightness contrast are perceived with equal speed (see Figure 7.11). However, when there is no lightness contrast between the color of an image and its background, response is faster to saturated colors.

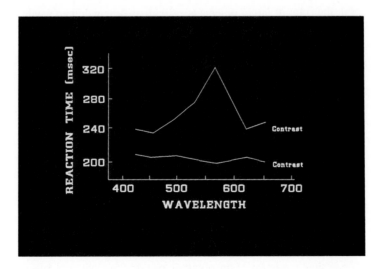

Figure 7.11 *Response Speed to Colors* Reaction time to detect a light (y axis) is shown as a function of wavelength of light (x axis). When the luminance of a wavelength is a constant increment against its background, reaction time does not change. When the test wavelength has the same luminance as its background, response time to middle wavelengths is fastest. (*Adapted from Nissan and Pokorny, 1975.*)

On most computer displays, luminance contrast determines response speed of equal size images. It is therefore possible to predict colors to which people will respond most quickly on a simple three-bit CRT display (see Chapter 9). For example, green, yellow, and white (which have a higher luminance contrast on a black background than other colors) will produce the fastest responses. However, on a white background, red, blue, and black have a higher luminance contrast and will produce faster responses than other colors.

READING SPEED   The color of text does not generally affect reading speed. However, as text size becomes barely perceptible (approaches the acuity limit), reading performance mostly decreases for blue (430 nm) and red (650 nm) characters. In addition, when the intensity level of color text and background of a different color are equal (generally not a desirable situation for reading but good for visual testing), reading rates are independent of wavelength in typical office lighting. Thus, provided the luminance contrast is equal between text colors, the color of text should not affect reading speed.

Effects of Ambient Light

Environmental (ambient) lighting and the adaptive state of the eyes play a significant role in determining the appearance of color. Both intensity and wavelength of a light source affect color perception.

Ambient lighting essentially adds light and desaturates colors on a display or a projection screen. With CRT colors which are already desaturated (like cyan and yellow), the effect of ambient light can be sufficiently strong to eliminate their color recognition and discrimination. Moreover, if the ambient lighting has a dominant color component, like the blue of fluorescent lamps, it can shift the adaptation state of the eye and reduce the ability to distinguish certain colors. These effects illustrate the importance of ensuring that colors assigned to display images, transparencies, and 35 mm slides are appropriate for the lighting conditions and that anti-glare filters are used on display screens (See Chapter 8).

Size and Color Recognition

In general, the color of larger objects is easier to distinguish than smaller ones. The color of extremely small images (less than one-quarter degree—see Box) cannot be resolved by the visual system. This occurs, in part, because the photoreceptors of the eye are located in different densities throughout the retina: Cones (which operate at high light levels) are most dense in the fovea, and rods (which operate at low light levels) are most dense in the periphery. If the images viewed are smaller than the spacing of the photoreceptors, their color will not be visible. Color sensitive neurons collect information from many photoreceptors scattered over a wide region; whereas neurons not sensitive to color collect from small patches. This means a strong color signal is only generated for larger colored images. Thus, the colors of area-fill bars in histograms and wedges of pie charts are easier to discriminate than the colors of text, data points, or lines on a graph.

VISUAL ANGLE

The critical measure of an object is not its physical size, but its size on the retina or "visual angle." This measure is also critical for determining the visibility of color (see Chapter 8). It is expressed as visual angle or the angle an object subtends on the retina (see Figure 7.12). The formula for determining the visual angle of an object is

---

(continued)

$$\theta = \arctan \frac{\text{size of object}}{\text{distance of object}}$$

Visual angles of some common objects are

- A thumb viewed at arm's distance $\quad\quad \theta = 2$ degrees
- Fovea (highest concentration area of color receptors) of the eye $\quad\quad \theta = 2$ degrees
- Full moon viewed from earth $\quad\quad \theta = 0.5$ degrees

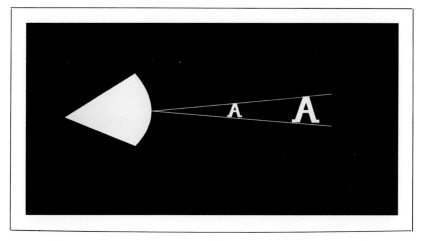

Figure 7.12 *Visual Angle* Although the two letters are different physical sizes, they subtend the same visual angle. Therefore, the viewer sees them as equal in size.

Spatial Contrast

Both image form (shape and size) and contrast contribute to pattern visibility, color, and resolution. In general, high contrast between the borders of images results in high visibility, low contrast results in low visibility. The visual system is very sensitive to a spatial pattern if only a small amount of contrast is required to see it; conversely, it is not very sensitive to a pattern if a large amount of contrast is necessary. Measuring visual responses to different color and spatial contrasts is one way to determine the perceptual quality of an image (see Box). The visual quality of a color image can be evaluated in terms of the frequency with which the contrast of an image varies over space.

EVALUATING RESOLUTION WITH SINE WAVES

The test patterns used to evaluate the eye's responses to different spatial and color properties of images are sinusoidal gratings. They are the same test patterns used by engineers to measure the spatial properties of visual displays. The defining feature of these patterns is that the luminance increases and decreases smoothly and periodically (sinusoidally) across distance (see Figure 7.13).

(continued)

Figure 7.13 *Sinusoidal Grating Patterns* The grating and its corresponding light distribution for a) a lightness-varying sinusoid and b) a color-varying grating.

Spatial frequency refers to the number of cycles per unit distance subtended across the retina of the eye (that is, one cycle per visual degree). Contrast refers to the highest and lowest (peak and trough) variation in light level relative to the average light level across the pattern.

The sinusoid is the simplest mathematical description of a light wave-form. Much like sound, a light distribution can be analyzed into its sinusoidal (or Fourier) components. Distributions of light imaged across the retina are composed of multiple sinusoidal frequencies, as are most naturally occurring sounds.

Fourier theory is used in vision and image processing to decompose complex visual images into less complex components. Studies show that the contrast of the lowest (fundamental) spatial frequency (Fourier) component in a visual pattern determines its visibility. In general, the spatial frequency content of an image does not vary with viewing distance.

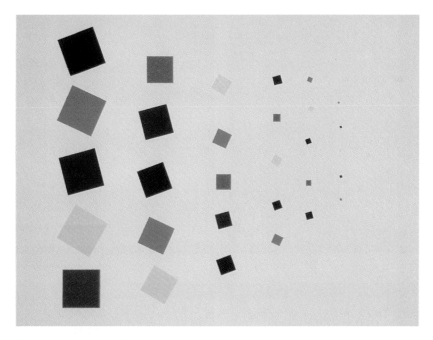

Figure 7.14 *Image Size and Color Perception* As the size of the colored squares decreases, the ability to identify and distinguish colors becomes more difficult. The color most susceptible to this phenomenon is blue.

In general, images have both high and low spatial frequency components. Their global shapes represent low spatial frequency content; boundaries represent high spatial frequency content. As the size of images decreases, their colors eventually become unidentifiable (see Figure 7.14). Some colors lose their identity before others.

The loss of color resolution due to the size of an image is determined by measuring the eye's response to patterns whose spatial and color properties (contrast spatial frequencies) can be systematically varied. Test patterns (or gratings) exist which allow testing of the eye's sensitivity to different spatial frequencies (see Box and Figure 7.15a, b, and c).

The contrast of each pattern is adjusted until the observer reports recognition of its colors. The test patterns vary in either lightness (such as black and white) contrast or in hue (such as red and green or blue and yellow) contrast. The purpose of the test is to separately evaluate the sensitivity of the black-white, red-green, blue-yellow color sensitive mechanisms of the eye. If the observer is very sensitive to the pattern, low contrast is sufficient to see its different lightness or hue values. Conversely, high contrast is necessary to see the values if the observer is not very sensitive to the patterns (see Figure 7.15d).

Data from tests like this indicate that the amount of contrast necessary to see a pattern depends on its color and spatial properties. The eye can detect high frequency black-white variations with low contrast. However, the eye cannot resolve the same patterns in saturated red-green or yellow-blue. In addition, the ability of the eye to spatially resolve red-green gratings is better than its ability to resolve yellow-blue gratings (see Figure 7.15). Thus, black and white high spatial frequency patterns are more easily seen at greater distances than the red-green and yellow-blue ones. This phenomenon has important implications for high spatial frequency computer images like line graphs and text.

The inferior ability of the eye to resolve high spatial frequency color patterns is due to the density of photoreceptors in the retina and neural connections of the color opponent cells. Since all these cells contribute to luminance perception, the eye can easily resolve high spatial frequency images which vary only in lightness. The distance between neural cells sensitive to blue and yellow lights is greater than those sensitive to red and green light, which are both greater than those sensitive to lightness differences. This results in

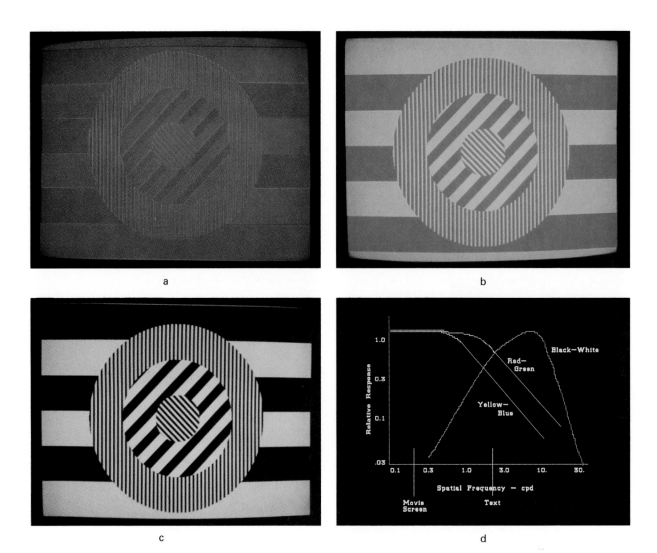

Figure 7.15 *Sensitivity of the Eye to Spatial Frequencies* a), b), c) Color patterns to test the eye's sensitivity to different spatial frequencies. (*Courtesy of R. De Valois.*) d) Threshold detection responses of the eye to different sinusoidal gratings as a function of spatial frequency (cycles per degree). (Relative response is reciprocally related to the amount of contrast modulation required to identify patterns and colors.) Also indicated is the fundamental frequency of the wave whose half-cycle equals the width of a typical alphanumeric CRT character viewed at 70 cm and a nine-meter movie screen viewed at 15 feet. (*Parts a, b, and c courtesy of Eugene Switkes and Russell De Valois; part d adapted from Granger and Heurtley, 1973.*)

the necessity for a larger area of light to stimulate hue sensitive mechanisms than that required to stimulate lightness sensitive cells.

These spatial limits of color vision are used by the television industry as a way to conserve their use of broadcast bandwidth. As the television signal is restricted to a specific bandwidth (7 MHz), the high frequency portion transmits brightness signals and the low frequency portion transmits color signals.

Improving Search with Contrast and Spatial Frequency

The spatial properties of visual neurons can help explain the advantages of color in visual search tasks. When searching for a target image, global characteristics (low spatial frequencies) are first perceived. Since color vision is good for low spatial frequencies, an image's color is a good feature for guiding visual search.

Color for Text

The visual characteristics just described show the spatial limits of color perception and are useful to determine the contrast and spatial requirements of color images to ensure their identification and resolution. For example, spatial frequency and contrast components can determine text legibility. The high resolution edge detection mechanisms of the visual system which determine text legibility also play an important role in readability.

Since low spatial frequency color patterns are easier to identify than high spatial frequency patterns, color coding words results in more efficient color perception than color coding single characters. In addition, color coding the background of a word results in faster color discrimination than coloring the word. However, the advantages of color coding a character, strings of characters, or their backgrounds depend on the application (see Figure 7.16). Using different background colors to code long rows of character strings

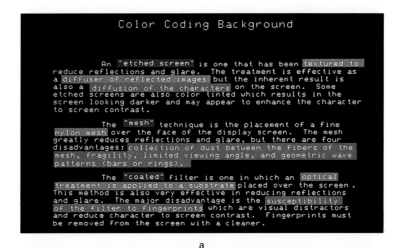

Figure 7.16 *Colored Text versus Background* (a) Coloring the background of dense text makes the paragraphs appear cluttered; (b) Colored text reduces this cluttered appearance.

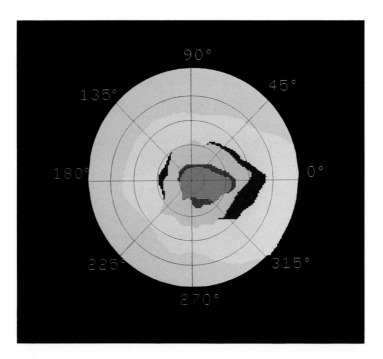

Figure 7.17 *Peripheral Detection of Color* Polar diagram of the ability to recognize the color of a spot (two-degree diameter) placed at different positions in the visual field. The center of the diagram signifies the foveal region, or the center of the visual field. Each concentric circle marks a ten-degree interval. Each color coded region corresponds to the visual area in which the hue of a corresponding wavelength is recognized. Spots appear colorless when located at a position more than 60 degrees from the fovea. (*Adapted from Hurvich, 1981.*)

(such as in a paragraph) can result in excessive screen clutter and interfere with reading performance.

Peripheral Color Recognition

Color perception is superior to acuity in the visual periphery. Locating color coded images in the periphery is superior to locating achromatic (that is, black, white, or gray) ones. Color identification and spatial resolution (acuity) are better directly in front of the eye (central vision) than to the side (peripheral vision). Blue is usually perceptible up to about 60 degrees in the periphery, yellow only to about 50 degrees, and red and green only to about 40 degrees. Colors are not recognizable if they are located in the far periphery (see Figure 7.17).

Contrast Requirements

In summary, the visual system determines the ultimate constraints for identifying the color of high spatial frequency and small images. Although a visual display or hard copy output device may be capable of producing high resolution images, their colors will not be identified unless they are a certain contrast, size, and spatial frequency. Thus, the resolution and color discrimination of high spatial frequency images, such as integrated circuits, may not be sufficient unless their lines are of sufficient thickness, contrast, and spacing (see Figure 7.18).

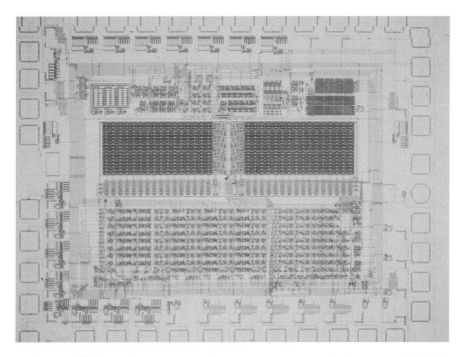

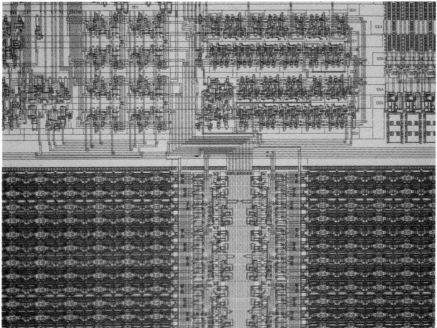

Figure 7.18 *Colors on an Integrated Circuit Design* Viewed at typical reading distance, the colors on the IC design cannot be discriminated and appear black. Viewed very close, however, it is possible to see that the lines are actually green and magenta. (*Courtesy of Hewlett-Packard.*)

Minimal Spatial Frequency for Edge-Dominant Images

Computer color images must thus have sufficient contrast to stimulate the color opponent mechanisms to assure hue recognition (see Chapter 6). In addition, the fundamental spatial frequency of a colored image should be no more than three cycles per degree (see Figure 7.19).

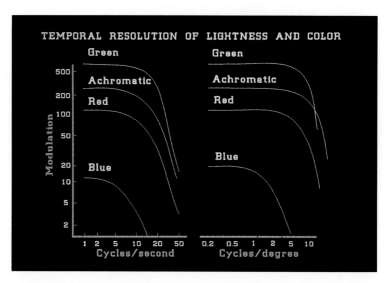

Figure 7.19 *Temporal Resolution of Lightness and Color* To discriminate the color of a blinking light, the blink rate should be slower, the lightness increased, and the image size larger for blue (and yellow) lights. (*Adapted from Bartleson and Grum, 1984.*)

Duration and Color

The length of time an image is visible also affects its color appearance (and whether it is presented as a steady or a blinking light). If the duration of an image is too short the color will not be visible (see Figure 7.19). In addition, alternating the colors of a flashing light (like red to green) at a rapid rate (for example ten cycles per second), will cause the colors to appear as one color (like yellow). This is due to blending or additive mixing of the lights by the eye. Similarly, if a yellow and blue light flash too rapidly, they will blend and appear white.

The blending or visual fusion point of two colored lights depends on several factors, including the illumination level in the visual field, the contrast and size of the images, and the viewer's sensitivity to this effect. It is therefore difficult to specify the exact rate at which two colors will fuse. To guarantee color recognition of a flashing image or two alternating colored lights in a typical office illumination of 500 lux, the flash rate should not exceed three cycles per second. This is an important consideration for computer display images like blinking cursors or flashing error messages.

Useful Facts

Factors Influencing Color Recognition and Quality	Color appearance depends on several factors, including size, shape, color contrast, spatial variations, color properties of adjacent objects, duration, and ambient illumination.
	Color quality judgments depend on the content of the scene.
Color for Different Forms of Images	Realistic scenes and pictures represent the most fundamental level of visual information, contain mostly area-fill, and usually form a larger

image on our retina than other images.

The use of color for pictorial information is usually constrained by our expectations of photorealism.

Colors for high spatial frequency based or narrow line images are more difficult to discriminate.

Contrast and Visibility	Most forms of contrast include differences in both lightness and hue. Contrast is one of the most important features in ensuring visibility and legibility.
Size and Color Recognition	The color of larger images is easier to distinguish than that of smaller ones.
Color for Text	Coding long text strings may be superior to coding their background. Color coding the background of short text strings may be better than coding their characters.
Contrast and Acuity	If the brightness of the image and the background is similar, the image may appear blurry. Closely spaced, thin colored lines appear more blurry than if they are in black and white.
Sharpening Edges	Blurred edges can be sharpened by a contrasting border around an image.
Lightness Illusions	Lightness illusions (Mach bands) at the borders of different shades of the same hue can interfere with image resolution and detection.
Peripheral Color Recognition	Colors are not visible in the extreme visual periphery. Blue is most visible in the periphery, yellow less so, and red and green are not visible.
Enhancing Saturation	The hue of an image will appear more saturated if it is located on a complementary color background.
Assimilation	If the size of the image is very small and if the image is a neutral color, it may look like a pastel version of the surround color.
Recognition and Duration	The blink rate of colored objects should be no greater than two to five cycles per second.
Color and Response Rate	Different colored items of equal brightness contrast will be responded to with equal speed. Darker colors on a light background are responded to faster than light colors. Reaction time

Color Recognition and Ambient Light	to saturated colors is faster than to those less saturated but of equal lightness contrast.
	High ambient light desaturates display colors and can therefore degrade the ability to identify and discriminate colors.
	The color of ambient lights can shift the adaptation of the eye, reducing the ability to discriminate colors.

REFERENCES

Ambler, B. A., "Hue Discrimination in Peripheral Vision under Conditions of Dark and Light Adaptation," *Perception and Psychophysics*, 15(3), 1974, 586–590.

Bartleson, J. C. and F. Grum, "Optical Radiation Measurements, Vol. 5, Visual Measurements," (Academic Press, San Francisco, CA, 1984).

Burnham, R. W., "Comparative Effects of Area and Luminance on Color," *Am. J. Psychol.*, 65, 1952, 27–38.

Burnham, R. W. and S. M. Newhall, "Color Perception in Small Test Fields," *J. Opt. Soc. Am.*, 43(10), Oct. 1953, 899–902.

Ginsburg, A. P., *Visual Information Processing Based on Spatial Filters Constrained by Biological Data*, Aerospace Medical Research Laboratory, Wright-Patterson Air Force Base, Ohio, AMRL-TR-78-129, 1978.

Gordon, J. and I. Abramov, "I. Color Vision in the Peripheral Retina; II. Hue and Saturation," *J. Opt. Soc. Am.*, 67(2), 1977, 202–207.

Granger, E. M. and J. C. Heurtley, "Visual Chromaticity-Modulation Transfer Function," *J. of Opt. Soc. Amer.*, 63, 1973, 1173–1174.

Harburn, G., C. A. Taylor, and T. R. Welberry. *Atlas of Optical Transforms* (Ithaca, NY: Cornell University Press, 1975.)

Hurvich, L. M. *Color Vision: An Introduction* (Sunderland, MA: Sinnauer Assoc., 1980).

Kaiser, P. K., "Color Names of Very Small Fields Varying in Duration and Luminance," *J. of Opt. Soc. of America*, 58(6), 1968, 849–852.

Lippert, T. M., W. W. Farley, D. L. Post, and H. L. Snyder, "Color Contrast Effects on Visual Performance," *SID Digest*, 1983, pp. 170–171.

McLean, M. V., "Brightness Contrast, Color Contrast, and Legibility," *Human Factors*, 7, 1965, 521–526.

Newman, K. M. and A. R. Davis, "Non-redundant Color, Brightness and Flashing Rate Encoding of Geometric Symbols in a Visual Display," *J. of Eng. Psych.*, 1, 1962, 47–67.

Nissan and Pokorny, *Optical Society of America*, 1975.

Tansley, B. W. and R. M. Boynton, "Chromatic Border Perception: The Role of Red and Green-sensitive Cones," *Vision Research*, 18, 1978, 683–697.

Tansley, B. W. and R. M. Boynton, "A Line, Not a Space, Represents Visual Distinctness of Borders Formed by Different Colors," *Science*, 191, 1976, 954–957.

Thorell, L. G. "The Role of Color in Form Analysis," Ph.D. Thesis Berkeley, University of California, 1981.

Uchikawa, H. and P. K. Kaiser, "Color Discrimination Perimetry," *Color Research and Application*, 7(3), 1982, 264–272.

Valberg, A. and B. W. Tansley, "Tritanopic Purity Difference Function to Describe the Properties of Minimally Distinct, Border," *J. Opt. Soc. Amer.*, 67(10), 1977, 1330–1336.

Van der Horst, G. J. C. and M. A. Bouman, "Spatiotemporal Chromaticity Discrimination," *J. of Optical Soc. of America*, 59(11), 1969, 1482–1487.

Wooten, B. R. and G. Wald, "Color-Vision Mechanisms in the Peripheral Retinas of Normal and Dichromatic Observers," *J. of General Psychology*, 61, 1973, 125–145.

8

Color, Visual Comfort, and Performance

The more harmoniously colors are combined, the more clearly outlines stand out. When color is at its richest, form is at its fullest.

Paul Cézanne

Visual Comfort

Color affects perception and interpretation of images and visual comfort. Viewing any images, including those produced by computers, should not require inappropriate or unnecessary concentrated effort or cause visual discomfort. An ideal viewing situation exists whenever

- The contrast, size, and shape of the images are easily visible and discernible
- There is no measurable decrement in visual performance (for example, in terms of reading speed or visual response)
- There are no reports of negative effects of viewing images

However, assigning color to ensure visual comfort is difficult because conditions that may be comfortable for one person may not be for another. Most tasks (like reading) that require intensive near viewing (a distance of less than 60 cm) become tiring or visually uncomfortable if continued for several hours. Since these types of activities are more frequent when viewing displays than other forms of computer output media, this chapter focuses on the effects of color displays on visual comfort. It describes how to apply color to display screens to optimize visual comfort and visual efficiency.

Ensuring Comfort and Efficiency

These techniques include

- Choosing the most appropriate color and numbers of colors for an application
- Optimizing color for legibility
- Using an image size that will optimize color recognition
- Minimizing unintended visual illusions

- Using appropriate brightness (image and background) contrast
- Using treatments that minimize glare and reflections from the screen
- Minimizing the inappropriate effects of ambient light

Media Changes and Image Appearance

For over three hundred years, we have printed our thoughts and messages onto paper. This medium has traditionally been in the form of dark ink on paper (like the text on this page). The quality of printed images has been traditionally defined by the differences in contrast between the light reflected from printed images and that reflected from the paper. Advances in both ink and paper quality have resulted in high contrast ratios which are now the visual standard against which other hard copy or soft copy media are compared. Familiarity with good quality print and its evolved standard of excellence influences our expectations and preferences for display image quality.

Unlike printed images, most computer display images emit light (see Chapter 2) and initially were brighter than their background (for example, white, green, or yellow on a black background). The resulting effects of this form of media and presentation are that the dispersion of light from characters causes the edges of thin lines and alphanumeric characters to appear more blurry than dark print. The type fonts of many older displays were originally designed to optimize quality of light images on a dark background. Although high resolution displays now have the capability to produce very sharp features and fonts on dark and light backgrounds, the quality of typeset print continues to have superior appearance (see Figure 8.1).

Technically, the difference in character sharpness between displays and paper is due to the number of dots that compose an image and the dispersion of light emission or reflection at its edges. Printed dots have a sharper edge profile than an equal size spot of light (see Chapters 2 and 3).

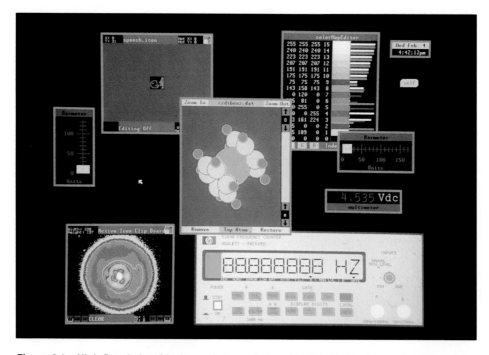

Figure 8.1 *High Resolution Displays* High resolution display allows sharp edge appearance of thin lines and small images on both dark and light color backgrounds. (*Courtesy of Hewlett-Packard.*)

Factors in Visual Discomfort

One source of visual discomfort appears to be the differences in light production (emission or reflection) of display and printed media and their contrast ratios.

The contrast of most printed media is almost 100 percent, which is optimal for visibility. In addition, the contrast of most of this media is constant regardless of the ambient illumination. On the other hand, the contrast of computer display media (typically between 30 and 85 percent) is significantly less. The contrast of images on displays also varies depending on the level of ambient illumination and glare sources reflected from screens.

Other sources of complaint are glare and reflections from the surface of the screen, inappropriate character size and spacing, inadequate image resolution, and lack of stability. Inappropriate design or adjustment of any of these factors can result in complaints of visual discomfort and/or annoyance.

Color and Eye Movements

Many users report that multicolor screens reduce symptoms of visual discomfort. Although the reasons for this are not yet clear, it may be that the correct assignment of color can reduce eye movements required for search tasks. Although muscles that control eye movements are evidently not susceptible to fatigue, very extreme movements can result in visual discomfort. (You can experience this effect if you rapidly shift your eyes from a far left position to a far right position several times.) Since color can reduce the number of eye movements in a search task (see Chapter 1), finding a particular colored item requires less work for the muscles controlling these movements. Thus, if visual discomfort results from excessive eye movements, less discomfort should occur with color displays.

In addition, people prefer viewing multicolor rather than single color displays (see Chapter 1). Whether this is because of aesthetic appreciation or the natural use of color sensitive mechanisms in the eye is not known.

Temporary Distortions of Color Appearance

Extended viewing of certain colors whether presented on a display or on other media can cause minor perceptual distortions (such as adaptation, afterimages, and movement illusions) which are sometimes erroneously assumed to be evidence of visual fatigue. However, they are all part of the normal visual function of adaptation rather than fatigue of the visual system.

Adaptation

Color adaptation is a visual distortion that occurs with concentrated, extensive viewing of colors. This phenomenon is associated with a temporary loss in sensitivity to colors. When *adaptation* occurs, colors appear less saturated due to a change in the sensitivity level of the eye's color sensitive mechanisms. For example, staring at two colors on a display that are similar in hue and brightness (like a desaturated cyan and white or yellow and white), will cause the color sensitive mechanisms to adapt to their average chromaticity causing their differences to become less apparent. However, by looking away from the screen for a few seconds and then looking back to the screen, the differences between the colors will once again be obvious. Color adaptation can be affected by the level and color of the ambient illumination. Color metrics are available to predict shift in adaptation (see Chapter 9).

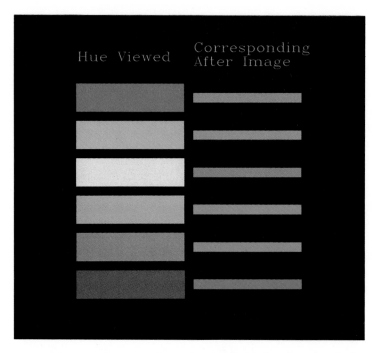

Figure 8.2 *"Afterimages"* When the eyes "adapt" to the colors in the left column, illusions of the lighter complementary colors in the right column might be seen when gaze is shifted away from the source color.

Afterimages

Color adaptation can also cause color *afterimages* (see Figure 8.2). For example, viewing a dense array of green characters may produce pink afterimages. The type of color after effects many display users notice most typically occurs after extensively viewing green text.

These afterimage illusions result from an increased sensitivity of the visual system to the complement of the color viewed. This phenomenon is also known as *successive contrast*, so called because the color of the afterimage is a direct contrast, or complement, of the original color. Color afterimage effects are considered temporary sensations as opposed to indicators of visual fatigue.

Movement Illusions

Color distortions can also induce the appearance of motion of static images. For example, lights composed of spectrally extreme wavelengths can appear to either proceed or recede as view shifts from one to the other. Thus, when the eyes view (and focus on) a red image and then a blue image, the blue image may appear to recede. When vision shifts again to the red image, it may appear to precede. These illusions are caused by the lens of the eye changing shape as it attempts to focus the colors on the retina (see Chapter 6). This refocusing causes the illusion of forward and backward movement and mostly occurs when simultaneously viewing extreme wavelengths of high purity.

These movement illusions can cause annoyance or discomfort depending on the individual's sensitivity to this phenomenon. Avoiding spectrally extreme color combinations or desaturating the colors will reduce or eliminate this effect. Some color-induced movement effects are desirable, and software techniques are available for animating with color (see Chapter 10).

Colors Optimizing Comfort and Performance

Colors and Visual Comfort

The choice of which color or combination of colors results in the best comfort or visual performance while viewing displays depends on three main factors:

- The image characteristics
- The viewer's visual ability
- The ambient illumination

Studies have not yet demonstrated that any particular color causes visual fatigue. In fact, visual fatigue is not scientifically characterized nor are the reports of its symptoms consistent between individuals.

Studies of visual comfort show that viewers report less visual discomfort with certain colors and their combinations. For example, more visual discomfort is reported when reading text in colors at the extremes of the visual spectrum (such as red and blue).

In addition, personal preferences for colors appear to influence visual comfort. These preferences appear to be a function of several variables, including the geographic location of users, their culture, and the advertising to which they are exposed (see Chapter 1).

The fact that the eye is more sensitive to the yellow-green portion of the visible spectrum (see Chapter 6) leads many people to believe that this color is best for display screens. In some northern European countries, the most popular color for single color (monochrome) display images is yellow. However, yellow images are not appropriate for all viewing conditions (see Figure 8.3). The color of characters is not as critical to visual comfort and good legibility as is their luminance contrast. The most critical variable for image visibility and legibility is thus luminance, not color contrast (see Chapters 6 and 7). So while yellow and green produce high luminance contrasts on black background display screens, their presentation on a light background is usually inadequate for good legibility and readability.

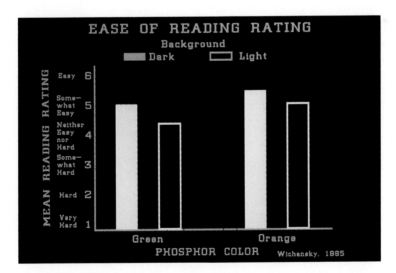

Figure 8.3 *Legibility of Commonly Used Monochrome Text* Legibility performance of different colored text (same brightness) as a function of standard viewing distance (50 cm) and far viewing distance (the farthest distance at which characters could be identified). Although the differences between legibility of orange and green texts on either light or dark backgrounds were not significant, more errors occurred when viewing the green images than when viewing the orange. (*Courtesy of Wichansky, 1986.*)

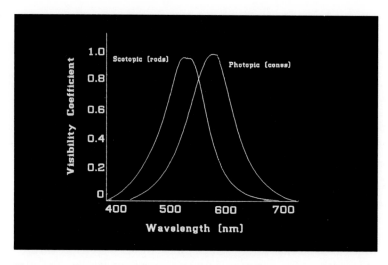

Figure 8.4 *Sensitivity of Rods and Cones* Sensitivity range of the cones and rods. Although cone receptor cells are sensitive to most wavelengths, they are most sensitive to middle wavelengths (perceived as yellow-green). Rod receptor cells which are used in dim environments are more sensitive to the lower end (blue-green range) of the visible spectrum. (*Adapted from Hurvich, 1980.*)

Visibility and Light Adaptation

Some colors are more appropriate for specific illumination levels and line widths. This is because of the differences in sensitivity of the eye's receptor cells to light levels and color. In natural or artificially lighted environments (*photopic* viewing conditions), the cone receptors are most responsive. Cones respond most strongly to wavelengths in the middle of the visible spectrum (such as yellow and green). Rod receptors are most active in dark environments (*scotopic* viewing conditions) and respond most strongly to short wavelengths (see Figure 8.4). Thus, some receptors process certain wavelengths more efficiently than others.

The best color for any medium partly depends on brightness of the light relative to the visual range of the eye and the adaptation state of the eyes to the particular hue. Since most displays are viewed in photopic conditions, any color can be used as long as there is sufficient contrast between the image and its background or surrounding images. For typical office ambient light conditions, the contrast luminance ratio of display images to their background should be at least three to one (3:1).

Brightness, Comfort, and Legibility

Background (Light versus Dark)

Background lightness has an impact on visual comfort and legibility by affecting contrast, glare, and thus the resolution between an image and its background. For CRT color displays with very small or fine-line graphics, colors are more visible and discriminable on dark backgrounds (see Chapter 11). For single color displays, there are usually no differences in reading performance between a dark and a light screen background when the text is equal in quality and perceived size. On multicolor displays, legibility scores are higher for light images on dark backgrounds. In addition, there is a general preference for viewing CRT colors on dark backgrounds for continuous reading and for applications where color appearance and discrimination are critical. This may be due to the large areas of high brightness and discomfort glare caused by very light screen backgrounds. In addition, light scattering on CRT screens (see Chapter 2) diffuses the spatial quality of display images. This causes the stroke width of fine-line dark images to appear thinner on light backgrounds which decreases visibility of thin fonts particularly at viewing distances greater than 50 cm.

With traditional types of CRTs, there are other disadvantages in using displays with a white background. One is the increase in flicker appearance on white and light background CRT screens (see Chapter 2) due to sensitivity of the eye to flicker of bright lights and large area-fill.

In spite of potential problems of light background CRT screens, many people prefer them because they are more similar to the appearance of images on paper and, screen reflections are less obvious. In addition, white background screens are convenient for reviewing the appearance of color images to be transferred onto paper or transparencies (see Chapter 3).

Changing View from Dark Screens to Paper

Extremely bright sources can cause discomfort glare. The differences in light appearance between a dark colored screen and paper are not normally sufficient to cause discomfort glare. In addition, the differences do not significantly change the size of the eye's pupil and do not cause excessive strain on muscles controlling pupil size.

The pupil adjusts its size to accommodate all the light within the viewing field (including the light surrounding the display and emitted from it). In typical office viewing conditions (display viewing distance is about 50 cm and illumination level is about 500 lux), there is normally no significant effect of the display luminance on pupil size. Even if extreme variation in pupil size did occur, the muscles that control the size of the pupil are virtually immune to fatigue (see Figure 8.5).

Optimal Color Combinations for Legibility

As previously mentioned, legibility on computer screens is primarily a function of brightness contrast rather than of color contrast. For black background CRT displays, brighter colors like yellow, cyan, green, and magenta are superior for recognition and

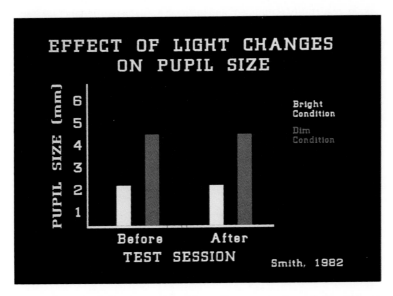

Figure 8.5 *Pupil Response over Time* The range of pupil size did not change after about 8,000 expansions and contractions to consecutive exposures to dim (20 cd/m²) and bright lights (960 cd/m²). (*Smith, 1980.*)

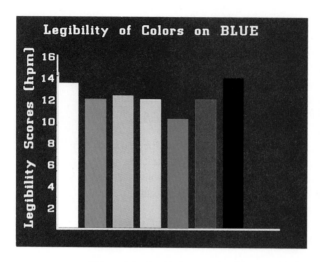
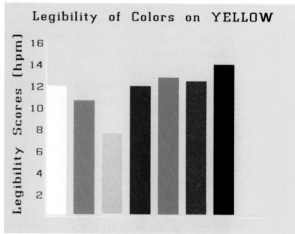

Figure 8.6 *Legibility and Preferences of Colors on Dark and Light Backgrounds* This study showed that legibility of the six typical CRT colors was better on a darker background (black, blue, and red) than on a lighter background (yellow and pink). Preferences are also for dark background screens. (*Adapted from Small, 1986.*)

readability than darker colors like black, blue, and red. When the background is changed to white, the reverse occurs: Legibility and readability are best for darker, saturated characters like red and blue and are reduced for the brighter colors like cyan and yellow (see Figure 8.6). However, when the brightness contrast of color pairs is equivalent, there are normally no significant differences in performance as long as the contrast between the images and their background is sufficient.

Unfortunately, color brightness between different displays is usually not consistent which results in variations in legibility between similar colors on different displays.

Number of Appropriate Colors

The number of colors that should be used at one time primarily depends on the application. If the number of colors is excessive or inappropriate, color confusions occur (see Figure 8.7), readability is reduced, and the time to find a particular color item increases (see Chapter 1).

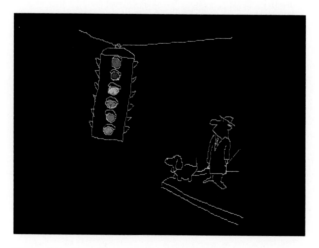

Figure 8.7 *Too Many Colors Cause Confusion* Too many colors can interfere with decision making and reduce performance. (Adapted from *New Yorker*, 1979.)

Color, Visual Comfort, and Performance Chap. 8

Choosing the number of colors for an application depends on several variables, including

- The visual demands of the application
- The apparent differences between the colors
- The size of the color images
- The technology producing the colors
- The number of color codes required

When meanings are assigned to colors, the number of colors should be limited. Studies in memory retention have demonstrated that five to nine items are relatively easy to remember at one time. Studies in memory for color meanings show similar results. However, when color is used only to differentiate information, any number of colors is acceptable as long as there are sufficient contrast differences (see Chapter 7).

Reflections and Glare

Reflections and glare from display screens are the most frequently reported complaints of visual display terminal operators. *Reflections* are mirror-like images of objects in the environment that appear on the surface of a screen. *Glare* is a source of light (emitted or reflected) that is significantly brighter than its surrounding light and results in annoyance (*discomfort glare*) or reduction in visual ability (*disability glare*).

Reflections of ambient light and glare on a display screen can cause a significant loss in image contrast (see Figure 8.8) and reduce image recognition and color.

Reflections are of two types: specular and diffuse. *Specular* (mirror-like) reflections appear on the front surface of display screens. *Diffuse* reflections are veiling luminances caused by light scattered through the glass surface of the screen.

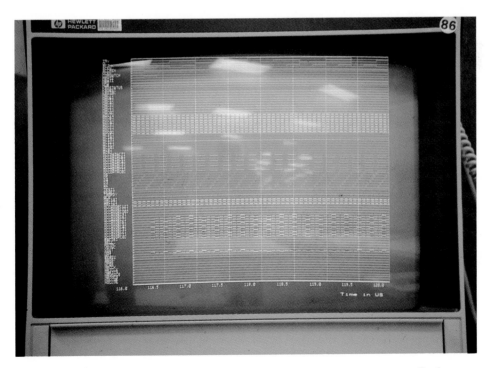

Figure 8.8 *Nontreated Screen* Without an anti-glare screen treatment, many reflections are apparent on the surface of the screen. (*Courtesy of Brian Benson, Hewlett-Packard.*)

Reflections and Glare

Display glare reduces color appearance because it adds light to image colors and reduces their saturation. Colors which are already desaturated (such as yellow and cyan) are usually further desaturated by glare. Moreover, if the glare source has a dominant color component, as do some fluorescent lights, the eyes will adapt to its color and be less able to discriminate values on the screen similar to that of the light. For example, blue fluorescent lights may reduce the number of discriminable shades of blue. This situation is particularly relevant in many computer display environments because of the use of "cool" white fluorescent lights.

Solutions to Glare and Reflections

There are several solutions available to reduce reflections and glare (see Figure 8.9). These include treatments to the display screen. The three most effective treatments are etching, woven fiber filters, and optical coatings. Each one has different effects on image resolution and color quality: Some reduce the brightness of colors, some reduce their wavelengths, others cause light dispersion which reduces edge sharpness. The effectiveness of a particular screen treatment depends on how well each works with the particular display technology. The effects on the optical characteristics of images and their spectral bandwidth should be carefully considered when selecting a screen treatment.

Some anti-glare–reflection filters attach to the front of the screen, other treatments are bonded directly to the screen. In general, the direct screen treatment is most effective.

ETCHED SCREENS   An *etched screen* has been exposed to a chemical process that roughens its surface. This diffuses or scatters specular reflections from the screen and emitted light passing through the screen (see Figure 8.10). Different degrees of etching, or granularities, produce differences in light scattering. Low granularity etch diffuses specular images and reduces the edge quality (and resolution) more than high granularity etching.

Low granularity etch can reduce breaks in lines or jagged edges caused by the visibility of individual pixels. Since diagonal lines are particularly susceptible to this jagged appearance, characters and symbols such as w, v, and s, 8, /, &, and $ have smoother appearing edges with an etched screen.

Applying an etch directly to the surface of the screen instead of placing a filter over the screen surface minimizes light diffusion.

Although etching affects resolution, it has little effect on the color quality. However,

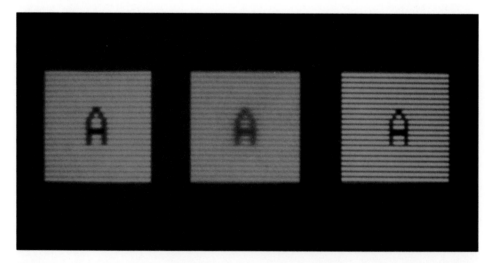

Figure 8.9 *Anti-Glare Treatments and Image Appearance*   a) Appearance of character with a nylon weave filter. b) Appearance of character with etch treatment. c) Appearance of character with quarter-wavelength anti-glare treatment. (*Courtesy of OCLI.*)

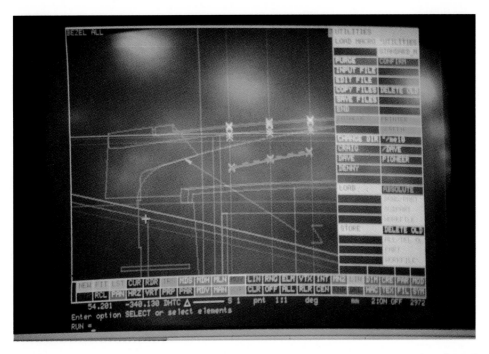

Figure 8.10 *Etched Screens* A chemical etch applied directly to the screen scatters the reflected light and the emitted light which causes a slight blur of the image. (*Courtesy of Brian Benson, Hewlett-Packard.*)

it improves the uniformity of the appearance of dithered colors (see Chapter 10) because it enhances the visual blending of individual pixels.

WOVEN FIBER FILTERS *Woven fiber* nylon *filters* are similar to Venetian blinds in that they allow light to reflect at different angles and can thus control the angle of light reflected from the screen and into the viewer's eyes. They usually attach to the external frame of the screen. They are a good solution to blocking all light reflected from the screen into the viewer's eyes except for low angle reflections (see Figure 8.11).

Figure 8.11 *Woven Fiber Screen Filters* The fiber material eliminates glare by directing the light at an angle away from the line of sight. Visibility of images at viewing angles other than perpendicular to the screen can be reduced depending on the thickness of the weave. (*Courtesy of Brian Benson, Hewlett-Packard.*)

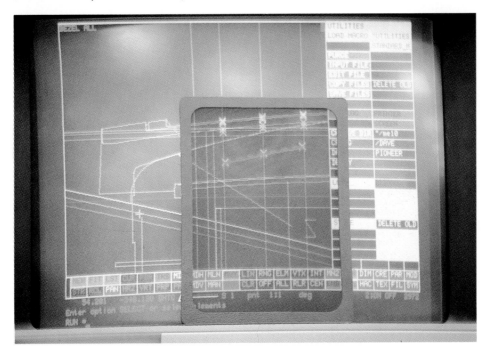

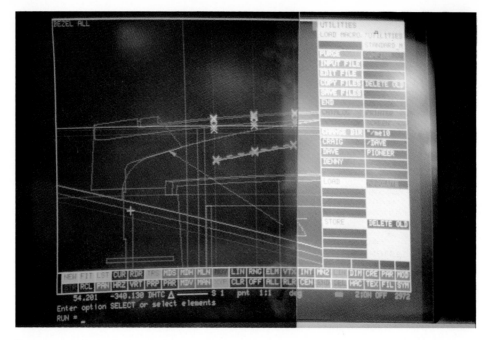

Figure 8.12 *Optically Coated Screen* An optical coating applied to the screen (left) makes the colors more vivid. The gray filter also enhances the contrast of the text. On the section of the screen not covered by the optical coating (right) the blue text appears white. This is because ambient light and reflections cause a reduction in saturation. (*Courtesy of Brian Benson, Hewlett-Packard.*)

However, the visibility of screen images is limited by the thickness of the weave and the user's viewing angle. In addition, patterns created by the weave of the nylon fabric can interfere with image resolution.

Also, dust collects between their fibers and, depending on their strength, depressions of the filter during cleaning can cause surface distortions. If extreme, these distortions produce visual illusions (such as Newton rings and moiré patterns) which can interfere with perception of screen images.

OPTICAL COATINGS   *Optically coated filters* are effective in reducing both reflections and glare. Optical coatings decrease specular reflections by reducing the differences between the optical properties of air and glass (see Box).

They reduce ambient illumination in two stages: by blocking light as it enters the screen glass and then by reflecting the light off the glass surface of the screen (see Figure 8.12). The amount of reduction of emitted and reflected light depends on the darkness of the tint in the coating.

REDUCING GLARE AND REFLECTIONS WITH OPTICAL COATINGS

Optical coatings are very thin films which reduce the first surface reflections from a display screen. These reflections are due to a difference in refractive index (RI) for air (R = 1.0) and glass (R = 1.5). Materials like magnesium ferrous oxide applied as a thin coating reduce the differences in refraction at the air/glass interface and hence reduce reflectivity to one percent. From Fresnel's optical law, the light from a display screen is calculated to reflect only four percent of the incident light. This amount of light reflection can be easily perceived.

Optical coatings do not reduce character resolution or cause visual distortions as much as other screen treatments. However, fingerprints can be easily seen which interfere with color perception due to the light they reflect.

Some optical coatings have a slight purplish tint that changes the appearance of certain colors. Coatings that allow transmission of only the wavelengths emitted by the display effectively improve a display's contrast.

The quarter-wavelength type coating appears to have the least negative effect on image quality and visual performance. Most quarter-wavelength coatings (particularly the thin-film type) are applied to a neutral gray glass panel that is bonded to the cathode ray tube. This gray tint (also known as a neutral density filter) can enhance the contrast of a display image.

COLORED FILTERS   A tinted filter which has low transmittance of wavelengths not emitted by the display and high transmittance of emitted wavelengths optimizes the hue contrast of the display. Color filters thus optimize the color contrast of colors to the filter on a multicolor display. For monochromatic displays which emit light over a narrow spectral band (such as LEDs), colored filters are often particularly useful because they can also increase color contrast. However, they also alter the appearance of other colors. The more spectrally different the image color from the colored filter, the greater will be its effects on image color. However, colored filters do not reduce reflections.

Brightness and Contrast Controls

The ability to control the brightness and contrast of images and their background can enhance color appearance. The resolution of edges of images is optimized when their effective contrast (the sum of the brightness and color contrast) is maximized. This can best be accomplished with brightness and contrast controls.

Contrast control is also important because the visibility of display images may vary dramatically in different lighting conditions. For example, the visibility of images on displays located next to windows is usually significantly less due to the reduction in image contrast.

If the eye is adapted to a dark environment, a ten percent brightness contrast on a display can be easily perceived. However, in a bright environment, a brightness difference as high as 70 percent may be necessary for detection. Thus, extreme lighting conditions require the ability to control brightness and contrast levels of lighted areas on a screen.

In addition, brightness and contrast controls are important because of the differences in visual abilities of users. People with visual deficiencies benefit most from the ability to change brightness and contrast. Older people and those with visual anomalies such as cataracts, require more brightness and contrast to see images, and particularly color differences, than those with normal vision. The ability to reduce brightness can also reduce flicker.

Flicker

Factors Affecting Flicker

Refreshing CRT display images often results in the appearance of *flicker* (see Chapter 2). Slower refresh rates result in more perception of flicker. Since CRTs in the United States are refreshed more rapidly (60 cycles per second) than those in Europe (50 cycles each second), the flicker of CRTs in Europe is more noticable than those in the United States.

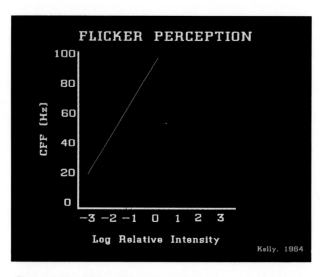

Figure 8.13 *Flicker Perception* Flicker is more apparent as the luminance of the light is increased. (Adapted from Kelly, 1964.)

The frequency at which a flashing light does not appear to flicker (known as critical flicker fusion frequency) is directly related to intensity. Low brightness values reduce flicker, high brightness values increase flicker (see Figure 8.13). In general, a refresh rate of about 85 Hertz is adequate to eliminate flicker for almost all viewers. However, flicker-free refresh rates actually depend on many factors other than refresh and intensity. These include phosphor characteristics (for example, decay rate), area of visual angle an image subtends on the retina, flicker sensitivity of an individual, ambient illumination, and viewing distance.

Flicker and Color

Thus, brighter colors and larger visual areas will result in more flicker perception. For example, large, brightly colored areas such as pie charts, dense text, and light color backgrounds are more likely to be seen as flickering. Desaturated, brighter CRT colors like yellow and cyan will thus induce more flicker than more saturated, darker colors like blue and green.

One of the advantages of color displays is that flicker is less perceptible than on achromatic displays because color phosphors usually produce lower luminances than white phosphors. However, hue has virtually no effect on flicker compared to luminance because the visual system is less sensitive to temporal changes in chrominance than to temporal changes in luminance. Flicker visibility is thus primarily a function of brightness and not hue.

It is easier to see flicker in the visual periphery. At a typical display viewing distance (such as 50 cm), a significant amount of a large screen (such as 48 cm) is in the peripheral area of view. Thus, flicker is more likely with these size displays.

In addition, flicker perception declines with age: People in their twenties are more sensitive to flicker than individuals in their sixties.

The illumination level of the area surrounding the display and the size of the eye's pupil also affect sensitivity to flicker. Higher levels of room illumination can reduce the contrast of the screen brightness and thus reduce the ability to perceive flicker. In addition, bright room lighting reduces the size of the pupil. A smaller pupil reduces the amount of light entering the eye, particularly from peripheral viewing areas (where the sensitivity to flicker is greatest). Dimly lighted work environments enhance the brightness contrast of the lighted portions of the screen, increase pupil size, and thus increase the perception of flicker.

Flicker Reduction and Measurement

There are a number of ways to reduce flicker. However, each solution can introduce other potentially more serious problems (see Table 8.1).

TABLE 8.1

Methods to Reduce Flicker*

Solution	Potential Problem
1. Use an anti-glare filter with a slight gray tint.	Increases brightness contrast; may cause noticeable decrease in brightness of some colors.
2. Reduce brightness of images or background.	Restricts maximum brightness contrast.
3. Use dark colors for backgrounds, pie charts, and dense text.	Limits color coding possibilities.
4. Increase viewing distance from screen.	Reduces the visibility and apparent size of image on the retina of the eye.
5. Increase room illumination.	Reduces brightness and color contrast of screen images.

* Listed in order of ease of implementation and effectiveness.

Useful Facts

Visual Comfort	Color can influence visual comfort (for example, focusing on spectrally extreme colors may cause reports of discomfort).
Ambient Light and Color Perception	Eyes adapted to typical computer display office illumination (such as 500 lux) are most sensitive to middle wavelengths (green and yellow).
	In very bright environments, the eyes are more sensitive to colors at the high end of the visible spectrum; in dark environments, the eyes are more sensitive to colors at the low end of the spectrum.
Adaptation	The loss in ability to discriminate colors after fixating on them (adaptation) is a normal, temporary phenomenon easily remedied by looking away from the colored images for a few seconds.
Afterimages	Continuously viewing colors can result in complementary color afterimages.

Colors for Good Readability	Colors for good readability on black background screens are yellow, light green, cyan; and for white background screens are red and blue.
Numbers of Colors	When the meaning of the color must be remembered, the number of colors should be limited to about four. Graphic applications usually require more colors than text and realistic imaging may require millions.
Background Color	The appropriate background color depends on contrast requirements for the visual task. Dark background CRT screens result in better visibility of colors. Light background screens can cause more comfort problems than dark screens.
Glare and Reflections	Glare and reflection can cause discomfort and reduce the ability to see color. There are several ways to solve this problem (in addition to eliminating the glare source).
Brightness Control	A brightness control should be available to optimize color in different light levels.
Flicker	Display flicker depends on the refresh rate, brightness, image size, sensitivity and age of the viewer, viewing angle, and ambient illumination.

REFERENCES

Bishop, H. P. and M. N. Crook, "Absolute Identification of Color for Targets Presented against White and Colored Backgrounds," WADD Technical Report 60–611, WPAFB, 1962.

de Corte, W., "High Contrast Sets of Colors for Color CRTs under Various Conditions of Illumination," *Displays*, 6(2), April 1985, 95–100.

Donohoo, D. T., "Accommodation During Color Contrast," *Society for Information Display*, XVI, 1985, 200–203.

Farrell, J. E., "An Analytical Method for Predicting Perceived Flicker," *Behavior & Information Technology*, 5(4), 1986, 349–358.

Fuchs, A. F. and M. D. Binder, "Fatigue Resistance of Human Extraocular Muscles," *J. of Neurophysiology*, 49(10), 1983, 28–34.

Hurvich, L. M. *Color Vision: An Introduction* (Sunderland, MA: Sinnauer Associates, 1980).

Kelly, D., "Sine Waves and Flicker Fusion," in *Flicker*, eds. H. E. Henkes and L. H. van der Tweel (The Netherlands: The Hague, 1964) 16–35.

Laycock, J., "Colour Contrast Calculations for Display Viewed in Illumination," *International Conference on Colour in Information Technology and Visual Displays*, IERE, Pub. #61, 1985, pp. 7–14.

Laycock, J. and J. P. Viveash, "Calculating the Perceptibility of Monochrome and Colour Displays Viewed under Various Illumination Conditions," *Displays*, 3(2), 1982, 88–98.

Legge, G. E. and G. S. Rubin, "Psychophysics of Reading. IV. Wavelength Effects in Normal and Low Vision," *J. Opt. Soc. Am.*, 3(1), 1986, 40–52.

Maas, J. B., J. K. Jayson, and D. A. Kleber, "Effects of Spectral Differences in Illumination on Fatigue," *J. of Applied Psychology*, 59(4), August 1974, 524–526.

Murch, G. M., "Visual Accommodation and Convergence to Multichromatic Visual Display Terminals," *Society for Information Display*, 24(1), 1983, 62–71.

Rupp, B., *Human Factors of Workstations with Display Terminals*, IBM Manual #G320-6102-1, 1978.

Small, P. L., "Factors Influencing the Legibility of Text/background Color Combinations on the IBM 3279 Display Station," Hursley, U.K., HF 066, 1962.

Smith, S. L., "Legibility of Overprinted Symbols in Multicoloured Displays," *J. of Eng. Psych.*, 2, 1963, 82–96.

Smith, W. J. Control of screen glare. *Proceedings of the Annual Conference of the International Society for Optical Engineering*, Jan. 1984, pp. 2–6.

Smith, W. J., "Research on the Impact on Computer Displays on the Human Visual System," *International Conference on Visual Psychophysics and Medical Imaging*, July 1981, pp. 40–42.

Smith, W. J., "A Review of Literature Relating to Visual Fatigue," *Proceedings of the Human Factors Society*, 1979, pp. 362–366.

Smith, W. J. *Physiological Correlates of Visual Fatigue*, Unpublished Thesis, Stanford University, 1980.

Sundet, J. M., "The Effect of Pupil Size Variations on the Color Stereoscopic Phenomenon," *Vision Research*, 12, 1972, 1027–1032.

Thorell, L. G. and A. Bradley, *Measuring Luminance on Displays: Tools and Analysis*. TR for Hewlett-Packard, Dec. 1983.

Video Displays, Work and Vision, National Research Council (Washington, DC: National Academy Press, 1983).

Walraven, J., "The Colours Are Not on the Display. A Survey of the Non-veridical Perceptions That May Turn Up on a Color Display," *Displays*, 1985, pp. 35–43.

Wichansky, A., "Legibility and User Acceptance of Monochrome Display Phosphor Colors," *Proceedings of Conference on Work with Display Units*, May 1986, pp. 216–219.

9

Specification of Color

A good painter needs only three colors.

Titian

Precise Descriptions of Color

We typically use words to describe a color: its appearance or its perceptual components (see Chapter 6). The basic color terms we use most often refer to hue (for example, red, yellow, or blue), whereas modifiers like ''muted,'' ''pastel,'' or ''bright'' describe saturation and lightness. These basic hue names and their descriptors help communicate relatively specific color perceptions. However, color names are inappropriate for objective specification due to their inherent ambiguity. For example, green can refer to emerald green, army green, or lime green. Each of us may have an image of army or lime green, but the image of their exact value varies from one person to the next. Color names are thus not sufficiently specific for producing and manipulating color on computer displays and hard copy devices.

To obtain a precise description of color, specifications and measurements of its physical properties (see Chapter 2) are necessary. Physical measurements reveal aspects of color not immediately obvious to the eye such as the fact that white is actually composed of many different wavelengths or that very colorful objects, like a banana or tomato, reflect a wide range of wavelengths. The same color sensations can be produced by dramatically different combinations of wavelengths. We cannot directly perceive these aspects of color, nor are they intuitively obvious.

Knowing the relationship between the physical and the perceptual aspects of color can help aid in the prediction of its appearance and reliable reproduction. The problem of accurately specifying color while relating it to perception occurs in the engineering of all devices that produce color images. Manufacturers must be able to describe the colors a display can produce and most would like to be able to develop a device that produces the range of colors that the eye can see. In addition, most would like to reproduce the same color appearance from a display onto a color printed hard copy.

This chapter addresses the objective specification of color. Specifically, it describes how to specify a subjective experience such as red or pale yellow by color systems in order to produce an identical color independent of the device. It also describes how these systems are useful to specify and predict color discrimination of display and hard copy images.

Colorimetric Systems

Numeric systems that specify mathematical relations between radiant energy entering the eye and colors we perceive are called *colorimetric systems*. Ideally, all colors that appear identical (despite any physical differences) should have the same numeric specification, and colors that have the same numeric specification (even if produced on different devices) should look the same.

USERS OF COLORIMETRIC SYSTEMS Anyone who wants to measure or communicate an exact color value needs to understand colorimetric systems. One of the advantages of these systems is that it is not necessary for users to understand colorimetric theory and implementation to use them. Artists, software designers, hardware engineers, and scientists can all use colorimetric systems to enhance efficient use of computer color. Artists can easily use them to select palette colors in a computer Paint program. It is important that people such as software designers who write color Paint programs understand color systems because their choice of which systems they use to select colors will affect not only color appearance but the ease of use of Paint programs. Understanding these systems is also necessary for hardware designers to specify the color tolerance (see Chapter 4) of display phosphors or to specify the range of display colors that a color hard copy device can produce.

Understanding color systems allows scientists to describe the physical aspects of color. The readings from light-measuring instruments quantify colors produced by displays, printers, or plotters. Describing the units of a standard color system is useful to reproduce a color by other color devices. Lastly, understanding these systems helps human factors engineers calculate colors that are maximally distinct in extreme lighting conditions (such as direct sunlight and dark environments).

Color Spaces and Trichromacy

Most colorimetric systems can be represented by orderly arrangements of colors in geometric solids or *spaces*. Practical uses of color spaces for designers and users of computer color include

- Specifying particular colors
- Calculating colors which are easy to distinguish
- Selecting highly contrasting colors
- Choosing colors which appear equally bright
- Selecting "easy-to-see" colors for people with color vision deficiencies

Most color spaces are three-dimensional and each color is represented by a point in the space. The three dimensions of color space best show *trichromacy* which is the basis of normal color perception (see Chapter 6) and the international standard for describing color (see CIE Color Systems). Trichromacy (three color values) means that mixing three specific wavelengths will match a white light.

TRICHROMACY Whichever system is used to specify color, its descriptive base is always trichromatic. Trichromacy is one of the cornerstones of color science theory and, as such, plays a major role in color perception and the engineering of color devices.

One of the advantages of trichromacy is that it allows considerable flexibility in the design of color devices because there are many sets of primaries which can produce the same specific color. The critical feature in specifying color is that its three components are independent, whether they relate to visual perception (hue, saturation, and lightness) or display or printer hardware primaries (such as red, green, and blue in displays or cyan, magenta, and yellow in printers).

TRICHROMACY AND COLOR MATCHING   The eye is easily fooled into seeing two physically different lights as the same indistinguishable color. This occurs because of trichromacy or, in physiological terms, the fact that the eye has three independent classes of color receptors none of which actually sends a color signal to the brain (see Chapter 6). Instead, each one generates an electrical response which is proportional to the total amount of light absorbed regardless of wavelength. Thus, there are a large number of different wavelengths whose intensities can be adjusted to create the same strength of electrical signal from a receptor cell. If the cell sends the same signal when the eye views two different lights, the brain cannot distinguish them and they look identical. For example, if we mix (or add) a 640 nm (red) light and a 540 nm (green) light, we will see pale yellow. As in the early experiments conducted by Isaac Newton (see Box and Figure 9.2), we see the same pale yellow when mixing a pure 570 nm light with a white light. In fact, adjusting the intensities of three primary colors can produce a match to any color. Thus, we can match colored lights (or ink pigments) whose spectral distributions are very different because for each color which matches another, the pattern of signals sent by the three types of independent receptors in the eye is equivalent.

EARLY COLOR SPACE AND TRICHROMACY

Three color values were used even in early modeling of color spaces. A classic example is the hue circle developed by Isaac Newton (see Figure 9.1). Although this shape appears simplistic, it captures Newton's greatest contribution to color theory: The correct representation of the order and relations of colors must be consistent with people's visual judgments of their appearance.

Using simple equipment consisting of a few glass prisms and the light from his window at Cambridge University, Newton conducted experiments to reveal the order and relations of colored lights. In one experiment, he observed that mixing a white light with a yellow light produced pale yellow. He also showed that this particular mixture of lights was not unique: Combining a specific ratio of red and green lights produced the same pale yellow.

Newton explained his observation by positioning the colors of the spectrum on a circle (see Figure 9.1) and explaining how the mass at the color's position on the circle represented the intensity of each color. With this simple diagram, he showed how the ratio of red and green intensities matched the addition of yellow and white intensities. The pale yellow color from either combination of color pairs was in the same location. In fact, there were many different color pairs which, when one member was combined with another, produced identical color mixtures.

Thus, even in this early color model, three numbers were necessary: two numbers to specify the center of mass and one to show the sum of the masses (representing their intensity).

(continued)

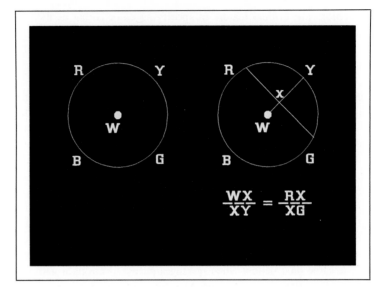

$$\frac{WX}{XY} = \frac{RX}{XG}$$

Figure 9.1 *Explaining Newton's Color Model* Newton's hue circle shows the results of his color mixing experiments: the ratio of intensity of yellow and white lights which match a mixture of red and green lights. The mixtures match and are located in the identical position in the circle.

EVOLUTION OF COLOR SPACES   Prior to 1931, most colorimetric systems were represented by simple geometric shapes and spaces that were only roughly based on color perception. As knowledge of color vision expanded, the number of dimensions and details of these spaces increased to include information from color perception studies. The shape of color spaces evolved from circular representations (see Chapter 6) to hexcones and cubic octahedrons (see Figure 9.2).

TYPES OF COLOR SPACES   There are many types of color spaces. They vary in their coordinate systems (or axes), scaling and, as a consequence, their shapes. *Perceptual color spaces* such as Munsell (see Chapter 6) are based on color vision data and experiments. *Computer color spaces* such as RGB are used for software and hardware specification and control of color (see Chapter 10). RGB space is not based on the visual perception of color but refers to direct hardware control of the CRT electron beams that illuminate the red, blue, and green phosphors (see Chapter 2). The resultant RGB color space is a cube with the maximal intensity primaries (red, green, and blue) and their full intensity binary combinations (cyan, yellow, and magenta) forming the corners. White (mixture of all primaries) and black (no primaries) are located at opposite ends of the central diagonal of the cube.

CIE Color Systems

The international standard for specifying color was developed by the Commission Internationale de l'Eclairage (CIE) which is a group of scientists and illumination engineers representing its member countries. Ever since its inception, the CIE color system has provided the primary description and specification for color. The foundation for this system occurred in the 1920s and has since continued expanding and developing its colorimetric

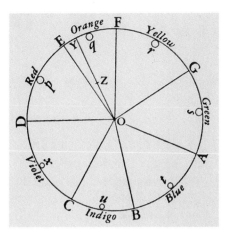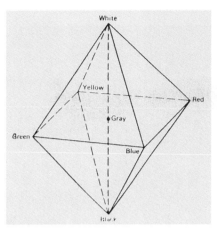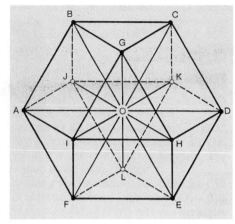

Figure 9.2 *Evolution of Perceptual Color Spaces* (left) Newton's color circle. The hue names of corresponding wavelengths border the perimeter of the circle. Upper and lower case letters mark points noted by Newton in his presentation. The width of the sectors was not based on vision data but from Newton's generalization from music theory. [*Adapted from Horsley's 1782 reprint of the second (1717) edition of Newton's* Opticks.] (middle) Runge's (1810) double pyramid, one of the earliest three-dimensional spaces. Here, the most saturated colors are midway between white and black. Saturated colors are not visible at the brightness extremes. (*From Wasserman, 1978.*) (right) The cubic octahedron of the Optical Society of America's Uniform Color Scale. In an ideal color space, the distance between colors should express their perceptual relations: Similar colors are close together, very different colors are correspondingly farther apart. In this space, the distance between nearest neighbor colors remains approximately constant throughout the color system. Letters refer to positions of colors which appear equal perceptual distances from one another. (*Adapted from Wyszecki and Stiles, 1982.*)

systems. Although initially intended for mixtures of pigments and lights, the CIE color standard is used for display and hard copy industry applications.

CIE XYZ Space

The main goal of the CIE is to create a standard tool to describe colors for all users, applications, and devices, to strive to make the calculations for specifying colors mathematically convenient, and to create a visual diagram that shows the order and relations of colors. The particular set of physical primaries for producing a color used in specifying the standard is not important because as previously stated, there are many sets of three primaries which create a particular color mixture. Thus, a particular red, green, and blue combine to create a specific gray value. Similarly, an orange, cyan, and blue combine to create the same gray color.

Although the CIE color space is a physical description of light, it also incorporates data from color vision experiments. However, as with all studies, the design of questions influences their answers. The original CIE color vision data were collected under very specific viewing conditions which imposed certain constraints in generalizing the system to typical viewing conditions of display and hard copy colors.

To accomplish the laudable goal of creating a color space which could be used to specify any perceivable color, the CIE reviewed color matching data from several different research laboratories. These data were collected by presenting observers with normal color vision, a circular two degree field of light divided into two halves on a dark background (see Figure 9.3). One half of the test field was illuminated by a test color of a specific wavelength while the other half consisted of a mixture of three primaries. The task of the observer was to adjust the proportion of the three primaries to create a visual match to the test light.

For test lights composed of more than a single wavelength, a match of the light by

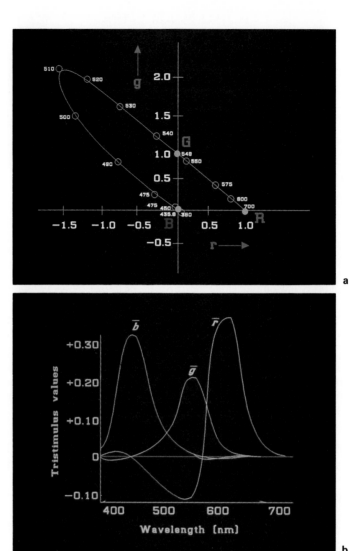

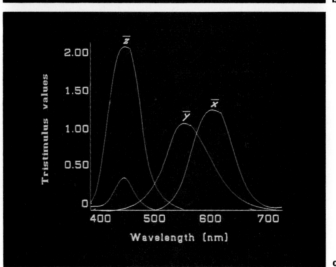

Figure 9.3 *Matching Functions* a) Guild's Color Matching Diagram. (*Adapted from Wyszecki and Stiles, 1982.*) b and c) The transformed color matching functions adopted by the CIE in 1931. (*Adapted from Wyszecki and Stiles, 1982.*)

some combination of the three primaries was possible. For single wavelength (pure monochromatic) colors, a match was not possible. The observer could often obtain a fairly reasonable match in hue, but the test color always appeared more saturated than the combination of primaries. To obtain a match, it was necessary to move one of the primaries to the other half of the field and add it to the test mixture. This desaturated the test color so that a visual match of the two field halves could be obtained. For example, if attempting to match a blue-green color of 500 nm, an observer would vary the mixture of the green and blue primary until a match in hue was obtained, then add enough red to the 500 nm test stimulus to desaturate it to look the same as the blue and green previously mixed.

By systematically obtaining matches across the entire visible spectrum, a diagram of color relations should be obtained. In a diagram produced by Guild in the late 1920s (see Figure 9.3a), the primaries used consisted of a red of 700 nm, green of 547 nm, and a blue of 436 nm. All the colors lying along the spectrum between 700 nm and 547 nm can be matched by some proportion of the red and green primary without adding any blue to the test sample. Conversely, all the colors along the spectrum from 548 to 437 cannot be matched by some mixture of the green and blue primary: The colors all require a desaturation by the red primary to the test sample. An extension to the left of the diagram resulted from calculating the amount of red required to adequately desaturate the test sample to match the primaries. In this system, color matches of test samples which were not monochromatic lights can be matched by some combination of the three primaries, provided they are within the boundaries of the triangle formed by the three primary colors. For Guild's matching experiments, it is possible to derive a set of color matching functions which indicates the amount of each primary required to match a specific point on the visible spectrum (see Figure 9.3b). The negative values indicate the amount of the primary which needed to be added to the test value to create a visual match.

As these studies were conducted before the availability of computers (and even calculators), the CIE decided to transform the color matching functions algebraically to eliminate the negative numbers. The resultant set (see Figure 9.3b) was adopted by the CIE as official color matching functions and termed X, Y, and Z. These new, transformed functions added several other nuances to simplify the specification of color. Most important, the color matching functions were transformed so that all visible colors could be described by some additive combination of X, Y, and Z. These color matching functions can thus be set equal as imaginary primaries (they lie outside the boundaries of the visible color space). In addition, the Y primary was equalized to the previously adopted CIE spectral luminosity function: the function which indicates the approximate brightness of lights of different wavelength distribution. The color matching functions can be used to calculate the chromaticity coordinates of any color (see Figure 9.4). The resultant color space can be used to assign names and locate all visible colors (see Figure 9.3) and has become known as the 1931 CIE chromaticity space.

Tristimulus Values Necessary for Matching Colors

With an estimate of the color matching functions, it is possible to specify any light in terms of the amount of X, Y, and Z contained in the mixture. The result is a tristimulus value and expresses the absolute amount of a primary necessary for a color match. The steps in deriving the tristimulus values X, Y, and Z can be shown graphically (see Figure 9.4). Two colors match when their tristimulus values are equal. Many different light distributions can produce the same set of tristimulus values.

The CIE tristimulus values can be expressed by

$$X = \int E_\lambda \, \bar{x} \, \Delta\lambda$$
$$Y = \int E_\lambda \, \bar{y} \, \Delta\lambda$$
$$Z = \int E_\lambda \, \bar{z} \, \Delta\lambda$$

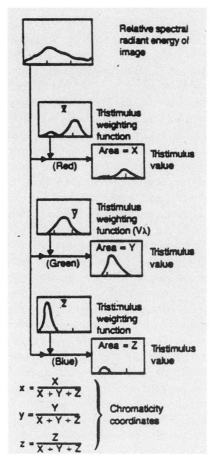

Figure 9.4 *Graphic Derivation of the CIE Calculations* The steps to calculate the CIE chromaticity coefficients are illustrated from top to bottom.

Chromaticity Coordinates: Color Plots in 2D Space

While a complete specification of color requires three numbers, three-dimensional spaces (see Figure 9.5a) are complex to use. For easier interpretation, CIE space can be converted into two dimensions because each of its functions (x,y,z) is a proportion of the total amount of energy or

$$x = \frac{X}{X + Y + Z}$$

$$y = \frac{Y}{X + Y + Z}$$

$$z = 1 - x - y$$

The sum of the primaries in any match will be one, or unity. The values of two primaries can be used to obtain the third value.

This two-dimensional representation is the CIE *chromaticity diagram* and is a two-variable or axis system (see Figure 9.5b) with a single luminance plane. The *chromaticity coordinates*, x and y, designate the position of a color. The CIE primaries X, Y, and Z are represented in the chromaticity diagram by x = 1, y = 0, z = 0; x = 0; y = 1, z = 0; and x = 0, y = 0, z = 1. As indicated, to simplify calculations, the imaginary X and Z primaries are set to zero luminance allowing the calculation of the luminance of a light from Y.

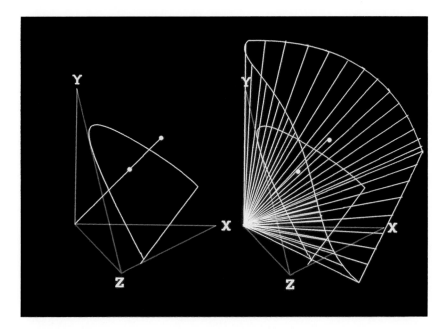

Figure 9.5 *CIE X YZ Space and CIE Chromaticity Diagram* a) Left: Each axis represents the amount of one of the three imaginary primaries. The horseshoe-shaped cone represents the outer boundary of human color vision. Points along this boundary mark the tristimulus values for spectral lights. b) Right: A cross section through XYZ space where each axis represents the proportion of one primary relative to the others. The x axis roughly corresponds to hue and the y axis to saturation. The spectrum locus is marked by points along the boundary of the horseshoe shape. Equal energy white is located at x = .33 and y = .33. The line of purples connects the blue and red spectral extremes.

While there are many three-primary color systems, XYZ space is unique because it is based on real color matching data. When these functions are located on the chromaticity diagram, they form a shape which bounds all the colors we can see.

Standard versus Large Field CIE Space

The appropriate choice of a particular color space depends on the level of accuracy necessary, the characteristics of the image, and the requirements of the task. For example, a hardware engineer may need to specify the color tolerance of a display, determine whether a white background will retain its appearance over time or measure the variation of a particular background color across displays. For situations where the color area is large and accuracy is very important, the *1964 Large Field CIE color space* is more appropriate.

However, for less stringent requirements, the standard two-degree 1931 CIE space is more appropriate because color device specifications are usually described in terms of the two-degree CIE space. In addition, more interfaces to computer color spaces (such as RGB and HSL) exist with the 1931 CIE space. Those who measure, manufacture, or sell computer color devices use the 1931 CIE space to specify colors.

Graphic Advantages of CIE Space

Advantages of the CIE color system for computer display image applications are as follows:

1. The CIE diagram is an international standard tool for comparing different color devices.

   The chromaticity coordinates (x and y) and the measured luminance (Y) of a light provide a complete psychophysical description of a color. The diagram specifies colors for displays, printers, plotter, and film color.

2. For additive devices (like emissive displays), the diagram predicts color mixing results (see Box).

   Any mixture of two colors exists on a line connecting the two chromaticity points (see Figure 9.6).

CALCULATING THE CHROMATICITY (x,y) AND LUMINANCE (Y) FOR A COLOR MIXTURE

MATHEMATICAL METHOD FOR CALCULATING x,y,Y   Given two colors, C_1 and C_2, with CIE specifications

$$(x_{C_1}, y_{C_1}, Y_{C_1}) \text{ and } (x_{C_2}, y_{C_2}, Y_{C_2}),$$

the equations for calculating the chromaticity "weights" of C_1 and C_2 where each weight is proportional to the absolute luminance (Y) and y coefficient are

$$T_{C_1} = \frac{Y_{C_1}}{y_{C_1}} \qquad T_{C_2} = \frac{Y_{C_2}}{y_{C_2}}$$

The equations for calculating the color mixture, m, are

$$x_m = \frac{x_{C_1} T_{C_1} + x_{C_2} T_{C_2}}{T_{C_1} + T_{C_2}}$$

$$y_m = \frac{y_{C_1} T_{C_1} + y_{C_2} T_{C_2}}{T_{C_1} + T_{C_2}}$$

$$Y_m = y_m (T_{C_1} + T_{C_2}) = Y_{C_1} + Y_{C_2}$$

We can predict the mixture of 580 nm and a 480 nm light added in equal amounts where the CIE specification of 580 nm and 480 nm is

$$x_{580} = .51 \qquad x_{480} = .09$$
$$y_{580} = .48 \qquad y_{480} = .13$$
$$Y_{580} = 10 \qquad Y_{480} = 10$$

The luminance weights are

$$10/.49 = 20.40$$
$$10/.13 = 76.92$$

The CIE specifications for the mixture are

$$x_m = \frac{(.51)(20.40) + (.09)(76.72)}{20.40 + 76.92} = .18$$

$$y_m = \frac{(.48)(20.40) + (.13)(76.72)}{20.40 + 76.92} = .20$$

$$Y_m = (.20)(20.40 + 76.92) \qquad = 19.46$$

(continued)

GRAPHIC METHOD OF CALCULATING x,y,Y   The mixture of two colors can also be calculated from a chromaticity diagram by connecting the coordinates of each color with a straight line. The mixture color is a point on this line and is at a distance inversely proportional to the amount of the component color in the mixture. If an imaginary weight is located at the end of the line, the mixture is the point (or fulcrum) where the line is in balance. (See Figure 9.6.)

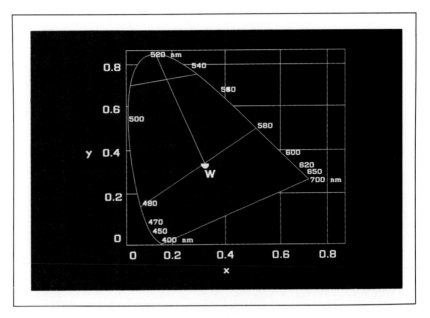

Figure 9.6 *Graphic Techniques for Showing Perceptual Relations among Colors* Predicting the results of color mixture. This example shows where a mixture of a yellow light (580 nm) and a blue light (480 nm) would plot if both lights were of equal luminance. The mixture color is indicated by the point W.

3. Color complements are easy to find in the diagram.

   The spectral complement of a color (the color which when added to another color produces white) can be located by connecting a line from a reference color through a reference white point in the CIE diagram (see Figure 9.6).

4. The hue and saturation of a color can be derived from the diagram because dominant wavelength and excitation purity are graphically obvious and wavelength directly relates to hue and excitation purity to saturation (see Table 9.1 and Figure 9.7).

5. Finding colors confused by people with certain types of color vision deficiencies is easy.

   Color confusions of red-weak (protanopic) observers lie along a *protan confusion line* in the CIE diagram and color confusions of green-weak (deuteranopic) observers lie along a *deutan confusion line* (see Figure 9.8).

   People with the common but less severe forms of color vision deficiencies will not confuse these colors. Nonetheless, these locations provide guidelines for color selection when accurate color discrimination is important and the color perception ability of the viewer is not known.

TABLE 9.1

Relations between Physical, CIE, and Perceptual
Descriptions of Color

	Properties of Color	
Physical	*← CIE Link →*	*Perceptual*
Wavelength	Dominant wavelength	Hue
Purity	Excitation purity	Saturation
Intensity	Luminance	Brightness and Lightness

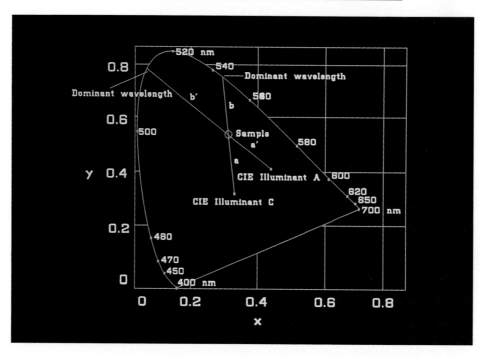

Figure 9.7 *Graphic Method of Determining Dominant Wavelength*   Dominant wavelength of a color is represented by a point which intersects the spectral locus when a straight line is drawn from a reference white and passes through the color to the spectral locus. Using the line extending to the dominant wavelength, excitation purity is the distance of the color from reference white relative to the distance of the dominant wavelength from reference white. (*Adapted from Bill-meyer, 1981.*)

6. The color capability of different hardware devices can be compared.

    The CIE tristimulus values provide a 3D coordinate system which encompasses an entire color solid. The CIE system is thus useful as a quality metric for comparing the range of colors of different hardware devices: the greater the percentage of the entire color solid encompassed by the colors produced by the device, the greater its color capability.

    Conventionally, a two-dimensional chromaticity diagram represents the color range of a computer ouput device. The triangle formed by the x,y values of the device primaries is its *color gamut*. Commercially available color producing devices (like displays) are not able to produce all perceptible colors (such as emerald green or deep purple).

7. The CIE 1964 color space describes the properties of color areas larger than two degrees and is thus more appropriate for evaluating the color of area-fill images in computer displays.

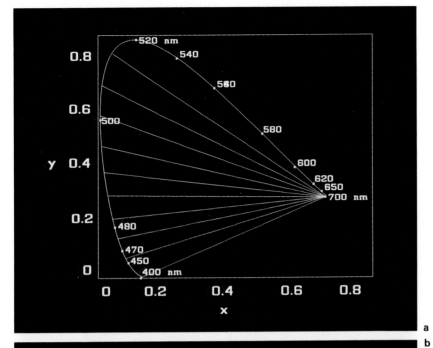

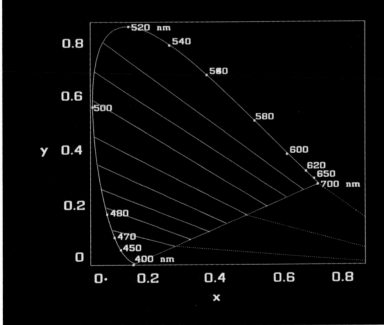

Figure 9.8 *Confusion Loci for Protanopes and Deuteranopes* In a), all the colors lying along a given line radiating from lower right portion of the diagram appear very similar to a protanope. In b), all the colors on a given line radiating from the right D look very similar to a deuteranope. (*Adapted from LeGrand, 1957.*)

The *1964 Large Field CIE space* is based on color mixing data obtained with ten-degree fields. It is very similar to the standard two-degree diagram except in the blue region.

Limitations of CIE XYZ Space

In spite of its usefulness, the XYZ space has some disadvantages:

1. The CIE system usually requires the use of expensive equipment to make color measurements unless color matching data are provided (such as phosphor or ink chromaticity coordinates).

2. The CIE XYZ system does not predict color appearance.

Matching the color of a small (two-degree) single spot on a dark background is an oversimplification and typically a misrepresentation of most computer color images. Normally, color judgments occur for larger images and in complex scenes. In fact, a CIE specification of color does not indicate its appearance or differences in appearance between colors. For example, the chromaticity coordinates for a chocolate bar are nearly the same as for red lipstick (see Figure 9.9). This similarity in appearance occurs because the CIE chromaticity coordinates are relative values which indicate information about the hue and saturation of a color, but not its brightness. In fact, red lipstick and chocolate bars would appear quite similar if the eye did not process luminance information. Thus, the inadequacy of the chromaticity diagram as a tool to determine color appearance is due to the exclusion of luminance in the CIE calculations. (However, the CIE tristimulus values for red lipstick and a chocolate bar are different.)

A limitation of the CIE chromaticity diagram is that colors with different chromaticity coordinates may be indistinguishable when viewed side by side. Colors reported to look identical on the CIE chromaticity diagram cluster in groups. The perimeters of each cluster resemble ellipses and are known as *MacAdam ellipses* (see Figure 9.10). Each ellipse represents the boundary of chromaticities which are a color match by an observer. In general, the boundary of each ellipse indicates colors which would appear different from the color in the center of the ellipse. The elliptical rather than circular shape of the color discrimination data demonstrates that CIE space is not perceptually uniform. Two points at a particular distance in one chromaticity region may appear exceedingly different; but the two colors associated with the same distance in another region may look similar. The ellipses are smaller in the red and blue corners of the CIE space. This indicates that people are much more sensitive to hue and saturation differences in the blue and red regions (see Chapter 6).

Because colors with different chromaticity coefficients may be indistinguishable, caution should be exercised in comparing the CIE color gamuts of different devices, even

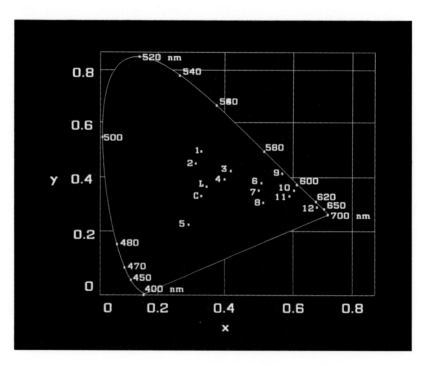

Figure 9.9 *CIE Space and the Chromaticities of Several Common Objects* Locations of chromaticities of green grass (1), green traffic light (2), banana (3), lemon (4), blue in US flag (5), orange (6), Hershey bar (7), clear red lipstick (8), amber traffic light (9), Coca-Cola (10), red in US flag (11), and red traffic light (12). (*Adapted from Farrell and Booth, 1975.*)

Specification of Color   Chap. 9

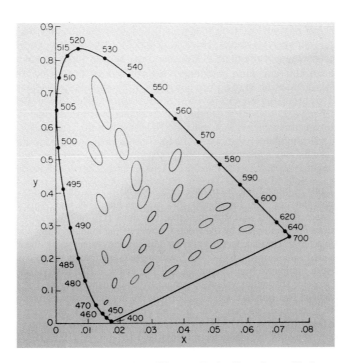

Figure 9.10 *MacAdam Ellipses* Each ellipse (magnified ten times) represents the boundary region of standard deviations from color matches to the central chromaticity within the ellipse. The boundary is an estimate of how many standard deviations correspond to a just noticeable difference (JND) in color. Each ellipse is about three JNDs in hue or saturation depending on the orientation of the ellipse. (*By permission from Butterworth Scientific Limited, 1982.*)

if the brightness of their colors is identical. The CIE system is a good indicator of color fidelity between devices as long as the differences between the color gamuts of the devices are large.

Extensions of CIE Color Space

Other color spaces have been developed to address the limitations of the CIE XYZ space. These spaces are generally known as *uniform color spaces* because they are more perceptually uniform. A uniform color space should allow:

- Prediction of similarities of two chromaticities
- Prediction of the amount of chromaticity change needed to create equal sized difference appearances (steps) in colors (for example, a graded scale of saturation for a given hue)
- Provision for choice of the number (N) of equally spaced colors for any N events or states

Extensions of the CIE space include UCS, CIELUV, and CIELAB. These three color spaces incorporate color vision data gathered under concentrated and sustained viewing. The appropriate space for color calculations depends on the task and the application.

1976 Uniform Color Space (UCS)

The 1976 UCS is a mathematical transform of the 1931 CIE space which linearly represents the discrimination of hue and saturation (see Figure 9.11). UCS is the culmination of many successive attempts to improve the CIE's uniformity and is the current recommendation by the CIE.

The conversion formulas for the 1976 UCS are

$$u' = \frac{4x}{-2x + 12y + 3} \qquad v' = \frac{9y}{-2x + 12y + 3}$$

The UCS transform modifies the CIE description by expanding the y axis to v' in UCS. This improves the underestimated wavelength discrimination along the blue-yellow axis of CIE space. (The compressed axis for the ellipses in Figure 9.10 occurs along the blue-yellow axis of the chromaticity diagram.) This conversion represents equally spaced color differences as points separated by nearly equal distances. It thus causes the MacAdam ellipses (see Figure 9.12) to become more circular. This means that three colors that appear equally different from each other are represented by three nearly equidistant points in the UCS space.

Because it is more nearly uniform, UCS space allows visualization of certain perceptual relations among colors. For instance, it allows predictions of colors which will appear similar or different in hue but equally saturated. Furthermore, it allows prediction of colors that will appear different in both hue and saturation.

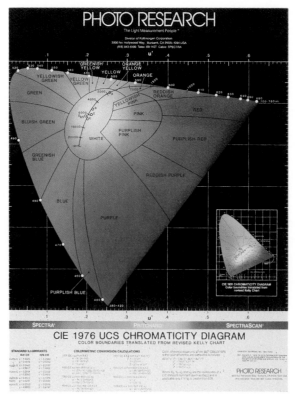

Figure 9.11 *1976 UCS Color Space* The larger space on the left is the uniform color transformation of the 1931 color space which is shown on the lower right. (*Courtesy of Photo Research.*)

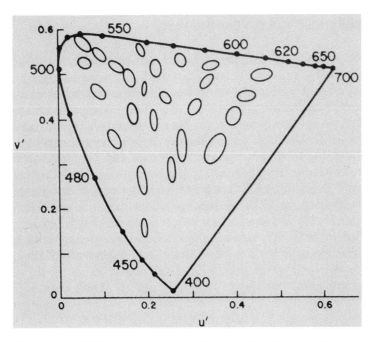

Figure 9.12 *UCS* Color discrimination data from Figure 9.10 transformed to UCS coordinates. The data have been replotted in UCS space for ease of comparison. Concentric contours represent lines of equal saturation separated by two JNDs. (*By permission from Butterworth Scientific Limited, in Laycock, 1982.*)

If a color space is truly uniform, we could impose simple polar coordinates on the color space. The spectrum locus would thus wrap around as a perfect circle with white in the center. Any radial line drawn from the origin would be a line of constant hue. Moreover, a circle would connect all hues of constant saturation. Concentric circles of increasing radius would connect colors of increasing saturation.

To use this analysis with a color diagram, it is necessary to know the white point or location of the chromaticity point where color appears neutral. This neutral point defines the origin of the polar plot. The appearance of white or neutral depends on the adapted state of the eye. Under natural daylight, a point near x = .33 y = .33 appears neutral. However, after staring at a green phosphor display, the neutral point will have different values.

Knowing the illuminant, we can use the UCS to define perceptible hue and saturation differences. For example (see Figure 9.13), lines of constant hue and saturation for an eye adapted to normal daylight can be shown by plotting hue lines at (arbitrary) five-degree intervals. Equal saturation contours can be separated by two JNDs (two times the threshold of a perceptible color difference). This type of graph provides a concise description of several features of color vision. For example, counting the number of JNDs (or circles) from the center to the spectrum locus shows there are fewer circles from white to yellow than from white to red or blue. Thus, spectral yellow appears relatively less saturated than spectral reds or blues. For a particular adaptive state, the graph can show which chromaticities will have a constant hue, as well as those which will appear equally saturated.

The lines of constant hue remain constant over a wide range of light levels. This is advantageous for the display designer because it does not require using control circuitry to compensate for hue changes over a range of display luminances.

Because the UCS better describes color appearance, it is very useful for display engineering specifications. For example, it provides a metric for assessing color shifts of display phosphors (see Box.)

Extensions of CIE Color Space

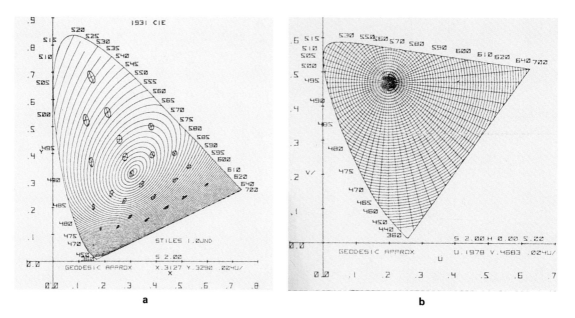

a　　　　　　**b**

Figure 9.13 *Lines of Constant Hue and Saturation Contours* Lines of constant hue are shown for an eye adapted to normal daylight. Hue lines are plotted at arbitrary five-degree intervals. Equal saturation contours are separated by two JNDs (two times the threshold of a perceptible color difference).

EVALUATING COLOR UNIFORMITY WITH UCS

Color tolerance refers to shifts of color appearance on a display. These shifts result from instability of the phosphor chromaticities. For most display users, this is not very important because precise color reproduction from a display is not usually necessary. However, color tolerance is important to color monitor manufacturers, their customers, and any application requiring precise color reproduction.

Color tolerance is usually specified as a color difference in UCS units. For color alphanumeric displays, the industry standard currently recommends that a phosphor color vary by less than 0.15 to 0.20 UCS units (see Table 9.2). This specification is probably too restrictive for computer graphics displays showing large area raster imagery.

These tolerances are empirically derived color differences and tolerance recommendations from several sources.

In summary, the UCS improves the CIE description of color appearance. However, it still leaves out important visual data. For example, it does not account for the lightness responses of the eye.

The lightness response of the eye can be measured by having observers estimate the percent of lightness change from one shade of gray to another. For example, a viewer may report that gray appears to be one-half or three-quarters of the value between black and white. Typically, a middle gray is judged to occur at 25 to 30 percent of the luminance range. As a result, lightness is usually expressed by a cube root formula.

TABLE 9.2

Recommended Color Tolerances for Color Text Displays

Source	Type	Original Distance Value(s)	Scale	$\sqrt{\frac{1}{2}D^2}$	u'	v'	CIE (1976)* USC Distance
MacAdam (1942)	Empirical	.00108 (Low Range)	CIE 1931	.000764	.001016	.002286	.002502
		.02754 (High Range)	CIE 1931	.019474	.0254861	.054861	.060035
Ward et al. (1983)	Empirical	.005 (2° Field)	CIE 1960	.003536	.003536	.005304	.006375
		.010 (.5° Field)	CIE 1960	.007071	.007071	.010607	.012748
Jones (1968)	Empirical	.004	CIE 1960	.0028	.0028	.0042	.0050
Boeing EFFIS (SCD)	Tolerance recommendation	.013	CIE 1960	.009192	.009192	.013788	.016571
Tektronix (Murch)	Tolerance recommendation	.015	CIE 1976				.0150
Sperry (Turner)	Tolerance recommendation	.020	CIE 1976				.0200

* To convert all units to 1976 UCS units, it was assumed that the tolerance values are composed of the formula: spacing $= \sqrt{\frac{1}{2}\text{distance}^2}$. (From Silverstein and Merrifield, 1985.)

Figure 9.14 *CIELUV Space* A color simulation of CIELUV, emphasizing its three-dimensionality. The three axes represent estimates of the red-green, yellow-blue, and black-white opponent systems. (*Courtesy of Maureen Stone, Copyright, Xerox Corp., 1987.*)

CIELUV

CIELUV is a companion to the 1976 UCS and is the primary uniform color space metric recommended by the CIE. It is a metric for expressing color differences and includes the lightness response of the eye. It therefore includes equations expressing the ranges of white-black, red-green, and yellow-blue (see Figure 9.14).

CIELUV thus incorporates more perceptual data than the CIE calculations and therefore better predicts color appearance. CIELUV also allows the specification of perceptual qualities that are not obvious in a CIE chromaticity diagram. For example, black does not have a discrete position in 2D CIE space, but in the XYZ system, black is at $x = 0$, $y = 0$, $z = 0$. However, since z factors out in constructing the chromaticity diagram, it is equal to zero at many positions in the diagram. In the CIELUV system, the coordinates are multiplied by L* so when L* is zero, so are u* and v*. Thus black has only one position in the CIELUV diagram, at 0,0,0.

CIELUV EQUATIONS

The equations for CIELUV components are

$$L^* = 116(Y/Y_n)^{1/3} - 16 \quad \text{with } Y/Y_n > .01$$
$$u^* = 13L^*(u' - u'_n)$$
$$v^* = 13L^*(v' - v'_n)$$

L* approximates a coordinate of the black-white opponent mechanisms. The u* and v* values respectively represent the red-green and yellow-blue systems.

The u' and v' values represent linear transformations of the CIE xy system. These coefficients are based on the magnitude estimates of the difference between lights of different chromaticity.

178

(continued)

$$u' = \frac{4x}{X + 15Y + 3Z}$$

$$v' = \frac{9Y}{X + 15Y + 3Z}$$

The red-green opponent coordinate is approximated by

$$u' - v'_n$$

where positive values denote redness and negative values greenness. The yellow-blue opponent response is approximated by

$$v' - v'_n$$

where positive values indicate yellowness and negative values indicate blueness.

Advantages of CIELUV

The main advantages of CIELUV include

1. CIELUV provides equations to specify both luminance and color differences.
   For any device using additive color mixture, CIELUV provides color difference equations useful for specifying differences in color appearance. The CIELUV color difference formula is simply the sum of the component differences or

   $$\Delta E^*_{uv} = [(\Delta L^*)^2 + (\Delta u^*)^2 + (\Delta v^*)^2]^{1/2}$$

   This formula is the basic tool recommended by the CIE for describing color differences. It allows a design engineer to select display colors for maximum discrimination.
   For example, for quickly searching and recognizing small (two-degree) color coded display symbols, colors should differ by at least 40 CIELUV units from the background and each other. Accurate and quick color discriminations are particularly important for critical applications such as air traffic control and nuclear control plant monitoring. For less critical tasks, this specification reduces to 12 CIELUV units.

2. Equal CIELUV distances represent equally distinct colors.
   To calculate equally saturated differences choose colors of constant ΔE along a line of constant dominant wavelength. To calculate equal hue differences choose chromaticities of constant ΔE along a line of constant saturation.

3. CIELUV retains the linearity of CIE space.
   Because CIELUV is a linear transformation of CIE space, it has several of the graphic advantages of CIE. For example, a light which is the sum of two chromaticities will lie on a straight line between the two colors.

Limitations of CIELUV

1. The accuracy of CIELUV predictions depends on how well the viewing conditions match the CIE experiments. CIELUV only estimates differences for colors of relatively high luminance on neutral colored backgrounds. The color difference equa-

tions will not predict differences between colors of very low luminance (less than about eight foot lamberts) and colors which differ greatly in luminance.

2. The L* metric is not entirely satisfactory because the appearance of brightness contrast is very dependent on viewing conditions. This problem is further complicated by the fact that there is no agreement on a reference white for displays. There is currently no standard for a lightness metric. However, recently a brightness metric has been proposed (see Box).

3. CIELUV color difference equations are not valid for very small colored objects (less than two degrees). This is a very practical problem for many visual displays where single characters or symbols may be as small as 16 minutes of arc.

However, the CIE metric can describe most display color images. Typical color text displays present a string of several colored characters, not single characters. Thus, the size of the entire word is large enough to allow the use of CIELUV to describe color discriminability.

DETERMINING PERCEIVED BRIGHTNESS OF A COLOR

This method determines relative brightness of two chromaticities by comparing brightness matches for different colors (see Figure 9.15).

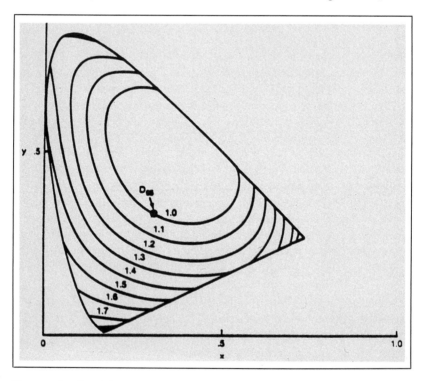

Figure 9.15 *Equal Brightness Contours for Colors Equated in Luminance* Each point on a curve represents the amount of luminance at which one color appears equally bright as another color of known luminance. For desaturated colors, luminance is a good predictor for apparent brightness. However, luminance and brightness diverge increasingly with colors of higher spectral purity. Curves shown assume the eye was adapted to daylight (D65). Each curve is the average of many observers. (*By permission from Ware and Cowan, 1983.*)

(continued)

The brightness for a given color (B_s) is estimated by

$$\log(B_s) = \log(L_s) + C_s$$

where

L_s is the measured luminance of the color

C_s is a correction factor based on data in Figure 9.15

$$C_s = 0.256 - 0.184\,y_s - 2.527\,x_s + 4.656x_s\,3 + 4.657x_sy_s\,4$$

The chief advantages of this method are

1. It requires only standard luminance measurement (Y) and CIE xy coordinates.

2. The method extends to all chromaticities not just spectrally pure colors (unlike other proposed luminance-to-brightness corrections).

The main disadvantage is that this approach describes relative brightness and not absolute brightness. Thus it cannot describe the amount of luminance necessary to identify a color as white or black.

CIELAB

CIELAB is the second uniform color space metric recommended by the CIE. This space is often used to capture the color appearance of subtractive color mixtures. It is the standard color descriptor tool of the paint and dye industries (see Figure 9.16).

Figure 9.16 *CIELAB Space* A 3D computer-graphic representation of CIELAB. As with CIELUV space, the axes correspond to the red-green, yellow-blue, and black-white opponent systems. (*Courtesy of Maureen Stone, Copyright, Xerox Corp., 1987.*)

As with CIELUV, CIELAB maps equally distinct color differences into equal Euclidean distances in the space. So equal distances in CIELAB space are useful for equally perceptible color differences on color plotters and printers or any subtractive color device. CIELAB retains many of the graphic advantages of the original CIE system. For example, we can find the mixture of two printer ink primaries on a straight line lying between them. In general, the advantages and disadvantages of CIELAB are much like those of CIELUV.

CIELAB EQUATIONS

LAB refers to the coefficients or coordinates of this space, L*, a*, and b*. While Lightness (L*) is the same function in the CIELUV equations, a* and b* are not linear transformations of the CIE. This is obvious in the following transformations of CIE XYZ space:

$$L^* = 116(Y/Y_n)^{1/3} - 16$$

$$a^* = 500[(X/X_n)^{1/3} - (Y/Y_n)^{1/3}]$$

$$b^* = 200[(Y/Y_n)^{1/3} - (Z/Z_n)^{1/3}]$$

where X/X_n, Y/Y_n, and $Z/Z_n > 0.01$

The CIE color difference formula resembles its CIELUV counterpart: It expresses the total color difference as the sum of squared differences or

$$\Delta E^*_{Lab} = [(\Delta L^*)^2 + (\Delta a^*)^2 + (\Delta b^*)^2]^{1/2}$$

Table 9.3 summarizes the various features of the color spaces described in this chapter.

TABLE 9.3

Usability Comparisons of Color Spaces

	1931 XYZ	1931 xy	1964 xy	1976 UCS	CIE LUV	CIE LAB
Color hardware	All types	All types	All types	Displays	Displays	Printers Plotters
Uses	Manuf. spec.	Manuf. spec. Predict color mixture	Same for larger fields	Selecting colors which are equally spaced apart in appearance; discriminable	. . .	. . .
				Any application where predictable color perception is required with sustained viewing	. . .	. . .
Requires photometric measurements	Yes	Yes	Yes	Yes	Yes	Yes

Specification of Color   Chap. 9

TABLE 9.3 (*continued*)

Usability Comparisons of Color Spaces

	1931 XYZ	1931 xy	1964 xy	1976 UCS	CIE LUV	CIE LAB
Provides easy to use visual diagram	No	Yes	Yes	Yes	No	No
Predicts color appearance	Poor	Poor	Poor	Fair	Fair	Fair
Provides color difference equations	No	No	No	No	Yes	Yes
Viewing conditions	2 deg	2 deg	10 deg	2	2	2
Accounts for brightness perception	No	No	No	No	Fair	Fair

Useful Facts

Color Representations	Representing colors in a three-dimensional space allows precise specification.
Describing Color	Color is described by three independent components which can be related to visual perception (hue, saturation, and lightness), display hardware primaries (red, green, and blue), or printer ink primaries (cyan, magenta, and yellow).
Color Matching	Any color can be matched as the sum of three independent wavelengths.
	Colored lights or ink pigments whose spectral distributions are very different can be matched because for each color which matches another, the pattern of signals sent out by three independent visual receptors is equivalent.
Standard Color Description	The CIE chromaticity diagram is the standard method to describe color used by display and hard copy industries.
Chromaticity Diagram	The chromaticity diagram is an international tool for describing the physical characteristics of a color. The chromaticity coordinates (x and y) and the measured luminance (Y) of a light provide a complete psychophysical description of a color.

CIE Applications	The CIE system is used as a quality metric to compare the range of colors of different physical devices (such as color CRTs, printers, plotters, and film recorders).
Spaces for Large Images	The 1964 Large Field CIE space is used to specify the color of colored images larger than two degrees.
Uniform Color Spaces	The UCS is a linear transform of the 1931 CIE space and more uniformly represents the discrimination of hue and saturation.
Predicting Color Mixing	The results of mixing any two colors can be predicted by connecting points in a chromaticity diagram.
Color Constancy	Color matches made at one luminance level are constant for a large range of luminance levels.
Specifying Color Values	CIELUV is a color description system that includes the lightness response of the eye. Its main contribution is to provide color difference equations which approximate the output of the black-white, red-green, and yellow-blue opponent mechanisms.
	CIELUV is used for display color evaluation; CIELAB is used for hard copy color evaluation.

REFERENCES

Benzchawel, T., "Colorimetry of Displays," IBM Technical Report #RC12590, 1987, pp. 1–42.

Billmeyer, F. W., "Optical Aspects of Color," *Optica Spectra*, Jan./Feb., 1968, pp. 43–47.

Cowan, W. B. and C. Ware. *Color Perception Tutorial Notes*, SIGGRAPH, 1983.

Farrell, E. J. and J. M. Booth. *Design Handbook for Imaging Interpretation Equipment* (Seattle, WA: Boeing Aerospace Company, 1975.)

Foley, J. D. and A. Van Dam. *Fundamentals of Interactive Computer Graphics* (Menlo Park, CA: Addison-Wesley Pub., 1982).

Horsleys, 1798.

Laycock, J. and J. P. Viveash, "Calculating the Perceptibility of Monochrome and Colour Displays Viewed under Various Illumination Conditions," *Displays*, 3(2), 1982, 88–99.

LeGrand, Y. *Light, Colour and Vision* (New York: J. Wiley Pubs., 1957).

Silverstein, L. D. and R. M. Merrifield, "The Development and Evaluation of Color Systems for Airborn Applications," U.S. Dept. of Transportation, FAA, Patusent River, MD, 1985.

Tansley, B. W. and R. M. Boynton, "Chromatic Border Perception: The Role of Red and Green Sensitive Cones," *Vision Research*, 18, 1978, 683–697.

Ware, C. and W. B. Cowan, "Colour Perception Tutorial Notes," *SIGGRAPH*, 1983.

Wyszecki, G. and W. S. Stiles, *Color Science*, 2nd ed. (New York: Wiley and Sons, 1982).

10

Manipulating Color on Displays

The division [of color] guarantees all the benefits of luminosity, color, and harmony.

Paul Signac

Complex Colors on Simple Displays

The sophistication of color images on computer displays is becoming increasingly more impressive. Although some of these images require complex graphics hardware and sophisticated programming skills, many can be created with simple color display systems and color manipulation techniques (see Figures 10.1 and 10.2). In fact, many colored images that appear to require high resolution displays can be created on low resolution technologies.

Several relatively simple software techniques are available for the manipulation of color to improve image quality on low resolution displays. They include:

- Color dithering, a method for increasing the number of colors on a display
- Hue smoothing, a method to improve edge quality of raster images
- Color animation

Knowledge of the fundamentals of programming color on displays is useful for creating effective color graphics. These fundamentals include the basic architecture of a simple raster graphics system, color models used by software designers to change colors on a computer display, and image processing methods which use color to reveal and highlight the structure of images.

The following sections briefly describes these basic principles, techniques, and their uses.

Figure 10.1 *Drawing on Low Resolution Bitmap Display* An artist's sketch created by manual drawing with an electronic paint program. Although the computer display only produces sixteen colors, the picture appears intricate and detailed. (*By permission from Daryl Anderson.*)

Figure 10.2 *Scene Rendering* A highly realistic scene rendering "Beach at Sunset" created on a computer and produced by calculations. (*By permission from Pixar, Copyright 1986.*)

A Simple Raster Graphics System

Pixels to Pictures

To create an image on a display, a color value is assigned to a location in a *bitmap*. A bitmap is an array of bits that represent an image (see Figure 10.3). Bitmapped displays are the most common type of computer display used for creating and enhancing images. In this type of display, a specific area of display memory stores an image. Bitmapped memory is also known as frame buffer memory, screen memory, refresh memory, or video memory. The different ways of writing to the bitmap memory are called *raster operations*.

In a simple display system, each location in a bitmap directly corresponds to a position, or *pixel*, on the display screen. A pixel (an acronym for picture element) is the smallest area on the screen that can be independently addressed and changed in intensity or color. The total number of pixels corresponds to the number of areas to which values can be assigned and independently displayed. A display screen with a 512 x 512 resolution will have 262,144 separate pixels or variable areas of intensities.

The relationship between a pixel and a screen image (see Figure 10.4) is easily understood by knowing a few basics about raster graphics. In a raster graphics display system like a CRT (see Chapter 2), the basic drawing element is a point (or pixel). In contrast, a vector display (or pen plotter) creates images with lines, not dots.

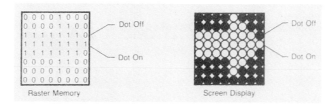

Figure 10.3 *Bitmap Memory* A bitmap stored in raster memory is shown on the left for the display image shown on the right. (*Courtesy of Hewlett-Packard.*)

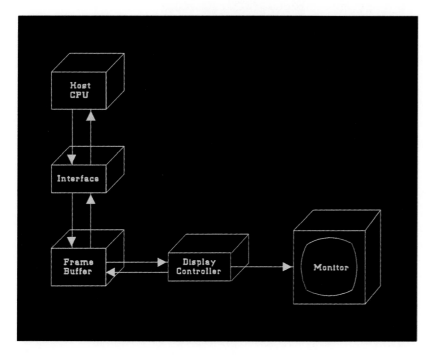

Figure 10.4 *Diagram of a Simple (Single-Port) Raster Graphics System* In creating a color image, a pixel's value is translated from bitmap memory to a screen color and a location on the screen through the use of graphics software that directly manipulates the display hardware. The software includes components such as the video (or refresh) controller and a color look-up table which translates signals into a form suitable for the display. The video controller reads the values of the color table and bitmap memory to determine the pixel's color. It then adjusts the timing signals and electron gun voltages to produce color images on the screen. (*Adapted from Conrac.*)

In some display systems, there are only a few bits and hence a small range of possible numbers for a pixel value. In more sophisticated graphic systems, the pixel value can be specified by as many as 32 bits. The number of bits available for describing each pixel is called the *depth* of the bitmap.

ONE-BIT IMAGE: MONOCHROMATIC SYSTEMS   In the simplest raster image systems, the bitmap memory is one bit deep allowing specification of two-pixel intensity values: either on or off. There is thus no other range of intensity values in a one-bit system, and intermediate grays or shades of colors are not possible. In an achromatic display, the pixels are thus either black or white, not an intermediate gray value. To obtain multicolors, more than one bit is necessary (see Figure 10.5).

THREE-BIT IMAGE: THE SIMPLEST COLOR SYSTEM   To obtain different colors on a display, there must be at least one bit for each color primary or three bits per pixel. Each bitplane controls the intensity of each electron gun (see Chapter 6) for each of the three primary colors in a color display like a CRT. Thus, in the simplest color systems, the bitmap directly specifies the color of each pixel.

```
F F F F F 7 5 A F F F F
F F F A 5 5 5 5 5 F F F
F F F A 5 5 5 5 5 F F F
F F C 5 D E 5 5 5 5 F F
F C 5 7 F F F 7 7 5 F F
F A 5 A F F F D F A 5 F
F 9 5 7 C F F D F F 3 F
C A 5 5 F 5 2 4 5 5 3 F
C F 5 3 C 7 2 A F 5 C F
F D F 3 F F F F F C F F
F C F 5 4 F F A 3 C F F
F F A 5 4 F C F C C F F
F F 7 2 3 9 A 3 3 D F F
F F 4 2 3 9 A F D F F F
F 4 2 2 C 2 2 2 2 F F F
2 2 2 2 2 2 4 4 3 F 2 2
2 2 2 2 2 2 4 4 3 F 2 2
2 2 2 2 2 2 2 2 4 2 F 2
```

a

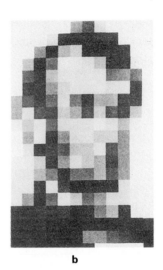

b

Figure 10.5   *A Digital Portrait and Its Bitmap Representation*   a) A picture of Lincoln on a bitmapped display. (*Courtesy of Leon Harmon.*) b) The corresponding pixel values arranged in a two-dimensional matrix. To create the different shades of gray, the pixels are set to one of 16 intensity levels. This bitmap thus has a pixel depth of 4 which means 2^4 or 16 possible intensity levels can be produced.

The simplest color frame buffer is typically implemented as three-bit planes in the bitmap thereby allowing 2^3 or 8 possible colors to be displayed. The number of intensity levels possible to display on a screen at any one time is determined by 2 raised to the power of the pixel depth or

Number of colors at one time $= 2^{\text{pixel depth}}$

A three-bit plane system (2^3) allows eight intensity levels. In a monochrome display this allows eight gray shades; in a color display, this allows eight color values. Typical three-bit CRT color values are RGB (red, blue, and green), CMY (cyan, magenta, and yellow), and white and black.

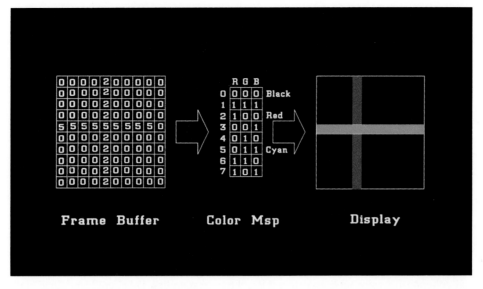

Figure 10.6 *Using a Color Look-up Table* Two color lines on a screen and their representation in the bitmap and color look-up tables of a simple color graphic system. The two short lines are drawn on a 10 x 10 pixel display, one in red and the other in cyan. The pixel values 2 (Red), 5 (Cyan), and 0 (Black) are stored in the bitmap at locations corresponding to screen coordinates. These values refer to color table addresses.

Adding a Color Table to a Graphics System

Most display systems use a *color look-up table* instead of directly referring to the intensity of the CRT electron guns. A color look-up table is a software matrix. Each row corresponds to a value from the bitmap and each column corresponds to an intensity level of a color primary. Each row index stores the table values of intensities of the electron beams (R, G, and B guns) of the color monitor. Entries in the color look-up table are frame buffer values. The pixel depth does not have to be equal to the width of the color look-up table and they are customarily different. A simple display system has eight rows and three columns (see Figure 10.6). The lowest bit controls the blue phosphor, the next bit the green phosphor, and the highest bit controls the red phosphor output via *digital-to-analog converters* (DACs). Interpreting the values within the color look-up table is the first step in converting memory values into screen intensities for the display.

The video controller transfers each pixel value into the color table using the pixel value as an index into the table. For example, the first four pixels of index 1 may refer to index 001 in the color table. The value 1 will thus be transferred into the red digital-to-analog converter (DAC), 0 into the green DAC, and 0 into the blue DAC. This is the simplest kind of color table because the gun voltages directly relate to the color index. More commonly, the color index does not directly relate to RGB values.

Color Quantity

There are two main limitations to the number of colors possible on a color display system. The first limit is imposed by the pixel depth of the bitmap memory. This determines the maximum number of different colors visible at one time.

There is a simple "power of two" relation between bitplanes in the bitmap and the number of screen intensities which can be displayed (see Table 10.1). For example, a three-bit plane system displays no more than eight colors at a time, a four-bit system up to 16 colors at one time.

TABLE 10.1

Relation of Bitplanes to Available Screen Intensities

Bit Planes	Colors or Intensities Available
2	4
3	8
4	16
6	64
8	256
10	1024

The second limit is set by the output bits, which are the number of bits stored in the color table for each color primary (see column 2 of Table 10.2). Output bits restrict the color resolution of each DAC. The DACs translate the binary values in the color table into gun voltages which, in turn, produce different screen intensities.

A comparison of pixel depth, output bits per primary, and number of colors for different color display systems illustrates the concept of color output resolution. If the red column of a color table has three bits, the corresponding DAC could produce eight unique voltage signals. If the red column has four bits, it would produce 16 distinct voltages. The number of intensity levels of primary colors controls the number of possible colors. The number of colors thus increases as the number of intensity levels increases.

The upper limit of possible colors depends on both the pixel depth and the number of bits per primary. The total number of colors is calculated by the following expression:

Total number of colors $= 2^{(\text{N bit planes} \times \text{N' bits out/primary})}$

The number of colors is dependent on the number of rows in the color look-up table. Some software techniques (such as dithering) can increase the number of colors beyond the number of rows.

TABLE 10.2

Number of Colors Available on Low, Medium, and High End Graphic Displays

Frame Buffer Type	Pixel Depth	Bits Out/Primary	Total # of Colors	Simultaneous Colors
Low	4	4	4096	16
Medium	8	8	16,777,216	256
High	24	10	1,073,741,824	16,777,216*
Very High	32	12	68,719,470,000	4,294,967,296

* A 24-bit system does not produce 16 million colors; it actually produces 16 million DAC levels.

Determining the Minimum Number of Colors

One of the primary limiting total factors in achieving a realistic computer image is the number of colors available. There are three main considerations in determining the minimum number of colors for computer-simulated imagery. These include the number of colors in the original image, the number available from the computer, and the total number of colors the eye can see.

Colors in the Original Image

For perfect color reproduction, a hardware device requires primaries that include the entire visual color space (see Chapter 9). However, from an engineering viewpoint, this is too strict a design criterion. A real image does not contain all the chromaticities

Figure 10.7 *Calculated Realism* The realism of this image from "Luxor Jr.," a computer generated film, is enhanced by mathematical calculations. (*By permission from Pixar, Copyright 1986.*)

in visual color space. In fact, most natural image colors are relatively desaturated. Measurements of light across a scene with a color sensitive device (like a *colorimeter*) produce chromaticity values which are significantly within the boundary of the CIE diagram indicating their distance from pure or highly saturated values (see Chapter 9).

More important, the chromaticities of images vary with different types of images. For example, the muted greens and blues of a landscape are very different from the highly saturated greens and blues needed for a glossy advertisement. This is why color maps in a computer are optimized for each scene.

In general, realistic images on a computer screen originate from two sources: scanning or computation. To preserve the original colors in a scanned scene, a scanner must have good color resolution. Scanners with 16 bits per pixel adequately transmit most detailed color images, like museum artwork.

Computed images include those where every object in the scene (including colors, lighting, and reflections) is computed by a programmer. The degree of realism and color accuracy often depends on mathematical calculations (see Figure 10.7).

Computer Color Fidelity

Even if a color hard copy output device could produce perfect color fidelity, it would not be possible to produce all the colors possible on a display because of the restrictions of the display technology. For most color display systems, a digital representation of a color space is not complete: The combined limits of (framebuffer) memory and primary output bits do not produce the range of colors in perceptual color space (see Figure 10.8).

Color Perception Economy

People with normal color vision can see an estimated 50,000 to 2 million colors. The number 50,000 is often a reference for framebuffer design. However, to produce this many colors requires a framebuffer of at least 16 bits per pixel.

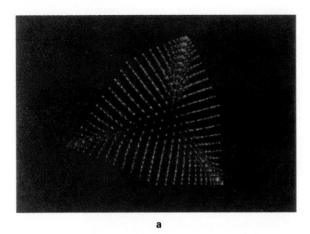 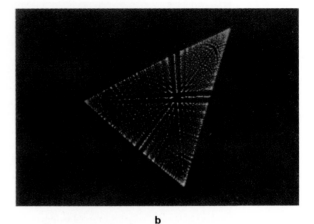

a b

Figure 10.8 *Display Colors Viewed in CIE Spaces* The set of 4096 colors that can be generated on a color graphic display in a) 1931 CIE space and b) 1976 CIELUV space. (The particular chromaticities are set by the gamma correction of the display.) The set of chromaticities possible for a medium quality color graphic display (pixel depth of 12; four bits per primary). Each point represents the xy coordinate corresponding to an RGB value in the computer's color table. The black regions indicate a missing color or gap in the color gamut of the display. (*From Santisteban, 1983, Courtesy of IBM.*)

Figure 10.9b shows a CIELUV representation of the same colors shown in 10.9a. Not all the points are equidistant. In fact, some of the distances are not large enough for the eye to discriminate the colors. Of the 4,096 points, the eye can resolve only 3,050. This means the display is actually only capable of 3,050 visually different colors.

Optimizing Look-Up Tables for Color

Adjusting the Look-Up Table for the Eye

To efficiently use color displays, the full set of possible RGB values should represent colors that the eye can discriminate. In principle, the values of colors in the look-up table should store these different colors. To use the widest range of intensity values, gamma correction is necessary (see Chapter 2). Once this is done, the color table can be adjusted to store perceptible color differences. The minimum chromaticity of a distinct RGB set should be at least one just noticeable difference (JND) in CIELUV space from the chromaticity value of the nearest adjacent chromaticity (see Chapter 9).

It is difficult to determine how well this criterion would apply to dynamic, animated color scenes. Colors which are easy to discriminate can look very similar when rapidly presented (see Chapter 7). This means the JNDs stored in the color table would have to be larger for color differences in dynamic color animation.

Color Fidelity of Digitized Images

Good color reproduction is ordinarily associated with pixel depths of 15 or 24 bits. However, it is also possible to produce good color fidelity with no more than eight bits. By using an image's color statistics (see Box), a color table can be adapted to the color gamut of the original image. This allows digitized pictures to achieve good color fidelity with only a few colors.

COLOR SELECTION METHODS

The "Popularity algorithm" is one technique to achieve good color fidelity with only a few colors. It builds a color table based on the frequency of occurrence of RGB values in a picture. In this approach, a *histogram* is created of all unique RGB values in the picture. In general, there are usually many more RGB sets than the color table can hold. To accommodate this restriction, the software designer selects the RGB values which occur with the highest frequency. This results in producing images that have almost the same color quality as the original image even though there are significantly fewer colors (see Figure 10.9).

Although this technique represents some of the image pixels very accurately, many others will be less accurate or less representative of the

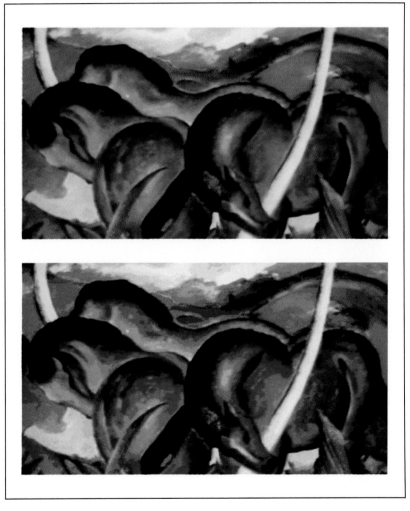

Figure 10.9 *High and Low Color Resolution Images of Marc's "Blue Horses"* A 24-bit digital image (top) and its eight-bit representation using the Popularity algorithm (bottom). (*Courtesy of Paul Heckbert, 1987.*)

(continued)

original image. It is thus not appropriate for small colored objects in the picture.

Another method, the "Median Cut algorithm," improves the accuracy of color representation. In this technique, each entry of the color table has an equal number of pixels from the original (input) image. The total number of pixels are sorted into equal sized groups (or bins) of a particular color range. The program first sorts all RGB values for all pixels into a bin whose length is as great as the minimum and maximum RGB values. This bin is then split at the median RGB value so that the resulting bins have equal numbers of pixels in distinct color ranges. This procedure iterates until K bins are obtained, each containing a nearly equal number of pixels. The average RGB value of each of these K bins is calculated and this value is then stored in one of K rows of the color table.

This technique results in a significant improvement in color reproduction. Although any given pixel may not be the RGB value of the original image, with the Median Cut algorithm, pixels are more similar to their original RGB values than those resulting from the Popularity algorithm. Both these methods partition RGB color space. Using a perceptually uniform space like CIELUV further improves the color selection.

Color Error Metrics

The fidelity of color reproduction by color digitizing techniques is usually evaluated by a color error metric: a measure of the differences between the original colors of an image and those on the screen. Perceptually based metrics are more appropriate than computer based metrics for quantitative estimates of the color error in a digitized image. The best approximation for color errors for color displays is the CIELUV difference equation; the appropriate metric for hard copy is the CIELAB difference equation (see Chapter 9).

Programming with Color Models

Color spaces (conceptual models of color order values and relationships—see Chapter 9) are useful to specify screen colors because they simplify calculations necessary for color transformations. Color spaces are either based on hardware color generation (like RGB—see Chapter 2) or on color perception (like HSL—see Chapter 6). The choice of which space to use depends on several factors: the accuracy with which the designer needs to control color, the requirement for interactive control of color, and the importance of computational speed to the application.

Thus, the screen color can be directly manipulated in terms of its RGB (red, blue, and green) values or by other color values such as HSL (hue, saturation, and lightness). If values other than RGB are used, additional look-up tables must be provided and the color values converted back to RGB values.

RGB Space

The color value specification model most commonly used with CRTs is RGB. The RGB space describes color in terms of the three phosphors (red, green, and blue) that produce colors on the screen (see Chapter 2). The system assumes that the intensity of the three color phosphors are a direct result of (or map to) the electron gun voltages.

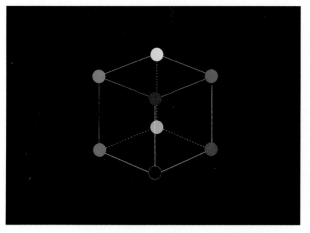

Figure 10.10 *The RGB Cube and Its Color Solid* (left) Arrangement of primary and secondary colors in RGB cube. Combining primaries produces the secondary colors (cyan, magenta, and yellow). (right) Cube showing results of all possible combinations of RGB. (*Copyright Xerox, courtesy of Rod Buckley.*)

Knowing the voltage values of the three color guns will thus allow prediction of color appearance on the screen.

RGB color space is usually represented as a cube where the main axes are represented by R (light emission by the red phosphor), G (light emission by the green phosphor), and B (light emission by the blue phosphor). In the RGB cube (see Figure 10.10), each primary is located in the corner opposite its complementary color. Thus, red is opposite cyan, green is opposite magenta, and blue is opposite yellow. Gray values (white to black) lie on a diagonal connecting the corners of the cube.

Usually RGB axes are normalized to 1. Combining two colors produces a color which is the vector sum of the component color values. Since phosphor intensity is not linearly related to voltage (see Chapter 2) or the DAC inputs, an additional look-up table must be used to obtain linear intensities (such as gamma correction) of the display (see Chapter 2).

Advantages of the RGB model are

1. RGB space is the industry standard for computer graphics. Even if color manipulations are calculated using another color space, the color values must eventually be converted to RGB space for screen display.
2. RGB conversions allow the use of several color spaces including: CIE, CMY, HSL, and HSV.
3. The RGB color system provides a straightforward description of screen color for hardware display engineers.
4. RGB color space simplifies certain computations. For example, a graded change in saturation for any color on the display is represented as a straight line in RGB space from a color to the black vertex. (This is useful for creating an easy-to-use color "slider bar" control where a value on each color axis can be directly mapped to an x,y screen location.) Transparency of an object can be varied as a point along a line extending from a color (opaque) to white (transparent).

However, there are some disadvantages to RGB space.

1. Using the RGB color space requires color monitor calibration for linear intensity output (see Chapter 2 for discussion of gamma correction). Since the voltage-intensity relations for most color monitors vary over time, it is necessary to repeat this calibration for good color reproduction.

Programming with Color Models

2. It is not possible to transfer the RGB values of a color from one color monitor to another. Thus, the RGB values for purple on one color monitor will not produce an identical color on another monitor.

3. RGB descriptions are only vaguely related to color appearance. Because RGB space is perceptually nonuniform, two points may or may not look like different colors. In addition, because it is not based on color perception, there is no direct mapping of RGB space to any perceptual dimension except hue.

HSL Space

The HSL (hue, saturation, and lightness) space refers to the same perceptual components as in color vision (see Chapter 6). Despite its name, the HSL color space is only an approximate perceptual transform of RGB space. Unlike perceptual color spaces (see Chapter 9), the HSL space is constrained by the CRT hardware and not color perception.

HSL space can be represented by a cylindrical coordinate system transformed onto a cube (see Figure 10.11). The resulting shape is a double hexcone. Hue (H) is represented by an angular coordinate, saturation (S) is represented by a radial coordinate, and lightness (L) is represented by the perpendicular axis. The most saturated hues are found at $S = 1$ and $L = 0.5$.

Advantages of HSL space include

1. HSL space is a relatively simple approximation to the perceptual attributes of color (Hue, Saturation and Lightness). Because hue is represented around the vertical axis, approximate color complements are easy to locate (at 180 degrees). Opposite lightness values (e.g., black and white) are at the extremes of the vertical axis.

2. HSL-based color controls appear to be easier for novice users of Paint programs and for artists to learn and manipulate.

The main disadvantages of HSL space are

1. The display must be gamma corrected (as with RGB space).

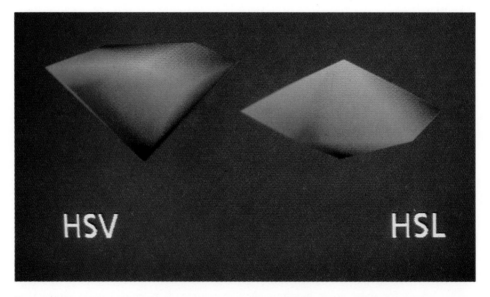

Figure 10.11 *HSL and HSV Spaces* Diagram of the location of primary and secondary colors in HSL and HSV color spaces. (*Copyright, Xerox 1987, courtesy of Rod Buckley.*)

2. Vector addition cannot be achieved by a simple addition of color components (unlike RGB space). Trigonometric operations required in the transformation may not allow the computational speed necessary for interactive color programs.

HSV Space

HSV (hue, saturation, value) is another transformation of RGB space. The HSV space is the RGB cube tilted onto its back corner. Hue is a radial angle around the Value axis. Saturation ranges from 0 at the center line to 1 on the side of the hexcone; the Value axis thus corresponds to the RGB white to black diagonal.

In viewing the corresponding screen color values of the HSV space, highest saturations are found at $S = 1$ and $V = 1$. In HSV, saturation is normalized to the color gamut of the display device.

There are two main advantages of the HSV space:

1. The color space easily adapts to color paint programs since the model is constructed to mimic artist's rules for color mixture of paints. For example, adding white to a pigment requires setting the hue to $V = 1$ and $S = 1$ and then decreasing the amount of S. The addition of black pigment is simulated by decreasing V with no change in S.

2. HSV has considerable computational advantages compared to the HSL space; there is no need for a trigonometric transform in converting its values to RGB space.

The main disadvantage is that, as with the other spaces, HSV requires gamma correction of the display. Table 10.3 shows various distinguishing features of these three color spaces.

TABLE 10.3

Comparison of RGB, HSL, HSV

RGB	HSL	HSV
Industry standard	RGB transform	RGB transform
Directly relates to display hardware	More related to color perception	More related to color perception
Final transform for all displays	Complex transform required	Simplifies calculation
Not transferable to other displays	Device independent	Device independent
Not mapped to color perception	Mapped to color perception	Mapped to color perception
Cube shape	Double hexcone shape	Single hexcone
Normalized to 1	Normalized to 1	Normalized to 1
Maximum saturation at 1	Maximum saturation at $S = 1$, $L = 0.5$	Maximum saturation at $S = 1$, $V = 1$
Color mixing not obvious	Mixing obvious	Mixing obvious

Color Enhancement Techniques

Color can radically change the appearance of an image, particularly on a display screen. It can create the appearance of more colors than the hardware will allow, smooth the jagged edges of images on low resolution displays, and produce animation.

Increasing the Number of Display Colors

Color displays with small framebuffers (e.g., pixel depths of three or four) allow the generation of only eight or 16 colors on a screen at one time. However, software techniques exist that extend the apparent number of colors.

INCREASING THE NUMBER OF COLORS WITH SOFTWARE INTERRUPTS   One technique for increasing the number of apparent colors on a display is to use software interrupts. This technique allows on-line changes of the color look-up table. This is accomplished by reloading the color table during the display's horizontal or vertical blanking period. With a four-bit framebuffer, 16 different colors per horizontal scan line can be produced. This would allow production of all 512 colors in one frame period.

DITHERING   Dithering uses unique combinations and patterns of a few elementary colors to produce additional colors, thus trading off spatial resolution for increased color resolution. This method uses the same principles as the pointillistic paintings of the Impressionists: A few elementary colors combine to create a composite color (see Figure 10.12). This effect occurs because the eye averages small spots of colors, whether they are dots of paint or display pixels, and perceives their blend or mix which is a different color.

Paint programs provide methods to allow manual creation of dither patterns. The dither pattern (called a "dither cell") consists of a matrix of pixels. Each pixel is assigned one color in a color table. For example, combining yellow and black pixels within a dither cell produces dark yellow or brown, and combining yellow and white pixels produces pale yellow (see Figure 10.13).

The total possible number of color shades is determined by the size of the dither matrix, the pixel size, and, in turn, the number of perceptually distinct colors. For example, a 2×2 dither cell uses a total of 4 pixels and produces three colors besides black. Using yellow, black, and white elements, 9 (or $4 \times 2 + 1$) different colors can be produced including pure yellow, white, and black.

A good dither color blend will produce a dithered pattern which is difficult to detect because the colors are processed by the color mechanisms of the eye which have poor resolution (see Chapter 6).

Figure 10.12 *Precomputer Dithering* "Moulin Huet Bay, Guernsey" by the Impressionist Renoir shows different colors made by combining small dots of only a few basic colors. (*Courtesy of the National Gallery, London.*)

Figure 10.13 *True Shading versus Dithered Shading* Different shades of yellow produced by a) a color graphic system which can produce different intensity levels of the color primaries (four bits) and b) a color graphic system (three bits) which uses dithering.

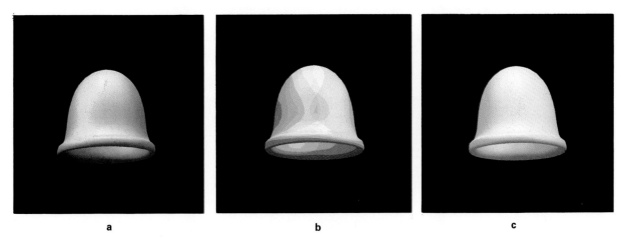

Figure 10.14 *Dithering to Improve a Computer Image.* (a) shows an undithered 24/plane image; an 8/plane version is shown in (b) without dithering, and in (c) with dithering. (*Courtesy Hewlett-Packard.*)

DITHERING APPLICATIONS   Both computer graphics production and digital image enhancement use dithering to enhance the appearance of color images. For an artist, dithering is useful for producing more colors in a graphic design (see Figure 10.14); for a software designer, dithering expands the range of colors available on a screen and hard copy device (see Chapter 8). For scanned or digitized images, dithering smooths color contouring effects resulting from a limited number of colors. Averaging values across neighboring pixels dithers an image. A picture displayed on a screen consists of these averaged values. In general, the production of an image by a set of color averages is more visually pleasing than a limited sampling of specific colors.

DISADVANTAGES OF DITHER COLORS   There are some problems with using dithered colors:

1. Although dithering produces more perceivable colors, dithered shades cannot be applied to single pixels because of the resulting loss in image and color resolution.

Color Enhancement Techniques

The smallest area painted with a dither color is the size of its dither cell: usually 2 × 2 pixels. Therefore, dither colors are appropriate for large-area graphics, but not single-pixel wide lines such as typical alphanumeric characters and thin lines.

2. Using a dithered color for small or thin-line area-fill can produce unexpected results. Area-fill images which are much smaller than the size of a dither cell will contain only a portion of the dither pattern.

3. The texture of a dithered color is often apparent. The individual pixel colors thus reduce the illusion of uniform color. However, careful choice of elementary colors can minimize texturing (see Box and Figure 10.15).

IMPROVING THE APPEARANCE OF DITHERED COLORS

The appearance of dithered colors can be enhanced by

1. Minimizing the luminance difference of the elementary colors in a dither pattern which reduces contrast variation within the pattern.
2. Using hues that have similar luminance values (such as CRT green and yellow or blue and red) to enhance the visual blending of the dithered colors.
3. Randomizing the luminosity of pixels within the dither cell.

Figure 10.15 *Bad and Good Dither Blends* The good dithered colors are green and yellow (top row), white and orange (second row), cyan (third row), and lavender and cyan (bottom row).

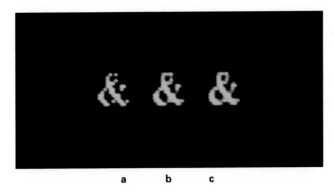

Figure 10.16 *CRT Character with Different Gray Levels* a) Two gray levels of a CRT image (one intensity level against a background intensity level) shows jaggies. b) The same image with three gray levels. c) The same image using four gray levels. (*Courtesy of Joyce Farrell, Hewlett-Packard.*)

Image Smoothing with Luminance

Using similar luminance values along an edge produces color blending, smoothing the jagged edges of diagonal lines and curves on low resolution displays. In addition, increasing the number of luminance levels (or *gray scales*) along an edge can smooth its jagged appearance (see Figure 10.16). Thus, using four different gray values for the edge of a circle will create a smoother edge than two levels.

Image smoothing (better known as *anti-aliasing*) is thus a technique that uses different levels of brightness to reduce the appearance of jagged edges. Like dithering, this method uses the spatial averaging properties of the visual system (see Chapter 6). At most viewing distances, an observer cannot resolve these individual brightness or gray levels. Instead, the different brightness levels of the image appear as smooth gradients. Even though the edges of these images appear slightly blurred, the quality of the image is usually judged to be superior.

Color Anti-Aliasing

Because of the low spatial resolution of the eye's color sensing and processing mechanisms, fewer levels of hue, compared to brightness, are necessary to smooth a raster image. For example, the jagged edges of images are less apparent when they are the same luminance as their background. Thus, more jaggies are apparent on the diagonal lines of a black ampersand on a green background than a cyan ampersand on the same green background (see Figure 10.17). Hue differences are thus useful to define the edge profile of a character. Since the color mechanisms of the eye have relatively poor resolving

Figure 10.17 *Soft Color Fonts* The ampersand accompanies a luminance difference. (The chromaticities are chosen from one of the lines of blurred colors shown in Figure 7.8.) In a) the jaggies are very obvious in this image. In b) the chromaticities are different but the luminance contrast is zero.

Color Enhancement Techniques

power, the pixel discontinuities are not apparent. Further research and use of this technique can improve the appearance of color fonts on color backgrounds for graphic and desktop publishing applications.

Color Table Animation

Simple forms of animation, like the cascading of a waterfall or the impression of rushing through a tunnel, are easy to create with color. Computer graphic animation typically involves changing the pixel values in the framebuffer. Redrawing thousands of pixels at video frame rates is time-consuming. A simpler method is to switch the color of pixels in the color table.

The basic concept in color table animation is to change the color by redefining the color entry in the color table. Using this technique, in a software Paint program, the blue of an afternoon sky can be easily changed to the orange of a sunset. Most paint programs provide a color menu where each pen color references a different color table entry. To recolor the sky usually requires redrawing the sky with a different pen. However, a simpler method is to change the color palette. Thus, instead of redrawing the sky, the user can replace a pen's blue value with an orange value. In this case, the entire sky would automatically change to orange without having to redraw every pixel. (However, any other item in the scene of the same blue value would also change to orange.) Most color Paint programs provide this feature.

This technique can also be used to create motion on a screen. Thus, to create the appearance of a growing square, it is only necessary to redefine the color table entries for particular pixels on the screen. No redrawing of the image is required (see Figure 10.18).

All of these methods (that is, color dithering, smoothing, and color table animation) can be used on inexpensive microcomputers.

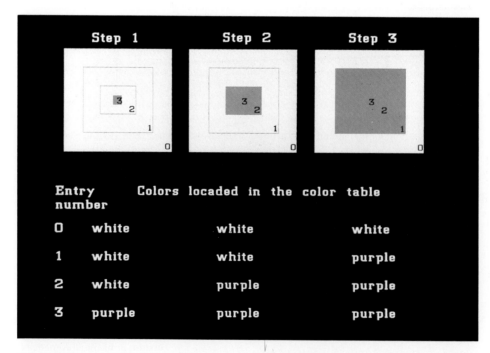

Figure 10.18 *Animation Using a Color Table* (top) Three stages in the animation of a growing purple square. (bottom) The corresponding state of the look-up table in each step in the animation.

Image Processing with Color

Some display images are photographs which are scanned into the computer system and then modified. This kind of programming is known as *picture* or *image processing*. It is a highly specialized technique of color use with computer displays. The use of color enhances the appearance of these images (see Figure 10.19). For example, in medical and satellite imaging, this process is used to reveal and highlight information that we may not or cannot otherwise see (for example, X ray film records radiation which is outside the visible spectrum).

Until recently, the only methods available to convert invisible wavelengths into visible images was through sophisticated photographic techniques and special film emulsifiers. With the advent of sophisticated image processing techniques and advanced display technologies, the details of low contrast images and invisible wavelengths are now visible. It is now possible to convert or scan photographic images (records) into a computer display system.

The class of programs which manipulates images is known as image processing software. This software not only converts the photographic record to displayed screen intensities, but also can enhance contrast, eliminate noise in an image, and change its magnification. This software allows changes to be more quickly produced than with photography.

There are now several processing methods for highlighting invisible or nearly invisible digitized images with color. All these methods either translate lightness (gray) values or invisible wavelengths into colors. One of the problems in viewing gray scale images is that the eye can only distinguish a limited number of values (between 24 and 36 on negative film). The advantage of converting these to color is that the eye can see many more colors (millions) than gray levels. Therefore, converting a gray scale image

Figure 10.19 *Satellite Imagery* The photograph of the Eagle Nebula in the Constellation of Serpens was made from "unsharp masked" negative copies of three black and white plates filtered for red, green, and blue sensitivities. The copies were then register printed using a three color additive technique. Red represents the hot gas radiating from this young cluster of stars. (*Courtesy of the Royal Observatory, Edinburgh, Copyright 1985.*)

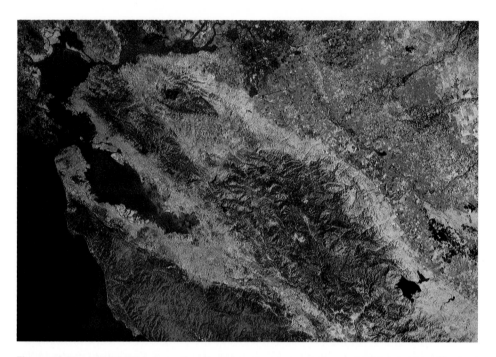

Figure 10.20 *LANDSAT Image* San Francisco bay area photographed from a satellite and enhanced by multiband image processing. Red represents growing vegetation, blue and green represent fields, and black represents water.

like an X ray into color can increase the visibility of an image's features (such as medical abnormalities) that would otherwise go undetected.

There are two general categories of images enhanced by image processing: single-band and multiband. Single-band are monochromatic images like medical X rays and consist of achromatic brightness values. Multiband images, like satellite (LANDSAT) pictures (see Figure 10.20), consist of contrast variations in multiple spectral pictures (called *records*). Some of their radiant emission values are within the visible spectrum, others are not. For example, although more sophisticated LANDSAT imagery is based on seven separate wavelength records, only four of these wavelengths are visible.

Pseudo and False Coloring

An example of single-band image processing is *pseudocoloring*. This technique transforms monochromatic (gray scale) images into color by assigning a different color to pixels of different intensity levels (see Figure 10.21).

A technique which converts extravisible spectra and multiband images to color is *false coloring*. This technique is similar to color photography except that the image processing is based on both visible and invisible spectra (see Figure 10.21).

These two techniques can reveal major features in an image and can be produced relatively quickly compared to other color imaging enhancing techniques.

Density Slicing

Density slicing is another image processing technique. It differs from pseudocoloring in that it assigns a specific color value to a group of gray scale levels, rather than to one gray value (see Figure 10.22).

In creating a density slice of an image, the boundaries of the gray scale values are not predetermined. Instead the user interactively selects a range of gray values and assigns

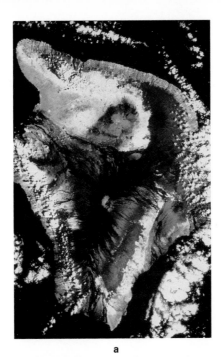

a

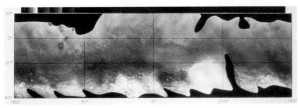

b

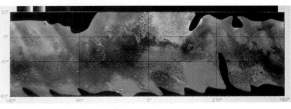

c

Figure 10.21 *False versus Pseudocoloring* a) False color photograph of the island of Hawaii. The infrared wavelength areas of radiation are shown in red, the green vegetation is shown in blue. (*Courtesy of Mike Carr, United States Geological Survey.*) b and c) Satellite photographic montage of Mars and pseudocolored representation enhancing differences in land elevation. (*Courtesy of Mike Carr, United States Geological Survey.*)

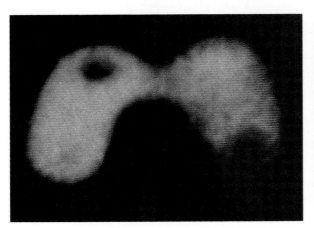

a

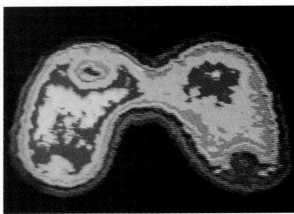

b

Figure 10.22 *Density Slicing* a) X ray of the Picker Thyroid Phantom. b) Result of density slicing into eight color regions. (*Courtesy of Addison Wesley.*)

them a hue and brightness. For example, darker colors may be selected to represent features of the structure farthest from view, and lighter colors for closer features. The increase in lightness from the farthest to the closest portion of the image results in pseudoshading: the colors are false in that they do not match the original lightness values of the unprocessed image.

Image Processing with Color

Density slicing is one of the simplest methods of pseudocoloring and is generally thought to produce superior image enhancement. This is not surprising, since density slicing is an interactive procedure which allows a user to fine-tune color and simultaneously enhance the visibility of features. By contrast, pseudocoloring relies on a predetermined mapping function (see Box). One of the major disadvantages of density slicing is that several gray scale values are typically combined into a single color slice and so some details of the image may be lost.

MAPPING PSEUDOCOLORS

The gray scale record of a single-band image (like an X ray) is converted to color by a pseudocolor mapping function (see Figure 10.23). Similarly, any one of the waveband records in a multispectral image can be mapped within a pseudocoloring function.

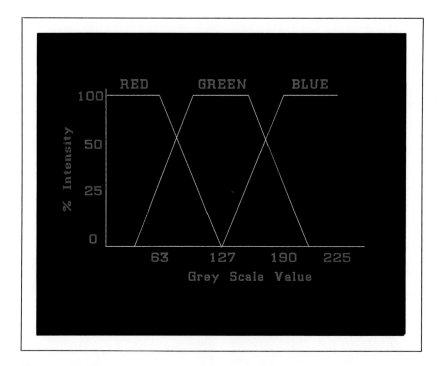

Figure 10.23 *Pseudocolor Mapping Function* This mapping function translates the lowest (lightest appearing) gray scale values to long wavelengths, middle gray values to middle wavelengths, and darkest gray values to short wavelengths. Higher values within a primary's range are assigned higher spectral purity; lower intensities within a primary's range are assigned less purity. Thus a low value for a red primary might be shown in orange, while higher values for this same primary set would appear an intense red. (*Adapted from Mather, 1983.*)

Color Composites

One of the false coloring techniques which transforms multiband images is color composites. This method respectively remaps each of three wave band records to the three CRT primaries. These color-mapped records of the image are then superimposed; the result is a false color representation (see Figure 10.24).

Figure 10.24 *False Colored Composite Image* The color composite photograph was produced from three photographic plates of the comet Halley. Three plates each representing either blue, red, or green were exposed, copied, and printed onto a positive photograph color material which colors the individual star exposures. The stars have trails because of the movement of the telescope as it tracked the comet. (*Courtesy of Royal Observatory, Edinburgh, Copyright 1985.*)

This method is often applied to satellite imagery. For example, LANDSAT pictures consist of independent wavelength records usually sampled across seven bandwidths of the electromagnetic spectrum. Of these bandwidths, some are outside the visible spectrum but, nonetheless, contain useful information. For example, differences in infrared reflectance of both natural and man-made objects in a scene convey a great deal of information about the characteristics of that scene.

The color composite technique converts this invisible wavelength information into visible images: near-infrared bands are converted to red, visible red to green, visible green to blue, and blue to black. For example, the infrared record of a terrain image might be remapped so that vegetation appears red and water appears black. Although the colors of the visible images are different from their natural appearance, people can learn to quickly interpret features imaged in this manner.

Useful Facts

Color Memory	Colors are arranged in computer memory in color maps.
Raster versus Vector Displays	Raster displays create images with spots; vector displays create images with lines.
Single Color Images	Two pixel intensities (on and off) produce a single color. There are no intermediate values.
Multiple Color Images	One bit for every color primary is required to produce a multicolor image.

Number of Intensity and Color Levels	Intensities and color levels are determined by 2 raised to the power of the pixel depth.
Color Quantity	The number of intensities of the electron beams, memory, pixel depth, or the number of bitplanes determine the number of colors.
Optimizing Color	Adjusting values in the color look-up table, digitizing the image, and color averaging (Median Cut or Popularity algorithms) optimizes color appearance.
Evaluating Fidelity	Color error metrics determine fidelity. It is preferable to use one that is based on color perception (such as CIELUV for displays and CIELAB for hard copy).
Color Spaces	HSL and HSV are useful color models to transform RGB color space.
Enhancing Image Quality	Techniques like interrupts, dithering, anti-aliasing and gray scaling are useful to enhance image quality.
Dithering	Unique combinations of pixels (dithering) are useful to expand the number of apparent colors. Dithering is better for area-fill images than thin lines or small images. As certain color combinations are better than others, its use is limited.
Gray Scales	Different intensity levels on the borders of an image smooths their appearance.
Smoothing Edges	The edge quality of images that appear jagged can appear more smooth by using gray scales. Additional smoothing is possible by using similar brightness values between the image and its background.
Making Invisible Wavelengths Visible	Several methods are available to permit visibility of invisible wavelengths. Colors assigned to enhanced images often result in the colors of the image not matching their natural appearance.

REFERENCES

Conrac Corp. *Raster Graphics Handbook* (New York: Van Nostrand Reinhold Co., 1985).

Foley, J. D. and A. Van Dam. *Fundamentals of Interactive Computer Graphics* (Menlo Park, CA: Addison-Wesley Pub., 1982).

Gonzales, L. *Digital Image Processing* (Menlo Park, CA: Addison-Wesley).

Heckbert, D., ''Color Image Quantization for Frame Buffer Display,'' *Computer Graphics*, 16(3), 1982, 297–307.

Meyer, G. W. and D. P. Greenberg, ''Color Education and Color Synthesis in Computer Graphics,'' *Color Research and Application*, 11, 1986, S39–S44.

Santisteban, A., ''The Perceptual Color Space of Digital Image Display Terminals,'' *IBM J. Res. Develop.*, 27(2), 1983, 127–132.

Stone, M. C., ''Color, Graphic Design and Computer Systems,'' *Color Research and Application*, 11, 1986, S75–S82.

Tanner, P., W. Cowan, and M. Wein, ''Color Selection, Swath Brushes and Memory Architecture for Paint Systems,'' *Graphics Interface*, 1983, pp. 171–180.

11

Computer Color Guidelines

Color, when once reduced to certain definite rules, can be taught like music.

Georges Seurat

This chapter contains color guidelines which apply to the types of computer images typical in text processing, process control, computer-aided design, and scientific instrumentation applications. These guidelines are based on visual characteristics that permit color perception and visual requirements necessary to successfully accomplish tasks in these as well as other types of applications.

Color Usage Goals

Color Guidelines and Standards

Regardless of the application of color, the ultimate goal of its use is to ensure its correct identification, image interpretation, appropriateness to the task, and acceptability. If these objectives are met, the result is enhancement in visual and mental processing of information, visual comfort, and aesthetic appearance.

One way to optimize performance and comfort is to use guidelines and standards that are based on studies of the effects of color on visual responses. Guidelines are generally more flexible than standards and they better accommodate different users, applications, and situations. In addition, guidelines are more easily updated to reflect the results of new research.

Traditional versus Recent Color Applications

Traditional color standards and guidelines were designed for lights on control and status panels for industrial, transport, and military systems (see Figure 11.1). Many of these more traditional guidelines are inconsistent and most are inappropriate for computer applications such as text processing, computer aided engineering, scientific analysis, and

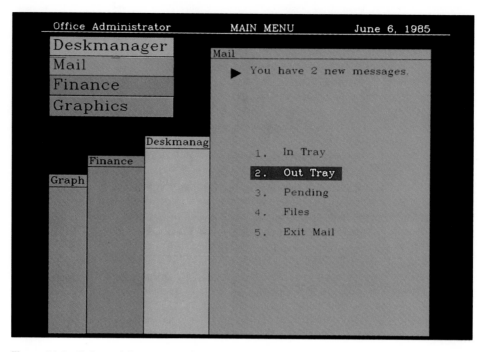

Figure 11.1 *Colors of Status and I/O Messages* Color coding screen backgrounds by office applications: Cyan designates mail, orange represents the desk manager, green designates finance, and pink represents graphics. (*Courtesy Hewlett-Packard.*)

medical monitoring. The primary purpose of color in traditional display applications is to enhance perceptual responses that are different from those required for office application images. For example, control and monitoring tasks often require rapid perception and reaction to changes and movements of images. The speed of response to these images often determines system or production efficiency (for example, in a manufacturing facility), sustainment of life (for example, at a medical monitoring station) or traffic flow (for example, in an air traffic control tower). These response characteristics either do not occur, do not occur as frequently, or are not important for display office image applications.

Most of the display images of business, engineering, and scientific applications are being created and manipulated, rather than monitored as in control systems. In addition, visual responses in these more recent display applications are not as critical. There are no tracking requirements and the changes in image appearance that occur are expected because they are generally controlled by the user.

Another major difference between color use for traditional and more recent computer image applications is the transfer of display images to hard copy. This has resulted in a fidelity problem because hard copy colors appear different from those on displays (see chapter 3). Although few guidelines exist for computer displays, even fewer exist to accommodate color transfer and color hard copy images.

Several national and international organizations are developing standards for user interface features of computer displays. The use of traditional color guidelines is being evaluated for incorporation into these standards. Some are appropriate for computer color applications (see Table 11.1). For example, the standard association of red for error may be used for screen error messages or critical commands like ''Delete,'' and yellow for caution conditions and messages like ''System going down.'' Other associations like green for ''go'' or white for a neutral message can be respectively used to indicate input fields or general information system status messages.

TABLE 11.1

Meanings of Colors for Display Applications

Red	Error messages.
Blue/Cyan	Standard title names of screens.
	Database information.
	Advisory or help messages.
Green	Input fields.
Yellow/Orange	Warning or caution messages.
White	System response messages.
	Neutral status messages.

General Guidelines

The following guidelines are based on color perception research and expand traditional color assignment. They should aid in choosing effective colors for business, engineering, scientific, and graphic applications. They were specifically developed for application to display and hard copy computer images and generally refer to saturated values.

Tasks Qualifying for Color Application

Images which best qualify to be presented in color are those which are to be located, grouped, coded, separated, changed, learned, remembered, associated, emphasized, or monitored, or those that represent a physical impression.

General Color Use Principles

The following general guidelines apply to any color application:

- Follow standards or established guidelines when they are appropriate for an application
- Maintain consistent color assignment
- Use a minimum number of colors
- Use brightness, hue differences, and color complements to maximize color discrimination (see Figure 11.2)

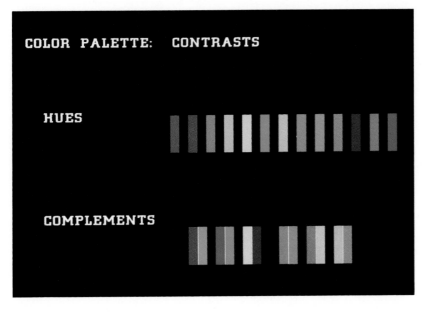

Figure 11.2 *Discriminable Hues and Complements* (top) Thirteen discriminable colors on a black background. (bottom) Complementary color pairs of primary and secondary colors maximize discrimination.

- Use colors with differences in more than one value (such as hue and lightness) to enhance discrimination
- Use different color values to enhance or reduce the visibility of a color or resolution of an image
- Use colors other than saturated blue for extremely small images
- Match hues with image colors, conditions, or actions being represented (such as red for hot and blue for cold)

Names

In general, names (instead of numbers) should be used to describe colors when confusions are not possible (see Figure 11.3).

- Use one word descriptors for basic colors (such as blue, green, red, or yellow)
- Use simple descriptors to indicate extreme values (such as light and dark)
- Use names from standard notation systems like the National Bureau of Standards Universal Color Language or the Color Naming System

Number and Size of Colors

The number of colors and size of color images depend on image characteristics and the requirements of the task.

- Use the number of colors appropriate for application
- Use no more than five colors when their meanings must be remembered
- Use fewer colors for abstract representations (such as formulas, graphs, text)
- As the number of colors increase, increase size of small images (such as data points and targets) to enhance detection and discrimination

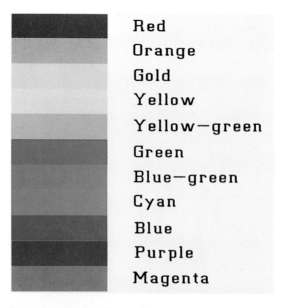

Red
Orange
Gold
Yellow
Yellow—green
Green
Blue—green
Cyan
Blue
Purple
Magenta

Figure 11.3 *De Facto Computer Industry Color* Assignment of single or combined de facto standard names for common CRT colors.

Computer Color Guidelines Chap. 11

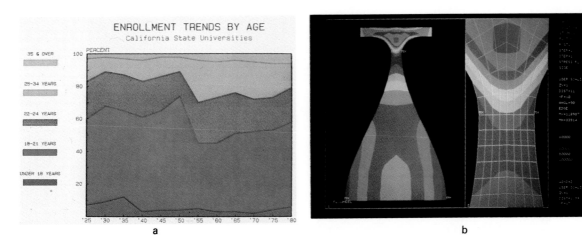

Figure 11.4 *Graphics with Color Legends* a) Color legend where hue segregates different age group categories. b) Color legend where hue is mapped to a scale of stress values.

Legends

Provide labels or legends with colors when

- Standard or commonly understood associations are not used (such as green for abnormal conditions or messages)
- The meaning of the color is not obvious (such as yellow for cool temperatures)
- The meanings of more than 5 colors must be remembered

Locate colors adjacent to their legends or color code the legends (see Figure 11.4).

Paper

- Use paper type recommended by manufacturer
- Use glossy paper to enhance saturated appearance

Environment Lighting

- Determine the effects of ambient illumination on color appearance
- Control ambient illumination that reduces contrast or distorts color appearance (with louvers, tinted windows, indirect lighting)
- Locate front of the display perpendicular to a window

Maximizing Color Harmony

Use color combinations that are opposite on a color harmony wheel (that is, color complements like red and cyan, blue and yellow, and green and magenta) to enhance harmony. Spectrally extreme color combinations not opposite on the color wheel (such as red and blue or red and green) and adjacent color combinations (such as blue and cyan, cyan and green, green and yellow, yellow and red, red and magenta, and magenta and blue) are less harmonious (see Figure 11.5).

To create a balance in lightness values of CRT colors, increase the luminance of CRT red and blue so that they appear equal in brightness to green and yellow.

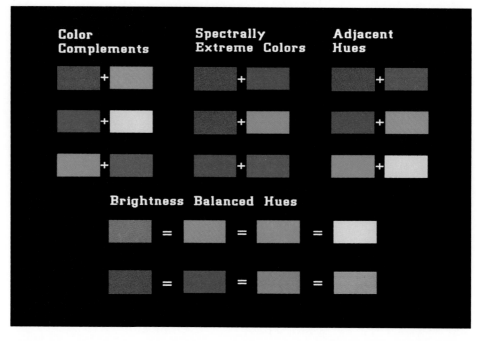

Figure 11.5 *Color Harmony Combinations* The pairs of squares on the left are color complements and are harmonious. The pairs in the top middle are spectrally extreme and the ones on
the right are adjacent combinations; neither are harmonious. The two rows of squares on the
bottom are lightness balanced so that none appears brighter, larger, closer, or attracts attention
more than the others.

Ensuring Color Recognition

To ensure color visibility, use wavelengths between 475 and 625 nm. Use complementary color combinations (such as red and cyan, blue and yellow, or magenta and
green) or spectrally extreme color combinations (such as red and blue, yellow and blue,
red and green, magenta and green) to maximize color contrast, recognition, and discrimination.

The appropriate lightness value of colors depends on the medium and color of the
background. For displays, the minimum luminance of the lighted image should be at least
35 candelas per square meter. The minimum contrast ratio between images and backgrounds
should be 3:1. The contrast between images and their backgrounds is more variable on
35 mm slides (than on paper or plastic transparencies) since their background can be any
color and lightness value.

Colors that can be easily discriminated in area-fill images do not necessarily ensure
good legibility or high resolution. The minimum size for blue and yellow images is larger
than for red and green ones. Minimum color and size requirements and color combinations
that optimize color discrimination and legibility are listed in Table 11.2.

Contrasts

High contrasts can be accomplished with either hue, saturation, or lightness values.
To ensure maximum color contrast, use combinations of light and dark colors, spectral
extremes and color complements. High hue contrasts are extreme spectral values and
complementary colors (see Figure 11.6). High saturation contrasts are hues most saturated
(highest purity) with those least saturated (lowest purity). High lightness contrasts are
colors which appear most white or brightest and those least white or darkest.

Use high color and luminance contrast ratios (>7:1) for bright environments, to

TABLE 11.2

Color Requirements

	Recognition	Discrimination	Legibility
Luminance			
Level	≥35² cd/m		
Contrast Ratio			
Image to	≥3:1	≥7:1	≥7:1
Background			
Wavelength	475–625 nm		
Color Differences		≥40 ΔE CIELUV	≥100 ΔE CIELUV
Small Images		≥40 ΔE CIELUV	
Image Sizes			
Blue and Yellow		≥20 arc min.	≥20 arc min.
Red and Green		>20 arc min.	>20 arc min.
Image color for			
Black Background	Desaturated bright colors	Magenta and green and yellow	Green, Yellow
			Cyan, yellow
White Background	Saturated dark colors	Red and green Blue and red Magenta and green Blue and magenta	Blue

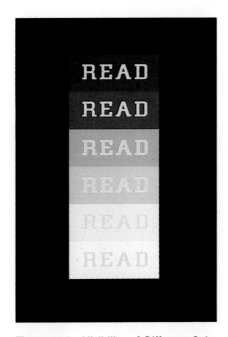

Figure 11.6 *Visibility of Different Color Contrasts* From top to bottom: The hue and lightness of the text color is constant, while that of the background becomes lighter lowering the contrast and visibility of the text.

attract attention, for far viewing, when legibility is critical. Use high luminance contrasts (>7:1) to sharpen edges.

Use medium contrast ratios (3:1 to 5:1) for continuous reading and dark environments. Use low contrasts (<3:1) to camouflage images or smooth edges.

Color on Achromatic Backgrounds

Use a black or dark gray background to maximize color visibility on displays and 35 mm slides (see Table 11.3 and Figure 11.7), especially at far distances, and to preview color appearance of 35 mm slides with the same background. With dark backgrounds,

TABLE 11.3

Discriminable and Legible Color Combinations on Achromatic Backgrounds

	Image Color					
	Red	Blue	Green	Cyan	Magenta	Yellow
On Black/Dark Gray Backgrounds						
Color Discrimination Combinations					X	X
				X	X	
			X		X	
				X		X
Legibility Combinations			X	X		X
On White Background						
Color Discrimination Combinations		X			X	
	X	X				
	X		X			
	X			X		
Legibility Combinations	X	X				
		X			X	
On Medium Gray						
Color Discrimination Combinations	X					X
		X			X	
Legibility Combinations	X					X

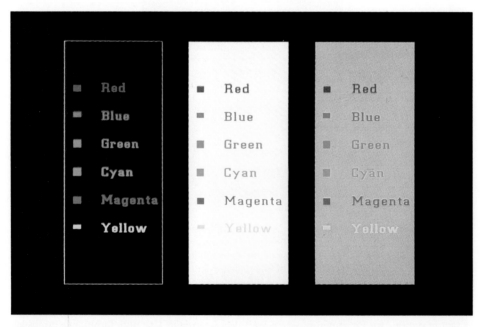

Figure 11.7 *Visibility of Colors on Black, White, and Gray Backgrounds* The blocks show color combinations that have maximum visibility and discrimination. The words show the colors of text with high visibility, color discrimination, and legibility. The lighter colors have high visibility on a black background and the darker colors have higher visibility on a white background.

use desaturated colors for thin lines or small images (such as yellow, green, cyan) and avoid dark saturated colors (such as red and blue) for text.

Use a white background to preview the appearance of color images to be transferred to paper, transparencies, and 35 mm slides with a white background. With a white background, use saturated colors for thin lines and small images to maximize legibility and produce sharp edges and avoid light, desaturated colors (such as yellow) for text.

Optimizing Discriminable Colors for Line Thicknesses

Thin Lines

To ensure color discrimination for thin-line graphics, single-stroke fonts, and very small images, special color palettes are required. Small images or thin lines which require sharply defined edges should have a high lightness contrast to their background. With very small images, darker colors (like navy blue and purple) will look black, and light colors (like yellow and light green) will appear less saturated. Similar hues on thin lines are difficult to distinguish. Examples of color combinations that are discriminable for thin-line images are shown in Table 11.4 and the top portions of Figures 11.8, 11.9, and 11.10).

TABLE 11.4

Easily Perceivable and Discriminable Colors for Thin Lines

	Background	
Number of Colors	White	Black
1	Red Green	Yellow Cyan Green
2	Red and green Magenta and cyan Red and blue	Green and magenta Yellow and magenta Cyan and magenta

3	Red, blue, and
	   green
		Cyan, magenta,
		   and yellow

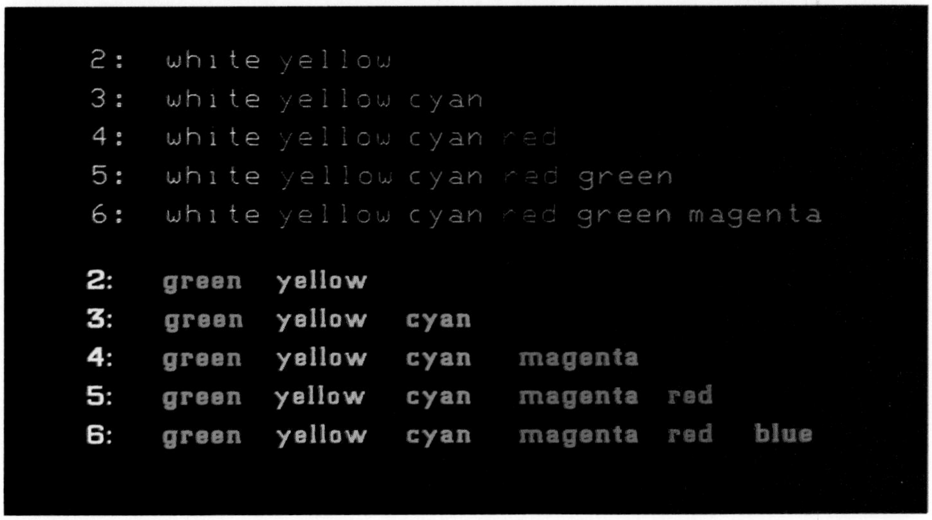

Figure 11.8 *Visibility of Colored Fonts* The colors of thin fonts (top rows) are difficult to perceive on a white background. The colors of bold fonts (bottom rows) are easy to see on both white and black.

Figure 11.9 *Color Visibility on Transparencies* Colors of dots (top row) and thin lines (second row) are most difficult to perceive; the colors of the blocks are easier to perceive and discriminate.

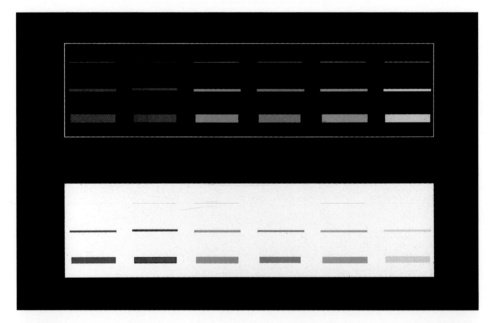

Figure 11.10 *Color Visibility on Slides* (top) Visibility of thin color lines on black is poor, but color visibility of the thick lines is good. (bottom) Visibility of thin color lines on white is not good. The colors of the thick lines on white is good (visibility of yellow is more difficult).

Thick Lines

Thick lines and area-fill images (such as bar charts, sectors of a pie chart, and bold fonts) allow more latitude for color assignment. They are more easily perceived and discriminated even at low saturation values than thin-line images (see Figure 11.8).

TABLE 11.5

Easily Perceivable and Discriminable Colors for Thick Lines and Area-fill

	Background	
Number of Colors	White	Black
1	Red	Yellow
	Green	Cyan
	Blue	Green
	Purple	Magenta
	Magenta	
2	Green and magenta	Magenta and cyan
	Red and blue	Magenta and green
	Red and green	
3	Red, green, and blue	Magenta, cyan, and yellow
	Magenta, green, and blue	Magenta, green, and yellow

Examples of color combinations that are discriminable for thick-line images are shown in Table 11.5 and the bottom portions of Figures 11.8, 11.9, and 11.10.

Viewing Angle and Distance

Color images located in peripheral vision are less perceptible and discriminable; colors located in the far periphery cannot be identified. For peripheral viewing, use area-fill, large images, bright saturated colors, and color backgrounds. Avoid using colors for images in the far periphery when identification and discrimination are critical. If color use in the periphery is necessary, avoid red and green beyond 40 degrees, yellow beyond 50 degrees, and blue beyond 60 degrees. Color visibility at different peripheral angles is shown in Table 11.6.

At close distances (for example, less than 60 cm), all colors either saturated or desaturated are acceptable, and are visible as long as they are at least 16 minutes of arc. For far viewing (greater than 60 cm), bright saturated colors are most visible and discriminable.

In general, for thin-line (single-stroke) images, dark colors produce better legibility and color recognition than light colors (orange and green) particularly at far viewing distances (see Table 11.7). Thin lines appear less saturated than thick lines, and spectral extremes are more discriminable than spectrally close colors. Optimal color values and image characteristics for extreme viewing conditions are shown in Table 11.8. Optimal colors for thin lines depend on contrast.

TABLE 11.6

Visible Colors for Different Viewing Angles

Peripheral Viewing	Red	Blue	Green	Cyan	Magenta	Yellow
0–40 degrees	X	X	X			X
40–50 degrees		X				X
50–60 degrees		X				
>60 degrees						

TABLE 11.7

Optimal Image Characteristics of Transparencies
and 35 mm Slides at Close and Far Viewing Distances

	Close (<60 cm)	Far (>60 cm)
Font		
Bold	X	X
Stick	X	
Graphs		
Bar, pie	X	X
Line, scatter diagram	X	
Colors for Transparencies		
Red	X	X
Blue	X	X
Green	X	
Cyan	X	
Magenta	X	X
Colors for Black Background Slides		
Red	X	
Blue	X	
Green	X	X
Cyan	X	X
Magenta	X	X
Yellow	X	X

TABLE 11.8

Color Values for Extreme Viewing Conditions

	Room Lighting Bright	Dim	Visual Angle Central	Periphery	Viewing Distance Short	Long
IMAGE COLOR VALUES						
Saturation						
Saturated	X		X	X	X	X
Desaturated		X	X		X	
Brightness						
Bright	X	X	X	X	X	X
Dim	X		X		X	
BACKGROUND VALUES						
Lightness						
Dark	X	X	X	X	X	X
Light	X		X		X	
IMAGE SIZE						
Very small	X		X		X	
Large	X	X	X	X	X	X
FONT WEIGHTS						
Font						
Stick	X	X	X		X	
Bold	X	X	X	X	X	X

Specific Media and Viewing Conditions

Transparencies and 35 mm Slides

On transparencies, use dark, saturated colors such as gold instead of yellow and blue instead of cyan particularly for text or thin lines. Use area-fill graphics (such as bar and pie charts) instead of edge-dominated graphs (such as line graphs and scatter diagrams).

To optimize image and color perception on 35 mm dark background (such as black and blue) slides, use desaturated colors (such as yellow, cyan, and green) for thin lines and text.

Maximizing Visual Comfort During Continuous Reading

For continuous CRT reading, medium contrast and desaturated colors that are not spectral extremes (such as yellow and green) are most appropriate. Use colors with obvious differences in hues and brightness levels (see Figure 11.11). If possible, use a dark gray rather than a black background and avoid a white background. Use a conservative number of colors at one time (say, four per screen).

Ratings of comfort of reading CRT color text on a color background are shown in Table 11.9.

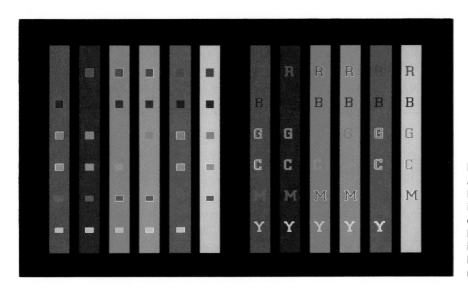

Figure 11.11 *Visibility and Legibility of Color Combinations* Each row shows two different images (a square and letter) in a constant color on different color backgrounds. Visibility and legibility are best when hue and lightness contrast are maximized.

TABLE 11.9

Comfort Ratings for Color CRT Text and Background Combinations

Text Color	Background Color					
	Red	Blue	Green	Cyan	Magenta	Yellow
Red	—	P	P	F	P	F
Blue	P	—	F	F	P	F
Green	P	F	—	F	F	P
Cyan	P	F	P	—	F	P
Magenta	P	P	F	F	—	F
Yellow	F	G	P	P	F	—

G = Good
F = Fair
P = Poor

CRTs use a black background to reduce flicker and glare. A white background reduces the perception of reflections, but increases the possibility of flicker and glare due to the large illuminated area fills. For displays with these problems, use a gray background for continuous viewing tasks such as reading. However, legibility of colors on gray is less visually efficient than on a black or white background because of the lower lightness contrast of color images to gray (see Figure 11.8). Bright colors (like yellow) are better to optimize legibility on dark gray backgrounds than dark colors (like blue).

Room Lighting

Avoid excessive room lighting when viewing color images on displays, transparencies, and 35 mm slides. Optimal room light level for viewing color displays is about 200 lux. When it is also necessary to read documents, the illumination level should be more than 200 lux. Anti-glare treatments should not distort colors on display screens.

In brightly lighted rooms, use saturated colors; in dimly lighted rooms, use low brightness and desaturated colors.

Reduce the light level for viewing transparencies because their optimum color visibility occurs in dark rooms. Transparency colors are usually visible in 200 lux but difficult to see above 500 lux. Adjust room illumination level to less than 200 lux for optimum color visibility of 35 mm slides.

Illumination recommendations for different media are listed in Table 11.10.

TABLE 11.10

Room Illumination

Media	Room Illumination Level
Displays	200–500 lux
Transparencies	<500 lux
35 mm slides	<200 lux

Creating Special Effects

Use different color values to create special effects like enhancing edge sharpness, attracting attention, showing a change, creating a physical impression of time, weight, height, distance, or size, and enhancing learning. Most of these effects are only apparent with certain color values and are easily reversed or eliminated if the values vary, sometimes even slightly, from those recommended.

Optimizing Edge Sharpness on Color and Achromatic Backgrounds

To produce sharp borders, use high lightness and spectrally distant or complementary color contrasts (such as red and cyan or blue and yellow). Although colors like yellow and cyan have both lightness and color contrast, their differences are insufficient to produce sharp edges. Avoid combining yellow with cyan, white with yellow, blue with red, cyan with white, and green with blue. Also, avoid extremely close spacing of thin-line color combinations, like blue and yellow or red and green.

To produce blurred edges (say, for smoothing jaggies), use low lightness and spectrally close color contrasts (such as green and cyan, red and magenta).

Image sharpness depends on color and luminance contrast. Primary CRT colors (red, blue, and green) appear darker than their secondary colors (cyan, magenta, and yellow) and thus produce sharper edges. Therefore, use primary (or darker) color images on secondary (lighter) color backgrounds to enhance edge sharpness (see Figure 11.12).

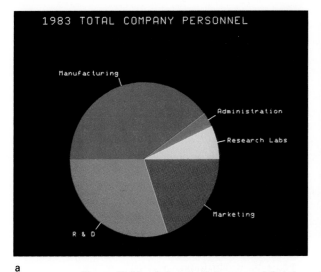 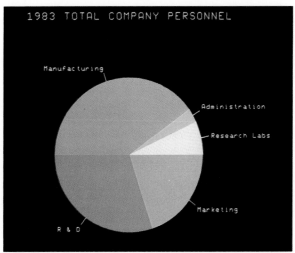

a b

Figure 11.12 *Colors to Enhance and Subdue* Application of saturated a) and desaturated b) color to pie charts which respectively enhance and subdue appearance.

Ratings of edge sharpness for CRT color images on color backgrounds are shown in Table 11.11.

TABLE 11.11

Ratings of Edge Sharpness of Color Images on Color Backgrounds

Image Color	Background Color							
	Red	*Blue*	*Green*	*Cyan*	*Magenta*	*Yellow*	*Black*	*White*
Red	O	L	L	H	L	H	L	H
Blue	L	O	M	H	M	H	L	H
Green	M	M	O	L	M	L	M	L
Cyan	M	M	L	O	M	L	M	L
Magenta	L	M	M	M	O	H	M	M
Yellow	M	M	L	L	M	O	M	L
Black	M	L	H	H	M	H	O	H
White	M	H	L	L	M	L	H	O

H = high edge sharpness
M = medium edge sharpness
L = low edge sharpness (blurry)
O = no edge visibility

Enhancing Edge Sharpness or Blur

The following is a list of techniques that creates special color effects.

- *SHARP EDGES*
  Enhance Resolution:

  Increase contrast.
  Use thin-line achromatic border around image.
  Use color complements and large brightness differences (such as red on cyan, blue on yellow).

- *SMOOTH EDGES*
  Create Blur/
  Smoothness:

  Decrease contrast between image and surrounding.
  Use gray scaling.

Creating Special Effects

Use equal brightness for image and background.
Use gradients in hue with constant brightness.
Use gradients in brightness with constant hue.

- *CONTRAST*
  Enhanced Contrast:

  Use saturated color complements (such as red with cyan, blue with yellow, green with magenta).

- *CAMOUFLAGE*
  Camouflage/
  Reduce Visibility:

  Use low contrast combinations.

- *REACTION TIME*
  Control Reaction Time:

  Use long wavelength colors for immediate action items (such as red, orange, magenta).
  Use short wavelength colors for nonimmediate action items (such as blue, green, cyan).

  Draw Attention/
  Quick Reaction:

  Use high brightness and saturation or contrast differences.

- *LEARNING*
  Enhance Memory:

  Use saturated primary colors (red, blue, green, yellow).

- *PHYSICAL APPEARANCE*

  Use hues and saturations to enhance the physical appearance of images (see Figures 11.13, 11.14, and 11.15). The physical impressions of different color values are shown in Table 11.12.

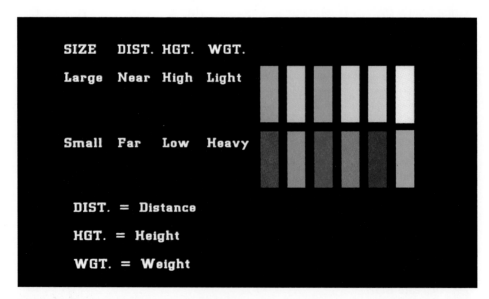

Figure 11.13 *Colors and Physical Appearance* The desaturated hues in the top row make images appear larger, nearer, higher, and lighter. The saturated hues in the bottom row make images appear smaller, farther away, lower, and heavier.

Figure 11.14 *Brightness and Size Appearance* The shapes in the top row are the same physical size as those on the bottom, although they appear different. Thus brighter colors appear larger.

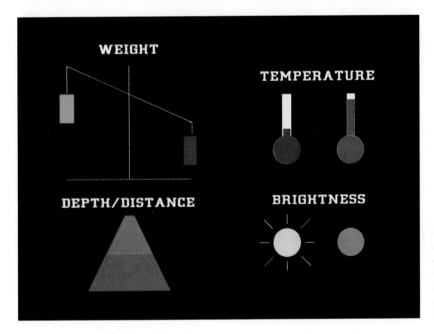

Figure 11.15 *Colors to Show Physical Properties: Weight, Distance, Temperature, and Brightness* The dark blue appears heavier than light blue; red appears closer than blue; red is associated with hot and blue with cold; yellow appears brighter than orange.

TABLE 11.12

Physical Impressions

	Image Appearance							
	Size		Weight		Height		Distance	
Color Value	Large	Small	Heavy	Light	High	Low	Close	Far
Saturated	X		X			X	X	
Desaturated		X		X	X			X
Light	X				X	X		X	
Dark		X	X			X		X

Creating Special Effects   **227**

- *SIZE*
  Enlarge Size: Saturate colors or brightness.
  Reduce Size: Desaturate colors or reduce
                                       brightness.
  Equate Size: Equate saturation and brightness.
- *WEIGHT*
  Show Heaviness: Saturate or decrease lightness.
  Show Lightness: Desaturate or increase lightness.
- *HEIGHT & DISTANCE*   Use spectrally extreme colors (such
  Show Height: as red and blue).
  Show Distance: Desaturated or light colors.
                                       Desaturated colors.

Three-Dimensional Effects

Palettes for three-dimensional effects require that colors be arranged according to spectral order and have equal brightness. Three-dimensional effects are possible with both saturated and desaturated color palettes (see Figure 11.16).

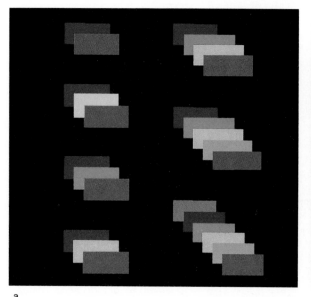
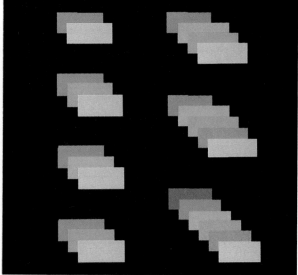

a   b

Figure 11.16 *Color Ordering Creating Three-Dimensional Impressions* Both the palettes are the same hue but a) is saturated values and b) is desaturated. The three-dimensional effect is created by spectral ordering and balancing brightness (for example, lowering the brightness of yellow to appear equal to the other colors).

TABLE 11.13

Color Combinations to Create Three-Dimensional Effects

	COLOR					
Number of Colors	Farthest Purple	Blue	Green	Yellow	Orange	Closest Red
2		X				X
3		X	X			X
		X		X		X
4		X	X	X		X
5		X	X	X	X	X
6	X	X	X	X	X	X

In general, short wavelengths (blue) will appear more distant than long wavelengths (orange and red). Color combinations that can produce depth and dimensional effects with different numbers of colors are listed in the order by which they should be located in Table 11.13.

Changes

To show change, link the degree of color change to event magnitude. For example, use small changes with small color value changes (for example, blue to green) and large changes with extreme color changes (for example, blue to orange).

SHADINGS   Shading is generally characterized by a gradual change in lightness or saturation of a color or change in its hue. It is well suited for indicating changes in value along a continuous variable. It is appropriate only for area-fill images such as bar charts, graduated bars, and simulations. However, when large or abrupt changes in a variable should be indicated, large hue changes are necessary. Different hues are more appropriate for discrete data than for continuous data; gradual changes in saturation or lightness are best to indicate continuous changes in data (see Figure 11.17).

SPECTRAL ORDERINGS   Thus to show continuous changes, arrange colors by either spectral or lightness order. The recommended arrangement of spectral orderings from short wavelengths (bottom or left) to long wavelengths (top or right) is shown in Table 11.14 (also see Figure 11.18).

Magnitude Changes

Use short wavelengths to code lowest magnitude of change and long wavelengths to code highest magnitude of change. For example, to show a progression or change in stress, use blue for lowest stress indicators to red for highest stress indicators (see Figure 11.19). Color should reflect the color of the object during state changes. Use of white on a scale indicating change depends on the appearance of the object (for example, a nonconductive material like paper is coded white at low temperatures and red at high temperatures).

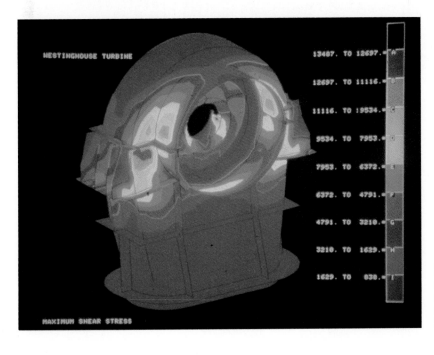

Figure 11.17 *Gradual Changes in Hue and Lightness* Increase in mechanical stress in the turbine is shown by gradual changes in spectral ordering of hues and their saturation.

TABLE 11.14

Arrangement of Hues and Lightness Values for Shadings and Gradings

Vertical Arrays		Horizontal Arrays
Wavelength	*Intensity*	*Wavelength*
Long	Light	Short ——————————— Long
│ red	│	(blue—cyan—green—yellow—red)
│ yellow	│	
│ green	│	*Intensity*
│ cyan	│	Dark ——————————— Light
│ blue	│	
Short	Dark	

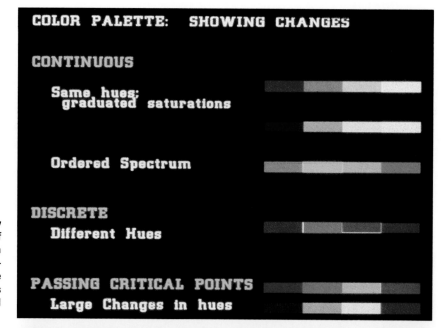

Figure 11.18 *Colors for Showing Change* Gradual saturation of same hue or ordered spectrum shows continuous changes. Different hues represent discrete changes. Large differences in hues can represent the passing of critical points.

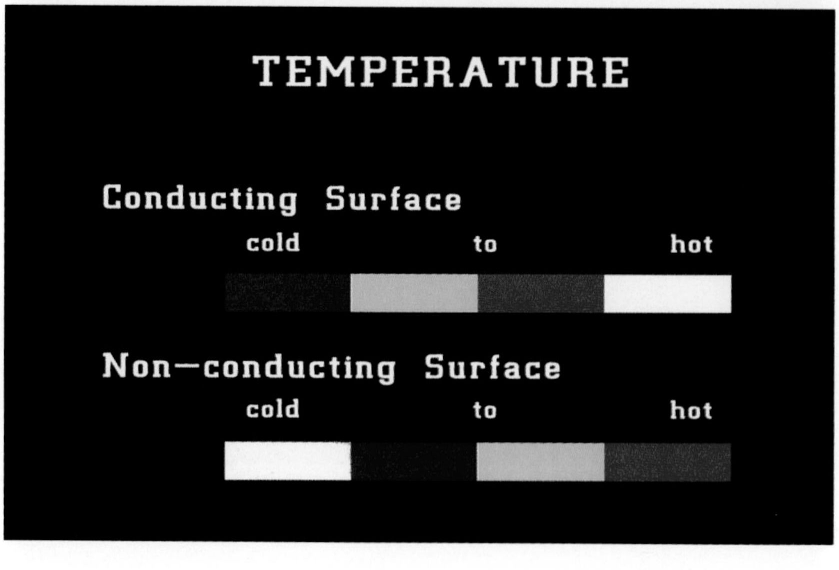

Figure 11.19 *Color to Indicate Temperature Changes* Ordering colors from short to long wavelengths shows increase in temperature. Assignment of white depends on appearance of material as it reaches flash point. Examples of ordering on nonconducting and conducting materials against a black background.

230

TABLE 11.15

Color Ordering for Physical Impressions

| Physical Impression | Magnitude | | | | | |
| | Lowest to Highest | | | | | |
	White	Blue	Green	Yellow	Red	White
Stress Simulation		X	X	X	X	
Height or Depth		X	X	X	X	X
Temperature						
Nonconducting Materials	X	X		X	X	
Conducting Materials		X		X	X	X

The order of colors to indicate magnitude changes of different types of states is shown in Table 11.15.

Color Problems and Causes

When colors do not produce the intended effects there can be a variety of reasons. They include inappropriate image size or contrast, inappropriate application, misunderstanding color meanings, inconsistency, and perceptual problems. A number of problems along with their most likely cause and solutions are listed in Table 11.16.

TABLE 11.16

Color Problems and Solutions

Problem	Possible Cause	Solution
Color Identification	Insufficient contrast	Use high lightness and hue contrast
	Images too small	Ensure images are at least 20 minutes of arc
	Color vision deficiency	Use colors that can be identified by all users
Color Discrimination	Insufficient hue differences	Ensure min of 40ΔE units between hues
	Insufficient saturation differences	Ensure at least 1 saturation JND
	Color vision deficiency	Use colors that can be discriminated by all users
In periphery:	Use of colors only visible in fovea	Use colors visible in periphery
Color Discrimination of Blue Images	Image size too small	Ensure images are at least 20 minutes of arc
Blurry Edges	High spatial frequency (small or thin images close together)	Increase image contrast Use combinations other than red-green and blue-yellow
	Low contrast	Increase lightness and hue differences
	Light image on dark background	Use dark images on light background
	Neutral images & color surround	Use dark images on dark background
Afterimages	Continuously viewing saturated color	Use desaturated colors
Color Fringes	Misconvergence	Align convergence
Depth Effects and/or	Extreme hues and high saturated values	Use similar hues and desaturated values
Equal Size Images Appear Unequal	Extreme differences in hue and saturation	Use similar hues, saturations and lightness values

Minimizing Color Interference

To minimize the effect of background on the appearance of image color, use an achromatic (white, gray, or black) background. Use bold fonts, thick lines, and large area-fill such as histograms, pie charts, and solid modeling. Avoid thin-line fonts, thin lines, and very small images such as those in text, line graphs, scatter diagrams, and circuit diagrams. If the background color is saturated, use white, not gray, for thin-line images like text.

Image characteristics which affect (minimize or enhance) color distortions are listed in Table 11.17. The characteristics of images that have low (small) and high (large) effects on color appearance are indicated. Fewer distortions occur with achromatic backgrounds, white text or lines, bold fonts, thick lines, and large images. To minimize the effects of adjacent colors, separate them.

TABLE 11.17

Image Characteristics Which Affect Image
Color Appearance

Image Feature	Magnitude of Color Interference	
	Low	High
Background	Achromatic	Color
Text/Line Color	White	Medium Gray
Font Weight	Bold	Stick
Line Thickness	Thick	Thin
Image Size	Large	Very Small

Specific Applications

Text and Graphics

Before colors are selected for text and graphics, it is important to determine the image size appropriate for the viewing distance by duplicating or simulating the viewing conditions and observing the legibility of the text or graphics. (Image colors selected without determining appropriate size may have to be later changed or resized to ensure legibility.) An alternative method is to test legibility using charts of various fonts, sizes, and colors (see Figure 11.20). Project transparencies and 35 mm slide images onto a screen and observe their legibility in the expected room illumination level and viewing distance.

Alphanumeric Strings

To ensure color recognition of text, color code long character strings rather than individual characters. Color code either characters or background of character strings for short, single-line character strings. Minimize the number of simultaneous colors and reverse video fields per display.

Text Processing

When possible, use conventional associations to color code text. For example, use the association of green (or cyan) with movement to designate text to be moved or copied. Use the neutral association of white for original or standard text. Use the association of magenta with danger to indicate text to be deleted.

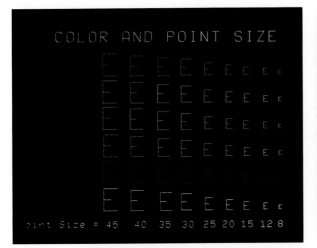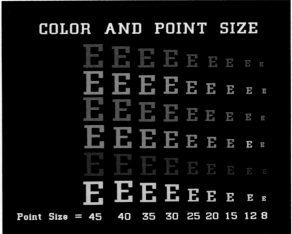

Figure 11.20 *Test Charts for Legibility of Colored Letters* The two charts can be used to determine the letters in the different fonts and sizes that can be seen correctly at different distances. (Note: one type point = .35 mm = .0135 inch.)

Although yellow is typically associated with caution, it can be used for new text or that which should be treated with caution.

CAD/CAM

Use spectral ordering to indicate depth appearance and magnitude. The ordering of colors to produce a layered appearance is shown in Table 11.18. Ensure that the colors of thin-line images like circuit diagrams meet minimum color requirements and preferably are values greater than these requirements (see Figure 11.21).

TABLE 11.18

Color Ordering for Image Layering

Integrated Circuits or Solid Modeling	Layer Depth First to Last		
	(Deepest)		*(Top Surface)*
Number of Layers			
1	white		
2	magenta		cyan
3	magenta	— yellow —	cyan
4	magenta — yellow — green — cyan		
5	magenta — yellow — green — cyan — blue		
6	red — magenta — yellow — green — cyan — blue		

Process Control

Use a graded scale of color values and spectral ordering to show progression or changes in a process. Use obvious hue differences to show different states and spectral ordering or shading to show state progression. Use saturated values to indicate maximum states (such as high chemical concentration) and desaturated values for minimum states (low concentration).

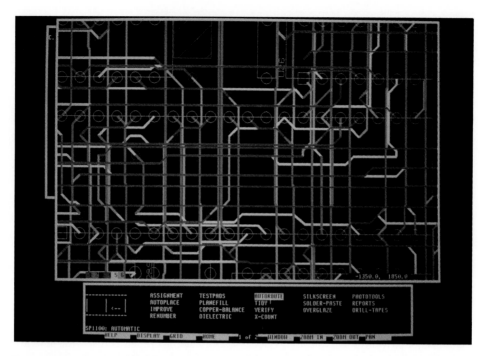

Figure 11.21 *Color for PC Boards* Examples using different colors to show ordering of circuit layers. (*Courtesy of Hewlett-Packard.*)

Scientific Graphs

Use a dark background and low contrast colors for grids and reference information (like axes labels) and high contrasts for data points and critical information (like out of specification data). Use high contrast and spectral extremes for combined wave forms and data points (see Figure 11.22).

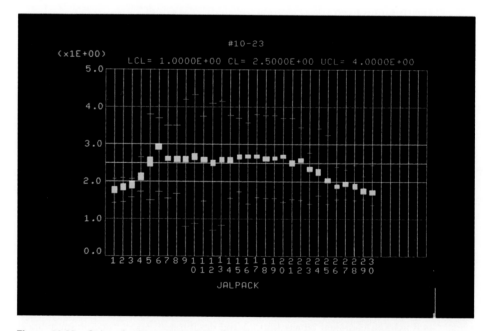

Figure 11.22 *Colors for Instrument Data Graphs* Rendition of quality inspection graph using colors recommended in Table 11.19.

Examples of colors for a quality inspection graph is shown in Table 11.19.

TABLE 11.19

Color Assignment for Data Graphs
for Instruments (Black background)

For	Use
Grid	Gray
Data Points	Yellow
Variance or Error Bars	Medium Blue
Out of Spec Data	Red
Labels	
X	Lavender
Y	Lime-green
Z	Cyan

Medical Monitoring

Use colors that can be easily identified at far viewing distances for surgical and bedside display monitoring tasks. Use dark background screens, high contrasts, appropriate blink frequencies, bold fonts, and colors perceptible in the periphery for images that should attract attention. Use colors that have associations commonly understood to indicate normal and abnormal conditions. For quick reference situations (such as surgical room viewing) color code background fields instead of characters to indicate physiological parameters. Colors to indicate medical status are shown in Table 11.20.

TABLE 11.20

Colors for Medical Status

Life Support Status	
OK	Blue/Green/White
Caution	Yellow/Gold
Emergency	Red
	(Flashing Option)

REFERENCES

Aggett, G. D., "Colours—Their Significance in Process Control," *Engineering Materials and Design*, 1968, pp. 1252–1253.

Birren, F., "Color Identification and Nomenclature: A History," *Color Research and Application*, 4(1), Spring 1979, 14–18.

Carter, E. C. and R. C. Carter, "Colour and Conspicuousness," *J. Opt. Soc. Am.*, 71, 1981, 723–729.

"Colours of Indicator Lights and Push-buttons," International Electrotechnical Commission Pub. #73, 1975.

Farrell, R. J. and J. M. Booth. *Design Handbook for Imaging Interpretation Equipment* (Seattle, WA: Boeing Aerospace Company, 1975).

Frome, F. S., "Improving Color CAD Systems for Users: Some Suggestions from Human Factors Studies," *IEEE Design & Test*, 1984, pp. 18–216.

Heider, E. R., "Focal Color Areas and the Development of Color Names," *Dev. Psych.*, 4(3), 1971, 447–455.

Heider, E. R., "Universals in Color Naming and Memory," *J. Exp. Psych.*, 93(1), 1972, 10–20.

"Human Factors Considerations for the Use of Colors in Display Systems," Snodd Scientific and Technical Reports, Jan. 1975, #NAST-TM-X-72196, T.R. 1329.

Hunt, R. W. G., "Measures of Color Appearance in Color Reproduction," *Color Research and Application*, 4(1), Spring 1979, 39–43.

Galitz, W. O. *Handbook of Screen Format Design* (The Netherlands: North-Holland, 1981).

Judd, D. B. *Contributions to Color Science* (Washington, DC: National Bureau of Standards, 1975).

Kaiser, P. K., "Color Names of Very Small Fields Varying in Duration and Luminance," *J. of Opt. Soc. of America*, 58(6), 1968, 849–852.

Kelly, K. L. and D. B. Judd, "Universal Language and Dictionary of Names," NBS Special Pub., 440, U.S. Govt. Printing Office, Washington, DC, 1976.

Konz, S., S. Chawla, S. Sathaye, and P. Shah, "Attractiveness and Legibility of Various Colours when Printed on Cardboard," *Ergonomics*, 15(2), 1972, 189–194.

Laycock, J., "Colour Contrast Calculations for Displays Viewed in Illumination," *International Conference on Colour in Information Technology and Visual Displays*, IERE Pub. #61, 1985, pp. 7–14.

Longley, W. V., "Color Difference Terminology," *Color Research and Application*, 4(1), Spring 1979, 45.

Moffitt, K., T. Cicinelli, and S. P. Rogers, "Color-naming Performance for Low-luminance Square and Line Symbols," *Anacapa Sciences TR 625–6*, August 1986.

Murch, G. M., "Perceptual Considerations of Color," *Computer Graphics World*, 1983, pp. 32–40.

Narborough-Hall, C. S., "Recommendations for Applying Colour Coding to Air Traffic Control Displays," *Displays*, 1985, pp. 131–137.

Payne, M. C., "Color as an Independent Variable in Perceptual Research," *Psych. Bull.*, 61(3), 1964, 199–208.

Post, D. L., "Effects of Color on CRT Symbol Legibility," *Society for Information Display*, XVI, 1985, 196–199.

Styne, A. F., "Color and Appearance—Bridging the Gap from Concept to Product," *Color Research and Application*, 1(2), 1976, 79–86.

Verriest, G., I. Andrew, and A. Uvijls, *Visual performance on a multi-color visual display unit of color-detective and normal trichromatic subjects*, IBM TR 11.241, March 1985.

Walraven, J., "Perceptual Problems in Display Imagery," *Society for Information Display*, XVI, 1985, 192–195.

Wolf, C. G., "Effects of Color on Legibility of Displayed Text," *Proceedings of the Human Factors Society*, 1982, p. 595.

Glossary

ABERRATION Failure of an optical lens to produce exact point-to-point correspondence between an object and its image.

ACCOMMODATION, VISUAL The adjustment of the lens of the eye to obtain maximum sharpness (focus) of an image.

ACHROMATIC Colorless; lights that have no definite hue.

ACTIVE DISPLAY Display that emits light.

ACUITY The ability of the eye to discriminate or see clearly (resolve) fine details.

ADAPTATION, CHROMATIC A change in visual sensitivity to hue, saturation or the ability to discriminate color differences.

ADDITIVE COLOR MIXING A process of combining lights so that the resultant color is brighter than the individual lights.

ADDITIVE PRIMARIES A set of colors (such as red, blue, and green) that produces a wide gamut of colors by additive color mixing.

AFTERIMAGE, COLOR Sensation of a complementary color that appears when shifting the eyes away from a color which has been viewed for an extended period of time.

ALOGRITHM Instructions which specify how to solve a problem.

ALIASING In a visual display technology, the perception of low frequency components or noise in an image when it is sampled at an insufficient rate. These low frequency components are really ''aliases'' of high frequency components in the image.

ALPHANUMERIC A character set that contains letters, numbers, punctuation marks, and special symbols (such as #, *, @).

AMBIENT LIGHT Total light in the visual field.

AMPLITUDE The height of a wave. The amplitude of a light wave is related to intensity.

ANOMOLOSCOPE An instrument (usually a tube) with a circular bipartite field half of which is illuminated in yellow and the other half a mixture (which can be varied) of red and green. Color perception is tested by having an observer mix the variable field to match the yellow field. Specific variations in combinations of the variable field indicate color perception ability.

ANALOG Representation of data as a smooth, continuous function.

ANALOG-TO-DIGITAL CONVERTER Device that converts voltage (an analog signal) to a digital pulse form for processing by a computer.

ANGLE OF INCIDENCE Angle between the axis of an impinging light beam and perpendicular to the surface of an object.

ANGLE, VISUAL The angle subtended by an image on the retina.

ANTI-ALIASING In computer graphics, the reduction of an "aliased" appearance (such as stairsteps along a diagonal line) by displaying an image as a series of gray scales.

ANTI-REFLECTION COATING Thin layer(s) of material on an optical surface which reduces reflectance.

APERTURE Opening through which light can pass. The effective diameter of the pupil aperature controls the amount of light passing through the lens which reaches the image plane of the retina.

APPLICATION PROGRAMS Software that addresses specific user-oriented tasks.

ASPECT RATIO, CHARACTER The ratio of the height of a character to its width.

ASSIMILATION, COLOR The perceptual illusion that occurs when a color appears to change its hue or saturation to a desaturation of the bordering color.

BANDPASS The specific range of frequencies, or wavelengths, that pass through a device.

BARREL DISTORTION The appearance of a bulging outward distortion (like a barrel) of the sides on an image caused by a decrease in effective magnification of points in an image distant from the center of the image.

BINARY IMAGE Representation of an image in computer memory as zeros and ones and appearing as two values, usually black and white.

BINARY PRINTING Technique where color values result from dot density.

BIT (BINARY DIGIT) The smallest unit of information possible to store and process by a computer. In image processing, a sequence of bits represents the quantized image brightness at a specific pixel.

BITMAPPED DISPLAY Display in which it is possible to program and store the characteristics of each pixel in memory. The number of bits per pixel determines the number of possible intensity values for a pixel.

BLINDNESS, COLOR Rare condition in which an individual is unable to perceive color.

BLOOM, CHARACTER The apparent increase in size and defocusing due to very high brightness levels of the background of an image. Bright characters on a black background appear larger than the same size dark characters on a white background.

BLURRING A form of degradation of an image in which the borders appear out of focus or "fuzzy."

BRIGHTNESS The perceptual (psychological) correlate of intensity which ranges from dark to bright.

BRIGHTNESS CONTRAST Perceived difference in luminance level of an image from its background.

BUFFER Temporary storage location for computer data.

CAD (COMPUTER-AIDED DESIGN) Software programs that allow the design, manipulation, and analysis of electronic or mechanical components.

CAE (Computer-Aided Engineering) Software programs which include computer-aided design, manufacturing, and instruction.

CAI (Computer-Aided Instruction) Interactive instructional software programs.

CAM (Computer-Aided Manufacturing) Software programs that aid the design, monitoring, and execution of manufacturing tasks.

Candela Unit of luminous intensity equal to one-sixth the normal intensity of a candle.

CAT Scan Computer Automated Tomography. A three-dimensional X ray constructed from multiple X ray views of an object.

Cathode Ray Tube Vacuum tube in which electron emission from a cathode focuses into a beam which is directed toward a phosphor-coated surface which becomes luminescent at the point where the electron beam strikes.

Central Vision The area of vision (a two-degree radius around the fovea of the retina) where acuity is sharpest.

Channel, Visual A series of light-sensitive cells (neurons) which sends a specific type of visual information from the eye to the brain.

Chroma Degree of saturation (percentage of pure hue content) of a color in the Munsell color system.

Chromatic Aberration, Visual Optical property of the lens which results in different wavelengths of light imaging at different distances from the lens.

Chromaticity The proportion of two of the three primaries necessary to match a color.

Chromaticity Chart or Diagram Two-dimensional chart of color space arranging colors according to physical specification and psychological data of observer's responses to colored lights. Color arrangements are such that saturated colors are on the boundaries (perimeter) of the space with decreasing saturations towards the interior.

Chromostereopsis Perception in which images of extreme wavelengths of the visible spectrum appear at different depths due to the chromatic aberration of the lens of the eye.

CIE (Commission Internationale de l'Eclairage) An international organization dedicated to measurement, specification, and standardization of color and lighting.

CIE Space A color specification model devised by the CIE.

CIELAB (CIE 1976 La*b*) Color relational system defined by three orthogonal axes representing luminance, red-green, and blue-yellow.

CIELUV (CIE Lu*v*) Color relational system based on the 1976 Uniform Color Space.

Color The psychological (perceptual) experience of varying wavelength distribution of light.

Color Coding Use of color to signify an attribute of an object or its meaning or color differences to indicate specific events.

Color Contrast The ratio of hue and saturation of an image compared to the hue and saturation of its surroundings.

Color Deficiency Reduction in ability to discriminate colors.

Color Differences Equations Metrics to establish the magnitude of perceived difference between pairs of colors.

Color Error Metric In computer graphics, a measure which indicates how different a display color is from the original color in a scanned image.

Color Fidelity The accuracy with which color can be reproduced.

Color Gamut Range of colors.

Color Look-up Table A software method for relating digital representations of a color to a set of RGB gun voltages.

Color Map Same as a color look-up table.

Color Opponency The process by which the visual system categorizes the amount of red, green, yellow, and blue in a colored image.

Color Quality A complex judgment relating to the appearance (either fidelity or aesthetics, or both) of a color.

Color Solid A geometric representation of the relationship between hue, saturation, and brightness of colors.

Color Space A relational representation of colors ordered along color difference dimensions.

Color Specification System A system for quantifying a color and its relation to other colors (such as CIE, CIELUV, and CIELAB).

Color Temperature The temperature of a Planckian radiator whose color most closely resembles that of a given stimulus at the same brightness and under a specific viewing condition.

Color Tolerance A measure of how closely a color can be reproduced.

Colorimetric System See Color Specification System.

Complementary Colors Two-colors that form white or gray when combined.

Computer Color Space A class of color spaces used in computer graphics, such as RGB, HSL, and HSV.

Computer Graphics Pictures or visual representations created on computer input and output devices.

Cones Visual photoreceptors in the retina that are active primarily in bright light.

Continuous Ink-jet Printing One ink-jet printing technique whereby a steady stream of ink droplets are emitted from print nozzles under pressure. A charge is selectively applied to the ink droplets causing droplets to be deflected either towards or away from the page.

Contrast (also see Color Contrast and Lightness Contrast) Range of difference (ratio between light and dark values in an image. Contrast Ratio: the ratio between the object and background luminance levels. Contrast Modulation: the difference between the darker of an object or background shade and the lighter of an object or background shade divided by their sum.

Contrast Enhancement Any image processing operation that increases the contrast of an image.

Convergence, CRT The alignment of the three electron beams of a CRT onto one point to minimize visible color fringes.

Convergence, Visual The lateral and synchronous inward movement of the eyes that occurs when viewing an image closer than 60 centimeters.

Coordinates A set of numbers representing different axes and corresponding to a point in a plane or space.

Cornea The transparent anterior portion of the eye, through which light bends (refracts) as it enters the eye.

Cortex, Visual The gray matter in the posterior lobe of each hemisphere of the brain; contains neurons that process visual information for complex pattern recognition.

Critical Flicker Fusion The frequency at which a flickering light appears to be steady and continuous.

CRT (Cathode Ray Tube) A tube containing a cathode which generates electron beams (cathode rays) that excite phosphors on a screen to produce visible light.

Cursor Small distinctive pattern (rectangle, crosshair, circle, or bar) used as a pointer to a specific area or image on a display and under user control via an I/O device.

DAC, Digital-to-Analog Converter A hardware device that converts a digital representation to an analog (such as a voltage signal).

Database, Computer A computer file of information on a specific or related topic(s).

Data File A collection of related records of information in a computer memory.

Density Slicing An image processing technique whereby a range of gray levels is mapped to one level, or density slice. Different density slices map to different gray ranges. The user can interactively set the low and high values of the range.

Depth of Field or Focus The range of focus of images from the distance where all the images are in focus.

Desktop Publishing A software application (and associated hardware) that allows the creation, manipulation, and combination of both text and graphics through illustration aids and high quality output devices (such as laser printers) which produce multiple fonts.

Deuteranope A type of color vision deficient person in which the middle wavelength sensitive pigment is missing.

Diffuse Reflection Redirection of incident light over a wide range of angles from a surface.

Digital Representation of incremental or discrete states by particular numbers like 0's and 1's.

Digital Imaging Conversion of a video picture into pixels by means of an analog (A)-to-digital (D) converter and storage of the brightness level of each pixel in a computer.

Digital or Digitized Image Creation of an image in digital format by partitioning its area into a finite two-dimensional array of small uniform, mutually exclusive regions and assigning a "representative" gray shade to each area.

Digitizing Tablet A data entry device which resembles a tablet and converts the position of a pen stylus to digital x,y coordinate information.

Diopter A measure of the refractive power of the eye equal to the reciprocal of the focal length in meters (for example, three Diopters is equivalent to focusing ability up to $\frac{1}{3}$ of a meter).

Discrimination, Visual Degree to which a visual system can sense differences in the physical characteristics of an image.

Dispersion Separation of light into wavelengths or colors by refraction or diffraction.

Dithering A process to produce intermediate colors by assigning one of eight colors to a specific pixel inside a matrix of pixels.

Dominant Wavelength For an object that emits or reflects multiple wavelengths, the wavelength of maximum amplitude.

Dot-Matrix Printing Printing technique that creates characters by depositing a two-dimensional array of dots.

Dot-on-Dot Printing Technique where ink is superimposed to create different colors.

Drop-on-Demand Printing One method of ink-jet printing in which ink droplets are formed in printer nozzles and ejected only through appropriate timing or electronic signals.

Drum Plotter A plotter whose paper is mounted on a cylindrical drum and is advanced by its rotation.

Edge Detection Process of finding edges in a scene through sensors that respond to the differences in the gray scale intensity in an image. Detection of an edge occurs when these differences exceed a specified value.

Edge Enhancement Image processing method to enhance the high spatial frequencies or sharpness of an image.

Effective Contrast The sum of the brightness contrast and the color contrast.

Electrode Conductor by which an electric current enters or leaves a conducting region.

Electroluminescent Display A type of light emissive display in which phosphors are energized by an electric field to emit light.

Electromagnetic Spectrum The entire range of electromagnetic radiant energy, including radio waves, radar, visible light, infrared light, ultraviolet light, and X rays.

Electromagnetic Wave A wave consisting of cyclic variations in the intensity of electric and magnetic energy fields traveling from a source.

Electron Beam Ray, or stream of particles with a negative charge.

Electron Gun Source of electron beams that activate phosphorescent material on a display screen, resulting in light emission.

Electronic Spreadsheets Computer software for presentation and manipulation of tabular data in which mathematical and statistical calculations are applied.

Electrophotographic Printer Device which reproduces color hard copy in a similar manner to a color copier where light exposure creates a charge on a photoconductive drum. Toner is attracted to the charged area and then fused to paper.

Electrostatic Plotter-Printer Device that reproduces images from a computer display into paper or transparency film by placing electrostatic charges on areas of treated paper. In turn, these form images by attracting toner to these areas.

Emissive Display Display which produces images by emitting light.

Ergonomics A multidisciplinary profession that studies the interaction between people, equipment (hardware or software), and the environment, emphasizing physiology and improvement of the work environment.

Etched Screen A computer screen treated with corrosive action to reduce the visibility of reflections through light diffusion.

Excitation Purity A quantitative measure of saturation; specified as the difference between a color's CIE xy value and some reference white relative to the difference between the white and the spectral locus.

Farnsworth-Munsell Hue Test A color vision test which entails sorting color chips into an order.

Film Recorder A device for reproducing a computer-generated image in 35 mm slide format.

Filter, Optical Device consisting of a transparent or translucent material which absorbs some wavelengths selectively while transmitting others.

Flicker, Screen A variation, over time, in the brightness of the lighted area on a screen associated with the screen refresh rate and phosphor decay.

Flat Panel Display Display typically not thicker than two inches.

Flatbed Plotter A plotter in which the paper is stationary and the pen is advanced for drawing across the surface.

Flow Diagram A graphic representation of system or program using conventional symbols and geometric shapes like process boxes and decision points.

Fluorescence Radiation emission resulting from the absorption of radiation from another source.

Focal Colors The four colors from a standard color chart that appear to best and most consistently represent a ''good'' example of red, blue, green, and yellow.

Focal Length Distance from a lens to the corresponding focal point.

Focal Point Point at which a lens or mirror focuses parallel incident light.

Focusing System The lens and the convergence muscles of the eye which allow the eye to resolve a clear image.

Font Specific type and size of alphanumeric character.

Footcandle Amount of illumination from one international candle falling on one square foot of surface at a distance of one foot. The same as lumen per square foot.

Footlambert Unit of luminance equal to one candela per square foot or to the uniform luminance at a perfectly diffusing surface emitting or reflecting light at the rate of one lumen per square foot. A lumen per square foot is a unit of incident light and a footlambert is a unit of emitted or reflected light. For a perfectly reflecting and perfectly diffusing surface (no absorption of light), the number of lumens per square foot is equal to the number of footlamberts.

Fourier Processing Mathematical technique of representing an image as a sum or the superimposition of sinusoidal functions.

Fourier Transform Mathematical technique to convert data from the space or time domain to the frequency domain. It represents data as sums of sinusoidal waves.

Fovea The central region of the retina where color vision and acuity are most accurate due to the high density of different classes of cones.

Frame Buffer Special image memory in a computer in which images can be stored and manipulated.

Frequency Number of times an event occurs per unit of time (temporal frequency) or space (spatial frequency).

Fresnel Lens Discrete, concentric, and circular composition of a lens.

Gamma The power exponent useful to approximate the curve of display-luminance output versus display voltage.

Gamma Correction An exponential correction to the signal input that allows a linear transfer function from a signal source to a display output.

Ghost Image Trails of light due to refreshing on long persistence phosphors.

Glare A relatively bright light, or the dazzling sensation of bright light, which interferes with optimum vision or produces discomfort; a distracting light source brighter than the surrounding illumination resulting from excess light uniformly distributed over the visual field which reduces contrasts and visibility.

Global Luminance Space-average luminance or the light integrated across the entire visual field.

Graphics The use of lines and figures (such as symbols and pictorial representation) to display images and data.

Gray Scale Arrangement of various shades of gray in a series of graduations from black to white.

Halftoning A process that creates more shades or colors by varying the sizes of dots in a matrix.

Hard Copy Permanent media onto which display images transfer. Computer hard copy is media like paper, plastic, or 35 mm slides.

Hardware The physical components that compose a computer system.

Highlighting Use of a video or graphic technique to draw attention to information (such as underlining, reverse video, blinking, and brightness).

HSL Model Hue, saturation, and lightness color model useful for specification of colors on a bitmap display.

Human Factors Engineering A multidisciplinary profession, originating in the United States, that studies the interface between people and equipment (hardware and software), emphasizing the improvement of productivity through enhanced machine and environmental design.

Hue The psychological attribute of color sensation associated with the physical property of visible wavelengths.

Icon A pictorial representation of symbolic information.

Illuminance Luminous flux incident on a surface.

Illumination Application of light to an object.

Image Optical projection of a brightness value or array or brightness values onto a plane.

Image Enhancement Any one of a group of operations which improves the detection of image details by enhancing contrast and edge resolution, spatial filtering, noise suppression, image smoothing, and image sharpening.

Image Processing Techniques that improve the appearance or resolution of images by transforming them. They include image compression, image restoration, image enhancement, preprocessing, quantization, spatial filtering, and other image pattern recognition techniques.

Impact Printing Impression of images onto paper by the impact of a hammer wire dot-matrix or character dye through a carbon ribbon onto paper.

Incident Light Light that falls directly on an object.

Infrared Region of the electromagnetic spectrum (from 0.75 to 1000 microns) which creates heat and whose wavelengths are beyond those visible.

Input Device Device which enters or manipulates information or images into a computer processor or terminal.

Intensity, Light The number of photons emitted by a light source.

Interactive Graphics User's dynamic control of the content of a display screen by means of a keyboard, mouse, toggle, roller, or other device.

Interface The device which allows the user to interact with a computer.

Interlaced Scanning Process in which an electron beam moves across the even rows and then the odd rows of pixels in a display.

Inverse Video Reversal of imaging polarity from positive (dark on light) to negative (light on dark) or vice versa.

I/O Acronym for input/output which describes all the activities of getting data in and out of a computer processor or the peripheral devices that receive data from, or transmit to, the processor.

Iris The circular pigmented muscular membrane between the cornea and lens, which can expand or contract to vary the diameter of the pupil.

Jaggies Uneven or step-like edges visible on single lines (usually diagonal or arc-shaped).

Jitter Spatial instability of a image on a computer screen.

Just Noticeable Difference (JND) A perceptual unit which specifies the amount of least physical change of an object so it will be perceived as different.

Keyboard A device consisting of a character set array of keys that allows a user to input information into a computer system.

Lambert Unit of luminance equal to one candela per square centimeter, and therefore equal to the uniform luminance of a perfectly diffusing surface emitting or reflecting light at the rate of one lumen per square centimeter.

LAMBERTIAN SURFACE Diffusing surface having the property that the intensity of light emanating in a given direction from any small surface component is proportional to the cosine of the angle. The brightness of a lambertian surface is constant regardless of the viewing angle.

LARGE FIELD CIE CHROMATICITY DIAGRAM Similar to the 1931 CIE chromaticity diagram, except that the diagram is based on data from color mixing experiments using a large ten-degree spot.

LASER Acronym for Light Amplification by Stimulated Emission of Radiation. Device that produces a coherent monochromatic beam of light.

LASER PRINTER Electrophotographic printing technology using a laser to produce images onto paper.

LATERAL INHIBITION The restraint of activity by a neuron, or group of neurons, on neighboring neurons or pathways in the nervous system.

LAYERED WINDOW The overlapping of software display areas which represent different components of an application program.

LCD (LIQUID CRYSTAL DISPLAY) A reflection-based display technology in which the variable transmission of certain crystals controls intensity.

LED Acronym for light-emitting diode.

LEGIBILITY Ability to identify an alphanumeric character or symbol. A criterion of image quality.

LENS Transparent optical component consisting of one or more pieces of optical glass (elements) with curved surfaces (usually spherical) that converge or diverge transmitted light rays.

LENS, VISUAL A highly tranparent, nearly spherical body in the eye that focuses light rays.

LIGHT EMITTING DIODE Semiconductor diode that converts electrical energy to light.

LIGHT, VISIBLE Portion of the electromagnetic radiation between 380 and 760 nanometers capable of stimulating the eye to produce visual sensations.

LIGHT PEN Photoelectric device in the shape of a pen that modifies information on a computer display when contact is made with the screen.

LIGHTNESS The perceptual sensation of the amount of white or black in an image.

LIGHTNESS CONTRAST Degree of difference between the lightest and darkest portions of images and their surround.

LIQUID CRYSTAL DISPLAY A type of passive display in which an external source of light is modulated to form an image. The device relies on the optical properties of certain organic compounds in response to an electrical field.

LOCAL LUMINANCE The measurement of luminance over a restricted part of the visual field.

LOGICAL RELATIONS A property (such as equal to or less than) that holds between an ordered pair of objects and an ordering of these objects.

LOGO An identifying representation usually in the form of a few letters or a symbol.

LOOK-UP TABLE (LUT) An area in computer memory in which one set of values is used to index another set of values (for example, one set provides the address of a place in the table where values for the R,G,B gun voltages are stored).

LUMEN Unit of luminous flux through a unit solid angle (steradian) from a point source of one candela.

LUMINANCE Luminous intensity (photometric brightness) of a surface in a specific direction per unit of projected area of a surface, measured in foot-lamberts.

LUMINOUS INTENSITY The amount of light radiation in a given direction per second.

LUX A unit of direct illumination on a surface that is located one meter from a uniform source of light equal to one light candle or one candela, or lumen, per square meter.

MACADAM ELLIPSE Clusters of colors on a chromaticity diagram which are reported to look identical when adjacently viewed.

MACH BAND Illusionary light and dark bands seen at the transition from a uniformly illuminated region to a region of graded illumination.

MENU, SCREEN Listing of text or graphic symbols on a computer screen that represent programs or screen functions available to a user.

METAMER Colors which perceptually match even though they have different spectral distributions.

MICROPROCESSOR A small central processor that performs calculations and controls functions of a computer system.

MIXTURE, COLOR Additive or subtractive combinations of two or more color stimuli to produce another color.

MODEL, COLOR Description of a geometric arrangement of colors useful for visualization of the relationship of psychological components (like hue, saturation, and lightness) of light.

MODULATION Process of varying a high frequency carrier signal with a lower frequency signal.

MOIRE PATTERN The perceptual illusion of repetitive patterns distinctly different from the components of the surface material.

MOLECULAR MODELING A computer simulation of the bonding and interaction of molecules.

MONITOR Display device for viewing computer of video images.

MONOCHROMATIC DISPLAY A computer screen that displays images in one color.

MONOCHROMATIC LIGHT Light energy of a single wavelength.

MONOCHROME One color.

MOUSE A device which fits in the palm of the hand that sends electrical signals to a computer to enter a command (such as to select or manipulate images on a screen). Its movement or depression of keys on its surface controls its signals.

MUNSELL SYSTEM Perceptual arrangement of a collection of hue chips along a lightness and chroma scale.

NANOMETER A unit of measure (one billionth of a meter) useful for description of portions of the electromagnetic spectrum.

NEGATIVE IMAGE OR VIDEO Light images on a darker background.

NEURON A cell with specialized processes that is the fundamental functional unit of nervous tissue.

NEWTON RINGS Patterns of rings that appear when the surfaces of transparent bodies enclose a thin film of air or other transparent medium. They occur from the reflections and interference of light from the sides of the air film.

NONEMISSIVE DISPLAY Display which produces images by reflecting ambient light.

NONIMPACT PRINTING Process of depositing ink onto paper by which the printing device does not contact paper but can print by means like squirting, heat impression, or electrostatic charge.

NONREDUNDANT CODING A method of applying codes such that no two codes (such as color and font) convey the same information.

Ocular Muscles Muscles that control movement of the eyes (extraocular) and size of the lens and the pupil (intraocular).

On-Line Power state of computer where it can send or receive computer information.

Opponent Color Cells or Mechanisms Antagonistic pairs of cells (such as red-green, blue-yellow, and black-white) that receive input from photoreceptors sensitive to different regions of the visible spectrum. They are opponent, or antagonistic, because of inhibitory connections between corresponding photoreceptors.

Optical Coating, Screen Deposit of a thin film of light-reducing material on a computer screen to reduce glare and reflection.

Optics The study of light and its nature, proportion, origin, propagation, effects, and perception. Also, the elements and design of an optical system.

Output Device Physical mechanism that produces images created with a computer.

Overplotting Plotting process in which inks are superimposed to create a darker shade of a color.

Paintbrush, Screen Software application program that allows a user to interactively use a palette of colors to choose colors for images created on a display screen.

Palette, Electronic A specific set of colors for application to electronic images.

Passive Display Display that reflects light.

Pattern Recognition Ability of a system to identify, discriminate, segment, classify, or screen patterns, and select, filter, extract, or enhance features, usually using statistical methods.

Pen Plotter (see Plotter) Device which draws with a pen and transfers images from a computer display terminal.

Pen Stylus A data entry device in the shape of a pen and used to point enter coordinate information via a digitizing tablet.

Perception, Visual Awareness of the elements of the environment through the physical sensation of seeing.

Perceptual Color Space A color space whose construction relies on reports of color perception.

Peripheral Vision Vision resulting from stimulation of the sensory receptors at, or near, the lateral perimeter of the retina.

Persistence Period of time a phosphor continues to glow after removal of stimulating radiation.

Phosphor A coating of luminescent material that emits light when a beam of electrons strikes the interior front surface of an evacuated glass tube such as a CRT.

Phosphor Decay The process in which a phosphor ceases to emit light over time.

Phosphorescence Fluorescence that persists for a certain amount of time after withdrawing the stimulating radiation.

Photon The basic unit of electromagnetic radiant energy. Particle of light.

Photopic Vision Vision which occurs in a lighted environment and permits perception of colors due to the sensitivity of cone photoreceptors in the retina of the eye.

Photoreceptors Cells in the retina that are sensitive to light.

Pie Chart Graphic figures resembling a pie, in which radial lines divide areas of a circle, indicating distribution of data.

Pigment An insoluble coloring material which can be combined with a binder so that the color will adhere to the material.

PINCUSHIONING Inward distortion of the images on the outer edges of a display resulting from an increase in the effective magnification of points in the image distant from the center of the screen.

PIXEL Smallest element that a computer display can illuminate and resolve.

PLASMA PANEL DISPLAY (PPD) Flat panel display in which electrical stimulation of small spots of neon gas illuminates different areas on the screen.

PLOTTER A device that draws images automatically by receiving digital electrical signals from the computer and converting it into movement of a pen across paper or plastic in minute increments and a specified direction.

PLOTTER INKS Black or colored dyes in plotter pens.

POINTILLISTIC PAINTING Technique of applying small strokes or dots of color to a surface so they appear to blend together when viewed from a distance.

POLARITY, IMAGE Positive (dark images on a light background) or negative (light images on a dark background) presentation of information on a display.

POLARIZED FILTER A filter that only passes light waves in a single oriented plane. A polarized filter may reduce the intensity of reflected light by allowing light waves in only one place to escape the field of the filter.

POSITIVE VIDEO Dark images on a light background.

PRIMARY COLOR Three colors that when combined in pairs produce a secondary set of colors and black when all are combined. No two primaries can produce a third primary.

PRINTER A device that deposits images from a computer display onto paper or film.

PRINTER CIRCUIT (PC) BOARD An insulated surface with electrical paths made by depositing conductive material in continuous paths from terminal to terminal.

PRINTHEAD Device that strikes paper or ribbon resulting in the transfer of a dot or an image to paper.

PRISM A triangular or transparent piece of glass or plastic which separates light into the spectrum of colors.

PROCESS CONTROL Programs which monitor a process and provide feedback for modification or corrective action.

PROCESSING STAGES The series of steps necessary to perceive, integrate, organize, and store information.

PROGRAM A sequence of numerically coded instructions or routines that direct executions of actions by a computer.

PROTANOPE A color-deficient person lacking the long wavelength sensitive photopigment.

PSEUDOCOLORING Translation of gray shades into different colors.

PSEUDO-ISOCHROMATIC PLATES Patterns used in a color vision test in which the person can only identify letters and shapes by discriminating color differences.

PUCK A digitized pointing device typically used with a computer tablet for transferring mechanical drawings to a computer system.

PUPIL The circular opening in the eye through which light enters.

PURE COLORS Highly saturated colors containing no visible trace of a mixture color.

PURITY The saturation or amount of white in a color.

PURKINJE SHIFT The change in appearance of colors due to reaction of the receptor cells (rods and cones) to differences in light intensities.

QUARTER-WAVELENGTH FILTER A vapor-deposited screen filter (with a thickness equal to one-quarter of one billionth of a meter) useful for reducing mirror-like reflections from a display screen.

RADIANCE A measure of the radiant flux emerging from a surface in a specific direction.

RADIANT ENERGY (RADIATION) Energy that travels from a source in the form of waves or particles.

RADIANT FLUX A measure of the energy (per unit time) generated from a light source in all directions.

RASTER A predetermined scanning pattern of the electron beam which provides substantially uniform coverage of a display screen.

RASTER IMAGING Method of creating images in a computer input/output device using dots, visually arranged as a series of rows.

RASTER LINE A horizontal line produced on a raster device.

RASTER-SCAN DISPLAY CRT display that generates an image by modulating the beam intensity as the beam moves through a regular pattern of horizontal lines, or raster. Used by TV cameras to create a video image.

RASTER SCANNING (See Raster Imaging)

REACTION TIME The amount of time between the presentation of a stimulus and a response.

READABILITY The ability to interpret the meaning of strings of alphanumeric characters.

RECEPTORS, VISUAL Light-sensitive rod or cone cells in the retina of the eye.

RECOGNITION Ability to recognize or interpret the meaning or association of an image.

REDUNDANT CODING Assignment of the same meaning to different codes.

REFLECTANCE OR REFLECTION COEFFICIENT The ratio of the energy per unit time per unit area (radiant power density) reflected by the object to the energy per unit time per unit area incident on the object. In general, reflectance is a function of the incident angle of the energy, viewing angle of the sensor, spectral wavelength and bandwidth, and the nature of the object.

REFLECTION Process by which incident light leaves a surface or medium from the side on which it is incident.

REFLECTION DISPLAY Display that produces images by reflecting light.

REFLECTONS, SCREEN Mirror images on a display screen.

REFRACTION The bending of the straight pathway of light from its original direction as a result of passing from one medium (like air) to another (like glass) with different transmission velocities.

REFRESH RATE The rate at which an electron beam completes a scan of a display screen, designated in Hz (cycles per second).

REFRESH TUBE A device which generates images on a screen surface by storing and re-illuminating phosphors at a specific rate.

RESOLUTION The smallest discriminable detail in an image or the proximity with which two points are visible and distinguishable.

RETINA The light-sensitive inner surface of the eye onto which images are projected by the lens; contains multiple layers of neurons that process visual information by converting chemical changes into electrical signals that are sent to the brain.

REVERSE VIDEO Reversal of imaging polarity from positive (dark on light) to negative (light on dark) or vice versa. Describes positive polarity on a display screen. (see Inverse Video)

RGB MODEL Acronym for red, green, and blue; a three-primary color system for representing color images.

SATURATION The degree to which a hue differs from a gray of the same lightness.

SCAN To move a sensing point around an image.

SCAN LINE A row of pixels which an electron beam scans in one horizontal pass.

Scattering Process by which light is redirected throughout a range of angles as it passes through a medium or reflects off a surface.

Scotopic Vision Vision which occurs in very dim light or in dark adaptation due to the sensitivity of photoreceptive rods in the retina of the eye.

Screen Density The number of images on a screen relative to background area.

Secondary Color A color resulting from mixing two primary (e.g., red, blue, and green) colors.

Sensitivity, Visual The capacity of the visual cells of the nervous system to detect light and wavelength differences.

Shading Gradual changes of the color of an image from light to dark, resulting in continued variations of brightness.

Shadow Mask Metal sheet that lies behind the phosphor coating on the display screen and determines (via fine holes in its surface) the arrangement of phosphor dots on the screen.

Shape Modeling The creation of images by a computer program to translate shapes into electronic impulses.

Simultaneous Color Contrast Contrast resulting from simultaneously presenting two colors in the visual field.

Sine Curve Graphic representation of a wave propagation that repeats itself at regular intervals.

Sinusoidal Waveform A spatial or temporal distribution of light that varies sinusoidally.

Slider Bar A continuous indicator of color values on a computer display.

Smoothing Technique using gray scaling or color contrast to reduce the irregular or jagged appearance of the edges of characters of other images on a computer screen.

Soft Copy Images on a computer screen.

Soft Keys Keys on a keyboard device performing a function under the control of a computer program or a user.

Software Programs that control the operations of a computer.

Spatial Frequencies The number of lightness cycles that occur in a set distance across space. High spatial frequency appears as a series of narrowly spaced, thin lines; low spatial frequency appears as a series of widely spaced, wider bars.

Spectral Colors The colors that appear in the spectrum of sunlight, from red to violet.

Spectrum of Colors The ordering of wavelengths (between 380 and 760 nanometers) or colors which occur when light is passed through a prism.

Specular Reflection Redirection of light from a surface on which it is incident.

Spherical Aberration Failure of the lens of the eye to produce point-to-point correspondence between the viewed image and its projection on the retina of the eye.

Split Screen Display in which information from different files or different information from the same file is divided into different areas of the screen via graphics.

Subtractive Color Mixing The production of colors by superimposing transparent color filters or by mixing dyes or pigments.

Successive Contrast The perception of a different color induced by successive presentation of visual stimuli.

Temporal Change, Visual Changes in the visual characteristics of images over time.

Terminal, Computer A computerized input/output device for receiving, transmitting, and displaying output of data on a commuication line.

Tertiary Color Color resulting from mixing two secondary colors.

Text Editor A special program that allows entry and manipulation of text.

Texture The regular or random repetition of spatial features across an image. Texture is dependent on the spatial distribution of the gray shades and discrete tonal features. When a small area of the image has little variation of discrete tonal features, the dominant property of that area is gray shade. When a small area has wide variation of discrete tonal features, the dominant property of that area is texture. The size of the small area, the relative sizes and the number of distinguishable tonal features are critical to the perceived texture.

Thermal Printer Device which sequentially transfers colored inks from a sheet or plastic ribbon onto paper by heating the ink and fusing it into the paper.

Three-dimensional Display A display whose images give the illusion of depth or varying distances.

Thumbwheel A rotating knob used to control movement or change of images on a computer screen.

Tiled Window A window which is adjacent to (as opposed to superimposed or over-lapping) other windows.

Time-Scheduling Program Diagram of flow of activity paths of a project.

Toner A dye consisting of organic pigments.

Touch Screen Display that uses a pressure-sensitive surface or light beams to sense impressions for input.

Trackball A circular device which when manually rolled causes movement of a screen cursor.

Transforms Various mathematical functions useful for image analysis.

Transparencies Clear plastic sheets from which plotted images can be projected.

Trichromacy A principle of visual perception based on the interaction of three primary receptors.

Tristimulus Values The amounts of the three primary color stimuli necessary to produce a color match by additive mixing.

UCS (Uniform Color Space) An ideal color space in which the order and distance between colors represents how these colors appear to observers.

Ultraviolet Radiation (Light) A form of electromagnetic radiation between .01 and 0.4 microns and continuous with the low (violet) end of the visible spectrum.

Unique Hue A hue which has no other color components, appears very saturated, and is not confused with other hues.

Value Munsell equivalent to lightness or brightness.

VDT (Visual Display Terminal) A computer display screen and associated input device (keyboard, mouse, light pen, table, data phone, voice interface, and so on) useful for receive, transmit, and display information.

VDU (Visual Display Unit) (see Visual Display Terminal)

Vector Imaging Method of creating images on a computer input/output device using points and lines.

Visible Spectrum The portion of the electromagnetic spectrum that contains wavelengths capable of stimulating the retina, ranging from 380 to 760 nanometers.

Vision Process of sensing light emission or reflection.

Visual Fatigue A condition of the eyes often associated with a decrease in visual function or physical discomfort.

Visual System Optics and neural pathways in the eye and brain that allow the perception of images.

WAVELENGTH The distance from one point in a waveform to the same point in the next corresponding wave.

WHITE LIGHT The results of adding red, blue, and green lights in roughly equal amounts.

WINDOW, DISPLAY Rectangular regions of a screen that display particular views of data objects in the computer; they allow the user to interact with multiple series of information at the same time.

WORD PROCESSING Computer processing of text consisting of functions for entry, manipulation, and formatting.

WOVEN FIBER FILTER A fine, cross-hatched webbing in front of or in contact with a display screen in order to reduce the visibility of reflections on the screen.

REFERENCES

Conrac Corporation. *Raster Graphics Handbook* (New York: Van Nostrand Reinhold Co., 1985).

Cowan, W. B. and C. Ware. *Color Perception Tutorial*, SIGGRAPH, 1986.

Judd, D. B. and G. Wyszecki. *Color in Business, Science and Industry* (New York: John Wiley and Sons, 1975).

Machine Vision Glossary (Dearborn, MI: Automated Vision Association, 1985).

Orr, J. N., "Mechanical CAD/CAM for Beginners," *SIGGRAPH Proceedings*, 1985, pp. 423–442.

Osborne, R. *Lights and Pigments* (London: John Murray, 1980).

Varley, H., ed. *Colour* (London: Marshall Editions Ltd., 1980).

Index